Translating Egypt's Revolution

This unique interdisciplinary collective project is the culmination of research and translation work conducted by AUC students of different cultural and linguistic backgrounds who continue to witness Egypt's ongoing revolution. This historic event has produced an unprecedented proliferation of political and cultural documents and materials, whether written, oral, or visual. Given their range, different linguistic registers, and referential worlds, these documents present a great challenge to any translator.

The contributors to this volume have selectively translated chants, banners, jokes, poems, and interviews, as well as presidential speeches and military communiqués. Their practical translation work is informed by the cultural turn in translation studies and the nuanced role of the translator as negotiator between texts and cultures. The chapters focus on the relationship between translation and semiotics, issues of fidelity and equivalence, creative transformation and rewriting, and the issue of target readership. This mature collective project is in many ways a reenactment of the new infectious revolutionary spirit in Egypt today.

Translating Egypt's Revolution

The Language of Tahrir

Edited by
Samia Mehrez

The American University in Cairo Press
Cairo New York

First published in 2012 by
The American University in Cairo Press
113 Sharia Kasr el Aini, Cairo, Egypt
420 Fifth Avenue, New York, NY 10018
www.aucpress.com

Dar el Kutub No. 11218/11
ISBN 978 977 416 533 7

Dar el Kutub Cataloging-in-Publication Data

Mehrez, Samia
        Translating Egypt's Revolution: The Language of Tahrir / Samia Mehrez. —Cairo: The American University in Cairo Press, 2012
        p. cm.
        ISBN 978 977 416 533 7
        1. Egypt—History—1981
        2. Revolutions
        I. Title

1 2 3 4   16 15 14 13 12

Designed by Adam el-Sehemy
Printed in Egypt

For Egypt: the revolutionaries and the martyrs whose
creative energy, unwavering courage, and enormous sacrifice
continue to inspire us all

Contents

Note on the Contributors

Chris Combs has a BA in Spanish and history from Mount Saint Mary's University in Maryland. Early in his career, he became fluent in Brazilian Portuguese and developed an interest in translation. Since he began learning Arabic in 2002, Chris has spent three years living and studying in the Middle East, and was pursuing a graduate diploma in Middle East studies at the American University in Cairo when Egypt's revolution began. He currently serves as director of international programs at a trade association near Washington, D.C., and aims to continue working with Arabic in his career.

Laura Gribbon has a first class bachelor's degree in international development with NGO management from the University of East London. She is currently studying for an MSc in Middle East politics at the School of Oriental and African Studies of the University of London. Her professional background is in youth and community relations, working in the United Kingdom and Northern Ireland on the politics of identity. Laura's work focuses on the discovery of unheard voices and she has a keen interest in conveying messages through images and the non-verbal. Arriving in Cairo in early January 2011, and living close to Tahrir, Laura was often in the *midan* speaking to people and taking pictures.

Sarah Hawas graduated from the American University in Cairo in 2011 with a BA in comparative literature. In the past, she has translated for creative writers, journalists, bloggers, and social movements in Palestine, Egypt, India, and the United Arab Emirates. Sarah is fluent in English and Arabic, with a reading knowledge of Hebrew and French. She is interested in the role of translation in the political economy of culture, with a special emphasis on gender politics, as well as contemporary literary and translation practices in the Arab world and Israel. She plans to pursue graduate studies in the near future.

Sahar Keraitim is a graduate student in the Middle East studies program at the American University in Cairo. Her main fields of research are the politics of the Middle East, conflict resolution, and gender studies. She holds both Egyptian and Norwegian nationalities and has three years' work experience in the field of translation, mainly from Norwegian into Arabic. She had the privilege of being in Egypt and experiencing the revolution from the very beginning.

Menna Khalil is an independent researcher and writer working between the Middle East and the United States, interested in pursuing further graduate studies in anthropology. She holds an MA in international human rights law from the American University in Cairo and a BA in international studies, French, and economic theory from DePaul University in Chicago. Menna's academic interests in anthropological approaches to language, semiotic mediation, and narrative production have guided her work on translation and forms of storytelling. She has been carrying out ethnographic work on the relationship between citizens and the Egyptian army following the ouster of former president Mubarak.

Samia Mehrez is a professor of Arabic literature and founding director of the Center for Translation Studies at the American University in Cairo. She has published widely in the fields of modern Arabic literature, postcolonial literature, translation studies, gender studies, and cultural studies. She is the author of *Egyptian Writers between History and Fiction: Essays on Naguib Mahfouz, Sonallah Ibrahim, and Gamal al-Ghitani*, and *Egypt's Culture Wars: Politics and Practice*. She has translated numerous Egyptian writers in her edited anthologies *A Literary Atlas of Cairo* and *The Literary Life of Cairo*, published in English by the American University in Cairo Press and in Arabic by Dar el-Shorouk.

Heba Salem has an MA in teaching Arabic as a foreign language from the American University in Cairo, where she also earned a BA in mass communication with a minor in psychology. She currently teaches various levels of Egyptian Colloquial and Modern Standard Arabic at AUC. She has participated in developing computer-assisted materials and a website for reading and listening materials for Aswat Arabia. She is co-author of a book on colloquial Arabic to be published by the American University in Cairo Press. Heba is particularly interested in the creative linguistic energy of the January 25 Revolution in Egypt.

Lewis Sanders IV is a graduate student in the Middle East studies program at the School of Global Affairs and Public Policy of the American University in Cairo. He received a BA in international and comparative politics with departmental honors from the American University of Paris in 2009. His research interests are identity formation in Egypt's cultural underground, the impact of space on identity, semiotic theory, and post-structuralist approaches to Middle East studies. He is proficient in Spanish and French, and has a working knowledge of Egyptian Arabic. His work on translation attempts to capture alternative narratives in the January 25 Revolution.

Amira Taha is completing her master's thesis on Egyptian and Tunisian civil–military relations in the Department of Political Science of the American University in Cairo, where she also received her bachelor's degree in international relations. Her professional background is in the field of governance and civil-society development. Amira took on this book project because the Egyptian Revolution, although still in progress, represents to her an epic period that ought to be documented, taught, and studied.

Kantaro Taira has an MA in area studies from Tokyo University of Foreign Studies, where he is enrolled in a doctoral program. For three years he has translated articles from *Al-Ahram* newspaper into Japanese for a Tokyo University project. He studied Japanese literature, but was impressed by Ghassan Kanafani's short stories and decided to shift to Arabic literature. He is also enrolled in the Department of Arab and Islamic Civilizations at the American University in Cairo, where he is pursuing studies in Arabic literature.

Mark Visonà has an undergraduate degree in Arabic language and linguistics from Georgetown University and is completing his master's thesis in the Department of Journalism and Mass Communication of the

American University in Cairo. In addition to poetry, he enjoys translating drama and has written an honors thesis comparing two plays of Yusuf Idris. As a dual Italian/American citizen living in Cairo, he studies both theoretical and practical journalism and writes anecdotal short stories in his spare time.

Note on Transliteration

In the Arabic transliterations in this volume, a capital H is used to represent the sixth letter of the Arabic alphabet (ح), in order to distinguish it from the twenty-sixth letter (ه, represented by lower-case h).

Acknowledgments

The editor and contributors of this volume wish to thank the following artists, photographers, bloggers, activists, and friends who generously shared their images of Egypt's revolution: Ahmad Saad Bahig, Amgad Naguib, Carlos Latuff, Ganzeer, Hossam El-Hamalawy, Huda Lutfi, Islam Azzazy, Joseph Hill, Karima Khalil, Lara Baladi, Madiha Doss, Mariam Soliman, Mia Gröndahl, Michael Kennedy, Nermine Hammam, Omar Attia, Omnia Ibrahim Magdy, Rania Helmy, and Sarah Carr. Their images constitute an integral and indispensable part of several chapters in this volume that would have simply not existed without their work.

The editor also wishes to thank several colleagues who have taken the time to read and comment on some of the chapters as they were being developed. Their insights have helped shape and further sharpen many of the arguments presented here. We are infinitely grateful to Professors Diane Singerman, Hanan Sabea, Huda Lutfi, Joseph Massad, Michael Burawoy, Michael Reimer, Mona Abaza, and Richard Jacquemond. We hope that the volume in its final form is now closer to their expectations.

Introduction

Translating Revolution: An Open Text

Samia Mehrez

By the time this volume is published, more than a year will have passed since the beginning of the January 25, 2011 uprising in Egypt that deposed former President Hosni Mubarak on February 11, 2011 and which continues to remap, in many complex ways, the future of Egypt as well as its position in both the region and the world. This is to say that the Egyptian Revolution, with its ongoing proliferation of narratives, and our attempt here to translate such plurality, each resists and defies unified or unitary meaning and closure. From *thawra* (revolution) to *fawra* (uprising) to *inqilab* (coup)—not to mention global translations of this uprising via the "Occupy" movement taking place in hundreds of cities worldwide, and which were all arguably inspired by the Tahrir model and experience in Egypt[1]—the very naming and framing of Egypt's revolution attest to the complexity of its meanings and significations. To use Umberto Eco's formulation, both the revolution and its translations remain "open texts" at the literal and semiotic levels.[2] Just as Egypt's revolution continues to unfold and accumulate new meaning and signification, so too does the endeavor to translate this remarkable moment in Egyptian modern history. Indeed, as a multilayered text, revolution and its translation(s)—not just in Egypt but in many countries in the region—is not to be read as a string of meaning or a single, linear line of signification, but rather, as layers of narrative and fields of meaning that are at once open and dynamic. On a certain level then, both the revolution and its translation(s) can be seen as "writerly" texts, in Roland Barthes's sense of the term, where the reader and translator are confronted with multiple undetermined signs and codes that challenge their expectations of narrative unity and call upon both to renounce the passive receptivity of the consumer and to embrace an engaged effort as producers of "a text" that continues to be written on several levels.[3] This is a particularly perilous task for the translator, since one of the basic rules of translation is to read the text to the end before embarking on its translation.[4] If we seem to stand in violation of this basic rule because we have embarked on translating the revolution, as text, when it continues to be written, it is precisely because it is a "writerly" rather than a "readerly" text with a predetermined beginning and end. Readers of the various chapters in this volume will therefore sense that the translations presented here offer a parallel text, one that has been produced alongside and not after the writing of the text of the revolution as it developed over the past year. The Egyptian Revolution and its meanings have not ceased to challenge its 'translators' at all levels. Consider, for example, a few pivotal moments in this fluid and volatile narrative: the January 28, 2011 Friday of Rage that ushered in the "Independent Republic of Tahrir"; Egypt's "Second Revolution," which erupted on Saturday, November 18, 2011 and left forty-four martyred and thousands injured;[5] the unprecedented participation in parliamentary elections that started on November 28, 2011; and the initial indications of an early victory of the Islamist parties and coalitions amid continuing demands for a national salvation government and an end to military rule by the Supreme Council of the Armed Forces (SCAF). It is precisely this incompleteness and un-determinedness of both the text of the revolution and its translation(s) in this volume that accounts for the intimacy between them and their shared moments of euphoria, innocence, and naiveté, but also anxiety, fear, and apprehension of what the 'end' of the text might be. If Egypt's revolution continues to be a narrative in progress, so too then are its translations.

Revolutionary Teaching, Revolutionary Translation

February 11, 2011, the date that marked the end of Mubarak's thirty-year presidency, coincided with the start of the spring semester at the American University in Cairo (AUC), whose students, faculty, and staff were regular participants in the demonstrations and the initial two-week-long sit-in at Midan al-Tahrir that had become the daily destination for hundreds of thousands of Egyptians. On February 12, 2011, one day after Mubarak was forced to step down, AUC reopened its gates for the spring session, to the great dismay of many members of its community who felt that their daily involvement in the raw, unfolding historic events would be substantially impacted, diverted, perhaps even severed by their university responsibilities. Fortunately, faculty members were invited to design courses that would address various aspects of the Egyptian Revolution and which would sustain the AUC community's involvement in and interaction with events—even if not directly on the ground—in Tahrir. Many of the courses proposed for this initiative were last-minute but intuitively crucial courses that were meant to respond to an urgent collective need on the ground. "Translating Revolution" was one of those courses and has since provided the members of this group with a solid anchor in Egypt's continuing revolution. The seminar attracted Egyptian and non-Egyptian students whose linguistic abilities and cultural competencies and experiences complemented each other in ways that were vitally important. Among them they commanded more than half a dozen languages—Arabic, English, French, Spanish, Portuguese, Japanese, and Norwegian—all of which helped them maintain an informed comparative perspective on their task as translators and a collective awareness of global linguistic, geopolitical, and cultural power relations. As the note on the contributors to this volume clearly indicates, the participants also came to the task of translation with their own histories, understanding, and perspectives on translation, all of which intersected throughout. There was the poet, the musician, the technical translator, the journalist, the photographer, the security translator, the activist, the creative writer, and the teacher. They had all experienced and lived through the revolutionary moment in Egypt and were all motivated by a desire to translate it—as the title of the seminar promised—even though it was not quite clear then perhaps what exactly such a perilous project might entail.

In many ways, therefore, "Translating Revolution" was itself a revolutionary seminar and it ultimately became a book project of revolutionary translation(s). Like the revolution itself, the endeavor to translate Egypt's revolution was motivated by a level of collective energy and commitment that were born of the moment. The seminar provided a communal platform to continue to engage the layers of revolutionary narratives and to translate these fields of meaning *to* each other and *for* each other in an attempt to understand, situate, and contextualize the historic events that enveloped us. During the semester, the group received a class visit from a journalist who was putting together an article about the Egyptian Revolution. In summer 2011 he published that piece and described the participants in the seminar in the following terms:

All of those present were in Tahrir from the start or very nearly so. There's an infectious urgency in the way they study and discuss their work. They know they have been, are still being changed, personally, directly, by what has happened. They digress, disagree, reminisce. They are not studying this as 'Middle Eastern experts' might. They are testifying, rather, to what they have seen and heard.[6]

This collective project is a reenactment of the new "infectious urgency" of the revolutionary spirit in Egypt today, which has manifested itself in an unprecedented production and proliferation of revolutionary cultural materials in various modalities—written, oral, visual, and performative—throughout the past several months that have decidedly remapped and redefined the contours and meanings of both public culture and public space. The participants in the seminar initially selected, read, and *collectively* translated some of this material, from chants, banners, slogans, jokes, poems, and street art to media coverage, interviews, video blogs (vlogs), presidential speeches, and military communiqués. They predominantly worked in groups and as partners, not as individuals. This is to say that their translations, even in the chapters undertaken by a single author, are the outcome of this collective and perpetual conversation and understanding. The range and scope of the cultural, visual, and performative material, and its different linguistic registers and referential worlds, presented a great challenge to any translator, not just at the immediate linguistic level, but more importantly at the discursive, semiotic, and symbolic levels within the local and global contexts. This volume, then, is the culmination of these revolutionary translation projects undertaken by the participants in the "Translating Revolution" seminar except for one contributor—Menna Khalil—who joined us at a later stage with chapter 7 in this volume ("The People and the Army Are One Hand: Myths and their Translations"), which seemed indispensable to any reading and translation of Egypt's ongoing revolution.

The content of the seminar itself and the projects undertaken by the participants were decided upon collectively at the beginning of the semester. My role as instructor was to inform these choices and projects through selected theoretical readings in the field of translation studies in order to broaden, redefine, and relocate the very notion of translation and its (dis) contents. At the core of our conversation lay the understanding that translation is not simply a linguistic process of exchange or transfer between two individual texts but rather a contextual operation that requires mediation and negotiation between texts within their cultural contexts. Translation is therefore engaged and undertaken as a perpetual process of decoding and recoding in which the translator transcends the purely linguistic level to one of creative transposition. This liberating understanding of the processes that lie at the heart of translation problematizes and questions the notion of 'full equivalence' between language systems. Further, it is informed by what Roman Jakobson argued more than half a century ago: synonymy between languages is never possible, for signification and meanings are always culture-bound; hence the impossibility of sameness in any translation.[7] This understanding of the centrality of the *politics of difference*—not sameness—in translation allowed us to go beyond arguments about 'loss and gain' and 'fidelity and betrayal' to come to think differently about the task and role of the translator and the very meaning and urgency of translation itself specifically within *this* revolutionary context.

Until quite recently, translation had been regarded as a professional, technical field, an instrument rather than a shaper of global relations and communication. It was historically shunned by the academy as a field of study despite its centrality to academic and humanistic endeavors. Translation, within the academy, had always been taken for granted, treated as a handmaiden, dealt with as transparent, and subsumed under the study of "World Fiction" or "Great Books" lists with practically no considerations at all to the processes and complexities of translation itself, not to speak of the very location of the translator and how he or she is ideologically, culturally, and socially constructed and reconstructed through the very process of translation. In his now classic *The Invisibility of the Translator*, Lawrence Venuti succinctly described this "illusion of transparency" and "invisibility" that is required by the translator "who is expected by market demands to ensure easy readability" that actually "conceals the numerous conditions under which translation is made."[8] Indeed, the illusion of "invisibility" also masks the real import and agency of the translator, who, through the process of translation, at once transforms the original text and is equally transformed by it. Hence, the "Translating Revolution" seminar involved what Michael Cronin has called the "de-schooling" of translation and an "empowering" of students that allowed each to bring to the seminar new theoretical and analytical tools and perspectives that became the lens through which they translated Egypt's revolutionary text.[9]

During the past thirty years, and particularly since developments in postcolonial translation studies, the very status of translation and its politics have witnessed a significant shift from a predominantly linguistic to a decidedly cultural orientation. As Susan Bassnett correctly argued, translation "is now rightly seen as a process of negotiation between texts and between cultures, a process during which all kinds of transactions take place mediated by the figure of the translator."[10] The centrality of the cultural turn in translation studies and the nuanced appreciation of the role of the translator have preoccupied a plethora of books, articles, conferences, workshops on translation studies, and translation training, predominantly focused on three main ideas: a redefinition of the understanding of translation as reproduction and equivalence, foregrounding the visibility of the translator, and theorizing translation as an act of rewriting.

The very role of the translator has been increasingly redefined and recast as one of creative endeavor. In "How to Read a Translation," Venuti suggests that "we should view the translator as a special kind of writer, possessing not an originality that competes against the foreign author's, but rather an art of mimicry, aided by a stylistic repertoire that taps into the literary resources of the translating language."[11] Similarly, in *Gender in Translation* Sherry Simon notes that

> The translator, the agent of language, faces the text as a director directs a play, as an actor interprets a script. This cannot be the case when translation is taken to be a simple matter of synonymy, a reproduction of syntax and local colour.[12]

Translation as interpretation of script, not as mechanical reproduction, is what informs developments in translation studies during the 1990s and brings about new alliances with various disciplines opening up uncharted areas of research in the history, practice, ethics, and philosophy of translation. It is precisely these new alliances that have enabled and shaped this book project. The contributors to this volume have called upon their own disciplines to inform their task of translation. They have deployed insights and perspectives from across the fields of literary theory, cultural studies, comparative literature, philosophy, gender studies, Arabic literature, Middle East history, political science, journalism, anthropology, and, of course, translation studies. In so doing, not only were they compelled to rethink the limits of their own disciplines but they were equally empowered by translating across boundaries and beyond linguistic, cultural, and disciplinary borders without surrendering to the homogeneity, transparency, and dominance of the monolingualism of the target language, English. This volume therefore engages and reflects the interdisciplinary nature of the field of translation studies and its multiple directions in research and analysis.

Between Translation and *Tarjama*

In English, as well as in other European languages, the word 'translation' has more than one derivation from the Latin: *translatio, traduco, transferre*, all basically connoting the notion of "carrying across" or "leading across." But what is it exactly that gets "carried across" and at what levels does this act of carrying across implicate the actor, the carrier, or in other words, the translator? Similarly, in Arabic, the word for translation, *tarjama*—also a loanword from Aramaic and beyond that, Sumerian—is equally ambiguous and fluid. Tarjama concurrently means to translate from one language to the other, to interpret or expound the words of an "other," but also to write the other (as in biography: *tarjama*), and to write one's self (as in autobiography: *tarjama dhatiya*). In both English and in Arabic, 'translation' and *tarjama* seem to be acts of interpretation in which the self, as interpreter, is heavily implicated. No wonder then, that the derivative cognates, dragoman and *turjuman* (translator, interpreter in English and in Arabic), as well as their variants in several other languages, should be entangled in histories of betrayal that are dominated by the Italian linguistic accident of "traduttore, traditore" (translator = traitor).[13]

The chapters in this volume represent a form of resistance to this history of collaboration and betrayal as their authors consciously confront, interrogate, and problematize their task of "carrying across" the layered meanings and significations of Egypt's revolution at the interlingual, intercultural, and interlocational levels. As they do so, the authors call attention to their location between two sources as well as the unequal power relations that exist between them, not to mention their awareness throughout the chapters of the pitfalls of the reification of the "foreign" as well as those of hegemonic universalizing abstractions that are "masked by the illusion of transparent language."[14] The eight chapters in this volume are predominantly co-authored by partner contributors for whom geographic, linguistic, cultural, and political displacement and dislocation have served as *the* anchor. In *The Location of Culture*, Homi Bhabha significantly uses the term "translation" not to describe a transaction between texts and languages but in the etymological sense of being carried across from one place to another.[15] This understanding redefines the very act of translation as well as the role of the translator so that the former becomes an act of perpetual migration while the latter is cast in the role of a traveler. In this particular project, the contributors are at once literal and metaphorical travelers, whose migratory movement between languages, texts, geographies, and cultures has involved an understanding that "the translation zone" they occupy, to use Emily Apter's formulation, is not neutral, but rather fraught with the politics and ideologies they bring to it.[16] Given the participants' collective plurilingual and pluricultural backgrounds and experiences, it was obvious to them that the challenge for any translator was not just to operate within and negotiate that space in-between as he or she carries across a text from a source to a target language, culture, history, and context, but rather that the real challenge lay in understanding and coming to terms with the very politics of that "space-in-between" that is determined by power relations between texts and cultural contexts both of which predate the very act of translation. It is with this awareness that they have worked together to identify a *third space* from which to translate, beyond binary oppositions of here-and-there, self-and-other, and original-and-copy.

The task of locating a third space from which to produce what I have referred to earlier as "revolutionary" translation lay at the heart of all the group projects throughout the seminar starting with the very first assignment that set the bar: the translation of a selection from Abdel Rahman al-Abnoudi's ode to the Egyptian Revolution that accompanied the lyrics to the popular revolutionary song "Sut al-Huriya."

أيادي مصرية سمرا ليها في التمييز
ممدودة وسط الزئير بتكسر البراويز
سطوع لصوت الجموع شوف مصر تحت الشمس
آن الآوان ترحلي يا دولة العواجيز
عواجيز شداد مسعورين أكلوا بلدنا أكل
ويشبهوا بعضهم نهم وخسة وشكل
طلع الشباب البديع قلبوا خريفها ربيع
وحققوا المعجزة صحوا القتيل من القتل
اقتلني قتلي ما هيعيد دولتك تاني
بكتب بدمي حياة تانية لأوطاني
دمي ده ولا الربيع الاتنين بلون أخضر
وببتسم من سعادتي ولا أحزاني

Since we had divided the class into three groups, the participants were confronted with the necessity of making collective decisions on translation by negotiating individual differences; the groups were also intentionally constituted of native and non-native speakers of both the source language (Arabic) and the target language (English) to foster a collaborative rather than competitive approach to the process of translation. Not only were the participants being asked to translate poetry—which of all the literary genres is probably the most challenging for any translator—but they were being asked to translate a poem in colloquial Egyptian Arabic intended to be heard not read, and performed not written. In addition, the poem had already been translated into English in two versions and the text of these translations was scrolled on the screen to accompany al-Abnoudi's recitation in Arabic on the YouTube clip of the song "Sut al-Huriya."[17]

Each group produced one version of the poem that was essentially a translation *against* the existing literal renditions into English, which not only followed the original Arabic almost word-for-word but in doing so had also sacrificed language register, tone, music, rhythm, and rhyme, not to mention figurative language as well as social and cultural signification. Here are the two versions against which the three groups were working.

Version I
Dark Egyptian hands that know how to characterize
Reach out through the roar to destroy the frames
(Two missing lines)
The creative youth came out and turned autumn into spring
They have performed the miracle and raised the murdered from murder
Kill me, killing me will not bring back your country
In my blood I shall write a new life for my home
My blood is it or the spring? Both in green color
Am I smiling because of my happiness or my sorrows?

Version II
Egyptian hands understanding how to differentiate
Breaking the mirrors of deception
(Two missing lines)
The beautiful youth showed up to change its winter to spring
And made the miracle and awoke the deadened country from its death

Kill me, killing me won't return your rule again
I'm writing with my blood a new life for my country
This is my blood or is it the spring
Both of them are green
And am I smiling from my happiness or my sadness?

All three groups posted their respective translations of the same lines on the class blog they created at http://translatingrev.wordpress.com/ followed by each group's comments on the myriad problems, issues, and challenges they encountered, how they resolved them, and why they chose such solutions. Some of their comments addressed the division of labor among participants and how, in working together, they had developed an awareness of the translator's subjectivity, an appreciation of their difference and diversity that lay at the forefront of decision-making, and the interactive process of translation that remained incomplete without a profound appreciation and navigation of audience.[18] Other comments focused on the process of translation itself: how they created individual versions and then negotiated a common one, the decisions they had to make and then adopt together concerning the music, meaning, and orality of the text, having to read modern popular poetry in other languages to negotiate linguistic registers and tone, the extent to which they needed to foreignize and/or domesticate certain moments in the poem with a view on cultural contexts and differences; the para-textual sources they had to consult and the basis on which they ultimately came to agree on a 'final' collective version. They did all this with the full conviction that they had *collective ownership* of the translated text and that their collaborative endeavor was not at all final, but open to more conversation and more reflection about the processes that govern translation.[19] More importantly, they came to confront their task of translation as one that implicated them in an ethics of selection: what gets left out, what is brought in, and why; how one justifies such choices; and how their "visibility" as translators implicated them in the politics of translation. Here is one of these 'final' versions produced by one of the three groups as it appears in chapter 6 ("The Soul of Tahrir") in this volume.

The Midan
Egyptian hands, tawny and wise
Smashing the frames, in thunder they rise

Flared in one voice, see Egypt in the sun
O state of old men, your time is now done
You ravaged our lands, rabid and old
One like the other, in greed, filth, and mold
Wondrous buds bloomed, turned fall into spring
Raising the dead, the miracle youth bring
Shoot me! My murder won't bring back your state
For my people I write in my blood a new fate
My blood or the spring, both they are green
I smile—in joy or sorrow, remains to be seen.

I have dwelt at length on this example because the experiment of translating al-Abnoudi's verse, challenging as it was, provided the economy of praxis for what I have referred to as "revolutionary" translation: a collective, not an individual, endeavor that amassed its strength, currency, and politics from informed negotiation, not erasure, of difference between individual positions that are shaped by individual histories as well as diverse cultural and linguistic backgrounds; negotiations that ultimately guided members of each group to that third space from which to translate collectively and against all odds, and they were many. This first experiment became the rule for all other assignments, including most of the final chapters in this volume. As they continued to work as a group they came to realize that behind each text they were translating (including chants, jokes, street art, banners) lay a myriad of other texts that had to be translated before that singular text in the source language could be carried across to the target language. As Octavio Paz rightly argued:

Every text is unique and, at the same time, it is the translation of another text. No text is entirely original because language itself, in its essence, is already a translation: firstly, of the non-verbal world and secondly, since every sign and every phrase is the translation of another sign and another phrase. However, this argument can be turned around without losing any of its validity: all texts are original because every translation is distinctive. Every translation, up to a certain point, is an invention and as such it constitutes a unique text.[20]

In other words, there is no single truth enshrined in a text, no single meaning that can be elucidated but rather, a multiplicity of meanings that will in turn produce other meanings in translation that not only ensure an 'afterlife' for the source text but also a new life for itself, as translation, in the target language.

The eight chapters in this volume understand and translate the text of Egypt's revolution as a translation of other texts and in so doing produce 'thick translations' (to borrow Clifford Geertz's formulation of 'thick description'[21] in ethnography) of that open text in which the task of the translator/traveler is to "carry across" the different narratives and layers of the revolution as part of a complex set of dialectical relationships with other texts (political, economic, social, and religious) that exist outside its immediate "readable" boundaries.

The Seduction of Translation and the Language of Tahrir

Even though translation permeates, defines, and shapes our very identities and collective human existence, our attempts to understand and theorize the processes that form it are quite recent. Translation theory tells us that translating a text means a rewriting of the original, no matter how invisible that process attempts to be. This act of rewriting does not happen in a vacuum but is rather fraught with decisions about "safety," anxieties about risk, and fears of violence as we translate from the source to the target language.[22] As Gayatri Spivak has described it: "Translation is the most intimate act of reading," where the task of the translator is "to facilitate this love between the original and its shadow" by surrendering to the text, and its language as rhetoric, logic, and silence. To surrender to the "text" rather than to the author is to effectively "be in a different relationship with language, not even only with the specific text,"[23] nor for that matter, the specific author.

How does one translate the language of the text rather than the language of the author? One might answer this question by retracing one's steps to Ferdinand de Saussure's model of *langue* and *parole* in his seminal work *Cours de linguistique générale*, where he uses *langue* to describe the social, impersonal phenomenon of language as a system of signs, while he uses *parole* to describe the individual, personal phenomenon of language as a series of speech acts made by a speaking subject.[24] For example, one could think of translating the slogan that swept the Arab world and continues to resound in several countries beyond the region, "*al-Sha'b yurid isqat al-nizam*" ('The people demand the downfall of the regime'), at the level of *parole*, that is to say at the level of this individual utterance as it has been translated on revolutionary banners, in the media, and in many image books about the Arab uprisings. But one can and *should* translate it at the level of *langue* where this one-line slogan becomes part of a system of signs, a metonymy for a myriad of levels of political, cultural, and linguistic phenomena that demand to be translated. What did it really mean for Egyptians, whose entire uprising continues to resound in colloquial Egyptian Arabic, to borrow this slogan in formal Arabic from the Tunisians? What affinities lay behind this borrowing? What poetics of resistance are written into it that conjoin these region-wide uprisings? What did it mean for people on the street to refer to themselves as "*al-sha'b*" (the people), a word that had been emptied of its signification through decades of abuse by the regime? Why was it significant for the people to will, want, demand *(yurid)*, when that "will" had been denied, compromised, and eradicated for decades on end? And what exactly was meant by the word '*nizam*'? Was this a reference to a 'regime,' a 'system,' or an 'order'? And which *nizam*: local, global, or both? How does this initial chant and slogan translate itself *horizontally*, over time, as the people continue to invest it with new signification, indeed new translations of power relations between *al-sha'b* and *al-nizam*? On November 18, 2011, which marked the beginning of Egypt's 'Second Revolution,' and after months of chanting "*al-sha'b yurid*," a slogan that placed the people in a position of demand and supplication, the chant transformed itself and repositioned the people as the sole authority and power: "*IHna al-sha'b, la gish wala shurta, wala aHzab bit'assim turta*" ('We are the people; no army, no police; no parties dividing the cake, each a piece') and "*Yasqut, yasqut Hukm al-'askar, iHna al-sha'b, al-khatt al-aHmar*" ('Down, down with military rule; we, the people, are the red line'). Likewise, what did it mean for protesters in Tahrir to put up banners on their makeshift tents that read "*muntaga' al-Huriya*" (Freedom Resort)? What significations and connotations does the word '*muntaga'*' (resort) carry in the context of an Egyptian neoliberal economy that excluded the vast majority of the people? How does one construct the complex history that lies behind this seemingly simple two-word sign once it appears in the reclaimed space of Tahrir? And what did it mean for the army and police to repeatedly dismantle and burn these makeshift "freedom resorts" every time they were pitched in Tahrir? The eight chapters in this volume are all committed to this level of *thick translation* that engages the language(s) of Tahrir at both a horizontal and a vertical level in order to render a synchronic and diachronic reading and interpretation of the unfolding revolutionary text. As we consider the symbolic and semiotic translations of revolution (chapter 1), the revolution's dramatic performative moments and discourses (chapter 2), the signification behind revolutionary signs and banners (chapter 3), street art and the contest over public space (chapter 4), the challenges of translating revolutionary humor (chapter 5), the polyphonic poetic tapestry of Tahrir (chapter 6), translations of encounters between the army and the people (chapter 7), and finally, global translations of revolt (chapter 8), we attempt to render thick translations of the language of Tahrir that resist the seduction of translating the revolution as *parole* at the expense of translating it as *langue*.

One of the most remarkable accomplishments of the various uprisings in the Arab World since January 2011 has been the radical transformation of the relationship between people, their bodies, and space; a transformation that has enabled sustained mass convergence, conversation, and agency for new publics whose access to and participation in public space has for decades been controlled by oppressive, authoritarian regimes. Like other uprisings and revolutionary moments whose histories have first been written in great public spaces—from the Place de la Concorde during the French Revolution to the Occupy movements around the world today—people in the Arab World have reclaimed the right to be together as empowered bodies in public space exercising their right to linguistic, symbolic, and performative freedom despite the enormous price in human life that continues to be paid.

In the case of Egypt, the successive waves of the January 2011 uprising with its initial mesmerizing eighteen days in Tahrir have had a dramatic, immediate, and continuing impact on Egyptians and their relationship to space (both public and private; real and virtual) as has been witnessed in unprecedented online social networking, campaigns, and solidarities, as well as mass demonstrations, repeated sit-ins, and persistent protests despite the heavy cost in human life. This newfound power of ownership of one's space, one's body, and one's language is, in and of itself, a revolution.

Over the past thirty years the Mubarak regime, which continues to be reproduced by the ruling military junta in post-January 2011 Egypt, has exercised increased control of both public space and public culture.[25] These constraints have been orchestrated through the enforcement of emergency laws that legitimated detention and torture, the erratic but relentless censorship of freedom of expression, the privatization and dismantling of physical public spaces, and the depopulation of the city center. Such policing measures of public space and culture have minimized the possibilities of collective political activism and mobilization, thereby stifling and constraining oppositional and democratic movements for decades.[26] The January 25, 2011 uprising has unsettled these measures and policies and continues to resist oppressive counterrevolutionary attempts to dispossess the people of their newfound freedom. The eight chapters in this volume translate this new language of *tahrir* (liberation) and how Egyptians have articulated their ownership of space, body, and language through a myriad of creative performative and cultural practices whose semiotics, aesthetics, and poetics have not only inspired parallel uprisings worldwide but have also created sustaining solidarities as well as challenging resistances to the unfolding text of Egypt's revolution.

Chapter 1, "*Mulid al-Tahrir*: Semiotics of a Revolution," explores the newfound relationship between Egyptians and public space as well as the emergence of resignified subjectivities that developed during the initial eighteen days of revolt in Tahrir through translating the multiple significations and connotations of the word *mulid* (in colloquial Arabic)/ *mawlid* (in formal Arabic), which means 'birth.' The chapter explores how Egyptians succeeded in *translating* and revolutionizing their cultural heritage of *mulid* celebrations—a popular celebration of the birthday of a venerated spiritual figure—which became an integral part of the semiotic processes and rituals that brought forth and sustained the birth *(mawlid/ mulid)* of the "Independent Republic of Tahrir." By showing how *mulid*s are occasions that disrupt and redefine not just public space but public order as well, the chapter maps out the continuing contest over the real space of Midan al-Tahrir that transcended its local physical meanings to become a global contest over space(s) of *tahrir* (liberation) worldwide. In addition, Sahar Kreitim and I argue that Tahrir is not just about resignified public space and public order but rather that it is equally about resignified subjectivities at both the collective and individual levels.

Chapter 2, "Of Drama and Performance: Transformative Discourses of the Revolution," translates some of the most decisive and influential discursive and performative moments that shaped the early drama of the unfolding text of Egypt's uprising. By drawing on analytical tools from the fields of translation, performance, and gender studies, as well as social movement theory, Amira Taha and Chris Combs translate—at both the linguistic and semiotic levels—selections from these transformative moments that impacted millions of Egyptians on social and conventional media networks by such diverse actors as activists Asmaa Mahfouz and Wael Ghoneim, former President Hosni Mubarak and General Mohsen al-Fangary, among others, molding and shaping the reactions of publics during various decisive moments of the uprising. The authors read these discursive interventions as theatrical performances, the impact of which can only be understood through a thick translation that attends not just to the linguistic but to the affective, emotive, and semiotic levels of these transformative discourses.

Chapter 3, "Signs and Signifiers: Visual Translations of Revolt," reads and translates the throng of revolutionary banners and signs whose visual immediacy both established the demands of protesters and responded to the emerging political discourse as it unfolded, thereby becoming, in and of themselves, a *translation* of the awakening of public consciousness and a remarkable and fearless articulation of the right to language. Laura Gribbon and Sarah Hawas trace how these visual public signs inscribed a narrative of resistance that drew on various symbols and layers of historical, cultural, and political memory to write the story of a people in revolt. As the authors correctly point out, "a palpable sense of guilt, responsibility, and complicity underwrote many of these banners, drawing on a collective memory of censorship and participation in silence, and paving the way for a new moral economy." Through a translation of the unprecedented politics of display in Tahrir, that combined humor, satire, and creative energy, the authors show how Egyptians used their individual and collective bodies as canvases to represent the demands of the revolution, to dismantle and expose a history of empire and global complicities, and to celebrate solidarities, exceptional valor, and enormously tragic sacrifice.

Chapter 4, "Reclaiming the City: Street Art of the Revolution," draws on the concepts of striated and smooth space in Gilles Deleuze and Félix Guattari's *A Thousand Plateaus* to translate the politics of street art of the revolution as "a performance and product of aesthetic smoothing that resists the dominant striated narratives of the state." As Lewis Sanders argues, street art becomes a way for Egyptians to reclaim and reappropriate urban space, and provides "a new understanding of the city as rightfully belonging to the people." From the first tags that called for the downfall of the regime, to the rock formations made from chunks of broken pavement in Tahrir, and the elaborate murals memorializing the martyrs, street artists have challenged the state's instruments of monopolizing public space and homogenizing Egyptian life and identity. Over the past months, Egypt's Supreme Council of the Armed Forces (SCAF) has mounted a "war on graffiti" targeting political artwork that is now widespread in Egyptian cities. Graffiti works inciting protest, critiquing the military junta and the Central Security Forces, or articulating the demands of the revolution, have systematically been painted over, dismantled, or 'cleaned up.' In addition, several artists have been harassed and arrested by the SCAF for bringing art to the street, in a clear showdown and contest over both public space and the space of visual consumption that Sanders identifies as "the active involvement of passersby, of interlocutors, to transform the signifiers of street art into signifieds, to participate in the production, assimilation, and claim of this new signification."[27]

Chapter 5, "*Al-Thawra al-daHika*: The Challenges of Translating Revolutionary Humor," focuses on the various problems and issues but also the subtleties, ambiguities, and subversive referential worlds that surround the translation of humor from a source to target culture and the extent to which notions of 'fidelity' and 'equivalence' may not necessarily 'carry over' in translating humor across cultures. Kantaro Taira and Heba Salem translate a representative selection from the avalanche of political jokes that the Egyptian Revolution has generated—which have qualified it as "the laughing revolution"—analyzing the structure and dissemination of these jokes that were predominantly inspired by both traditional and social media discourses, forms, and languages. One of the most revolutionary aspects of some of these jokes is that they are being constantly updated and made relevant to the latest events on mobile phones, Facebook, and Twitter. Despite the challenges of translating jokes and other emerging forms of humor and satire on social media networks (videos, cartoons, Photographshop imaging, and so on) these new forms of comic relief have come to represent some of the most important weapons that have sustained Egypt's revolution in its most difficult and tragic moments while continuing to provide some of the most eloquent sources for historicizing it. The wrenching black humor of the jokes that circulated after the October 9, 2011 "Maspero Massacre" is a case in point.[28] Despite abundant evidence from video footage and eyewitness reports, the military junta continued to deny its responsibility for the attack that left twenty-eight dead and hundreds injured, providing contradictory statements and claiming that the military vehicles that ran over the demonstrators were not driven by army personnel but by a "third party," who basically leveled their bodies to the ground. Egyptians immediately turned this horrifically tragic incident and the junta's transparent denial of responsibility for the massacre of peaceful demonstrators into a joke that ridiculed the SCAF's incredible claims by parodying and satirizing the language and discourse of the SCAF's Facebook communiqués while mixing language registers in Arabic for further comic effect:

تحذير من انتشار ظاهرة سرقة المدرعات بتاعت الجيش:
رقم واحد : حاول ماتنساش مفتاح المدرعة في الكونتاكت.
رقم إتنين: ماتسبهاش دايره وتنزل تجيب حاجة.
رقم تلاتة : ماتسيبش المفتاح أبدا لسايس الجراج.
رقم أربعه : تركيب جهاز إنذار للمدرعة.

Warning: Widespread Theft of Military Armored Vehicles
Article I: Try not to forget the key in the ignition.
Article II: Don't leave it running while you go fetch something.
Article III: Don't ever leave the key with the garage attendant.
Article IV: Install an alarm system in the armored vehicle.

Likewise, after hundreds of demonstrators were deliberately shot in the eye by the Central Security Forces in January 2011 and again the following November, social media groups circulated a joke saying that the digital smiley sign— :) —would now be changed to .) —a joke that once more demonstrates the resilience of the revolutionary humorous spirit in the face of an orchestrated military machine set on maiming an entire people and their vision both physically and metaphorically.

Chapter 6, "The Soul of Tahrir: Poetics of a Revolution," shifts our attention to the aesthetics of a different register of language of Tahrir, namely the polyphonic tapestry of the lyrical and poetic life of the *midan* that served to sustain the transcendental effect of the revolutionary experience and unite Egyptians from all walks of life through chants, songs, and poems. As Lewis Sanders and Mark Visonà translate selections from this open epic of Tahrir, they situate individual texts within a larger inter-textual poetic context, reading the singular poem or song in the source language as one that draws on a myriad of other texts at a structural or thematic level. By doing so, they are able to capture how certain poetic elements became part of a common narrative across the lyrical tapestry of the revolution, particularly through the concepts of 'al-sha'b' (the people) and 'al-watan' (the homeland/country). The selections in this chapter map out the transformations of these signifiers, as they were given new meanings and new significance during the January 25, 2011 uprising through a perpetual process of appropriation and historical relocation. Significantly, many of the poems chanted, tweeted, and exchanged on scraps of paper during the January uprising against Mubarak have already acquired new meaning during the "Second Revolution" against the SCAF. The most prominent examples have been Abdel Rahman al-Abnoudi's lines, translated above, as well as Tamim Al-Barghouti's "Ya Masr hanit wi banit" (O Egypt, We Are So Close), both of which had been written in January against Mubarak, but, more than a year later, have come to speak to the SCAF's violence and counterrevolutionary design.

Chapter 7, "The Army and the People Are One Hand: Myths and Their Translations," addresses the question of how to translate the use of slogans in simultaneous support and opposition to the army from January 2011 well into the time of writing in August 2011. Egyptians have chanted *"al-Gish wa-l-sha'b id waHda"* ('The army and the people are one hand'), but they have also chanted *"Ya 'askari y abu bundu'iya, inta ma'aya walla 'alaya?"* ('You, soldier with a rifle; are you with me or against me?') and *"al-Sha'b yurid isqat al-mushir"* ('The people demand the removal of the field marshal'), among many other chants, songs, and banners with and against the *'askar* (military), all in less than two months from the beginning of the uprising in January, 2011. As Menna Khalil argues, the initial popular discourse of declared unity and anxious expectation that bound the people and the army showed the relationship between them as "contradictory, in flux, but necessary and somewhat inescapable." However, after ten months of SCAF violence, military trials, virginity tests for detained women protesters, mismanagement, stalling, and opaque maneuvering against the demands of the January 2011 uprising, these oscillating chants have finally culminated in a single unanimous demand in Tahrir and elsewhere in Egypt: *"Yasqut, yasqut Hukm al-'askar"* ('Down, down with military rule'). Through the varying terms of language (slogans, gestures, songs, and images) the author maps out how the fetishized myth of "the army and the people are one hand" is historically constructed and gradually undone even as demonstrators continue to differentiate between the army as 'family' with its historic allegiance to the people and the authoritarian SCAF that is generally viewed as part of Mubarak's regime, which continues to ally itself with the interests of the United States and Israel instead of the demands of the people.

Chapter 8, "Global Translations and Translating the Global: Discursive Regimes of Revolt," seeks to understand the discursive politics of translating Egypt's uprising by simultaneously situating its adaptations and appropriations as well as its deliberate mistranslations within a global neoliberal moment. Several interdependent nodes of translation inform this project: the traveling representations of Tahrir actively used in the global north as a framing device from Wisconsin's labor strikes in February 2011 to the "Occupy" movement worldwide; international official discourse, civil society movements, and western media employing "a politics of the intelligible" that "domesticate" translations of the uprising; and the continuing, deliberately constructed misrepresentations of the revolution and the revolutionaries by a counterrevolutionary political regime in Egypt whose "illegitimacy and increased lack of sovereignty has become nakedly visible." By focusing on a limited number of sites of translation, Sarah Hawas investigates the political possibilities and stakes inherent in (mis)translating the Egyptian Revolution as she attends to what gets left out, compressed, managed, and (re)packaged in the concurrent processes of reification, reinterpretation, and reframing of Egypt's uprising within a globalizing context that not only "depends on and requires the localization and containment of citizenship" but imposes a dominant "imaginary whose constituents include, but are not limited to: cosmopolitanism, multiculturalism, diversity, democracy, pluralism, co-existence, and most intriguing of all, *tolerance*."

Together, these chapters offer open and thick translations of the language of Tahrir as it continues to be written. Through the very choices of topics and texts, as well as our conscious "visibility" and location as translators, these chapters also bear testimony to the politics of selection that implicate us (as individuals and as a group) in a very particular "version" of the revolutionary text in translation. Many other layers have yet to be translated: narrative literary texts that bear eyewitness representations of the uprising, emerging forms of graphic and visual humor, the open epic chants of the revolution, translations of Islamist and of Coptic discursive and performative representations of revolt, the language(s) of electoral politics, to mention only a handful of subtexts. Given developments on the ground, and the discourses surrounding the very meaning(s) of Egypt's revolution, both local and global—not to mention the ongoing contest over public space, freedom of expression,[29] public culture, and cultural production—there is no doubt that this early collective and selective effort represents but the beginning of many more "versions" of the revolutionary text that have yet to be translated.

Notes

1 For affinities and differences between Tahrir and other global uprisings in public spaces see Mohamed Elshahed, "Occupied Spaces," *Architectural Record*, December 2011, http://archrecord.construction.com/features/2011/1112-Occupied-Spaces/

2 Umberto Eco's *Opera aperta* (Milan: Bompiani, 1962) has become one of the seminal works in the field of semiotics due to the enduring relevance of his concept of "openness" to literary and cultural theory and specifically for its insistence on multiplicity, plurality, and polysemy in art. For a detailed discussion of Eco's theory of the open work see Umberto Eco, *The Open Work*, trans. Anna Cancogni (Cambridge, MA: Harvard University Press, 1989).

3 Roland Barthes's distinction between the "readerly" *(lisible)* and "writerly" *(scriptible)* texts is one that marks the difference between traditional literary works, such as the classical realistic novel, and those works that violate its conventions, forcing the reader to produce a meaning or meanings which are inevitably open. In *S/Z* Barthes defines the "writerly" as "ourselves writing," thereby insisting on the infinite play and plurality of entrances, and the infinity of languages that this understanding might imply.

4 Lawrence Venuti, "How to Read a Translation," *Words without Borders*, October 9, 2009, http:// www.wordswithoutborders.org/?lab=HowTo

5 On November 18, 2011 the families of the martyrs and the injured of the January uprising, who had been camping in Tahrir to claim their rightful belated compensations, were attacked by the Central Security Forces. This brutal violation of their rights drew thousands of protesters back to Tahrir in Cairo and several other cities nationwide and escalated into street war on Muhammad Mahmud Street, right off of Tahrir, where Central Security Forces used tear gas, rubber bullets, and live ammunition against the rock-throwing protesters. See Mostafa Ali, "Death Stops Overnight in Tahrir," *AhramOnline*, November 23, 2011, http://english.ahram.org.eg/News/27448.aspx

6 Horatio Marpurgo, "Translating Egypt's Revolution," *Quarterly Review* 5 (Summer 2011): 40–47.

7 Roman Jakobson, "On Linguistic Aspects of Translation," in *The Translation Studies Reader*, ed. Lawrence Venuti (London: Routledge, 2000), pp. 113–18.

8 Lawrence Venuti, *The Translator's Invisibility: A History of Translation* (London: Routledge, 1995), p. 1.

9   Michael Cronin, "Deschooling Translation: Beginning of Century Reflections on Teaching Translation and Interpreting," in *Training for the New Millennium*, ed. Martha Tennent (Philadelphia: Johns Benjamins, 2005), pp. 249–66.

10 Susan Bassnett, *Translation Studies* (London: Routledge, 1992), p. 1.

11 Venuti, "How to Read a Translation."

12 Sherry Simon, *Gender in Translation* (London: Routledge, 1996), p. 143.

13 Elliott Colla, "Dragomen and Checkpoints," in *ArteEast*, Virtual Gallery Special Feature, September 2009, http://arteeast.org/pages/generate?id=64

14 Lawrence Venuti, *The Translation Studies Reader* (London: Routledge, 2000), p. 336.

15 Homi Bhabha, *The Location of Culture* (London: Routledge, 1994), p. 38.

16 Emily Apter, *The Translation Zone: A New Comparative Literature* (Princeton, NJ: Princeton University Press, 2006), p. 9.

17 To listen to "Sut al-Huriya" (Voice of Freedom) and part of Abdel Rahman al-Abnoudi's poem go to http://www.youtube.com/watch?v=HcZAJRcOtY; to listen to al-Abnoudi's recitation of the entire poem go to http://www.youtube.com/watch?v=kV_q7qlw1gU

18 See "Unsettling the Dust: 'Translating Revolution' Class Blog" at http://translatingrev.wordpress.com/

19 For a complete reading of all the 'Translating Revolution' group comments on this assignment, as well as many others, see the "Translating Revolution" class blog at http://translatingrev.wordpress.com/

20 Octavio Paz, "Translation Literature and Letters," trans. Irene del Corral, in *Theories of Translation: An Anthology of Essays from Dryden to Derrida*, ed. Rainer Shultze and John Biguenet (Chicago: Chicago University Press, 1992), p. 154.

21 In anthropology and other fields, a 'thick description' of a given human behavior is one that explains not just the behavior itself, but its context as well, such that the behavior becomes meaningful to an outsider. The term 'thick description' was used by anthropologist Clifford Geertz in his *The Intepretation of Cultures* (1973) to describe his own method of doing ethnography. Since then, the term and the methodology it represents have gained currency in the social sciences and beyond.

22 Gayatri Chakravorty Spivak, "The Politics of Translation," *The Translation Studies Reader*, ed. Lawrence Venuti (London: Routledge, 2000), pp. 397–416.

23 Spivak, "The Politics of Translation," p. 398.

24 See the Wikipedia article on Ferdinand de Saussure's *Cours de linguistique générale*, http://en.wikipedia.org/wiki/Course_in_General_Linguistics

25 For examples of censorship cases in the cultural field (literature, the visual arts, media, film, and the academy) see Samia Mehrez, *Egypt's Culture Wars: Politics and Practice* (London: Routledge, 2008).

26 For a more detailed reading of the control of urban public space and the impact of the January 25, 2011 uprising see Mohamed Elshahed, "Tahrir Square: Social Media, Public Space," *The Design Observer Group*, February 27, 2011, http://places.designobserver.com/feature/tahrir-square-social-media-public-space/25108/

27 See Mohammad al-Khouly, "Egypt's New Rulers Declare War on . . . Graffiti" (edited translation from the Arabic edition), *al-Akhbar English*, November 10, 2011, http://english.al-akhbar.com/node/1330/

28 The "Maspero Massacre" refers to the attack by military forces on Coptic demonstrators, joined by Muslims in solidarity, marching from the Shubra neighborhood to the Television Building in Maspero to protest the burning of a church in Aswan. Protesters were brutally attacked by the Military Police, leaving twenty-eight people dead and at least 325 injured, eleven of whom had been deliberately run over by military armored vehicles.

29 See Robert Springborg, "What Egypt's Military Doesn't Want Egyptians to Know," *Foreign Policy*, December 10, 2011, http://www.foreignpolicy.com/articles/2011/12/09/what_egypt_s_military_doesn_t_want_its_citizens_to_know#.TuKLxPD9HN4.facebook

1

Mulid al-Tahrir:
Semiotics of a Revolution

Sahar Keraitim and Samia Mehrez

Friday, January 28, 2011 marked a crucial turning point in the history and narrative of the Egyptian Revolution, which began on January 25, 2011 with massive demonstrations in several major Egyptian cities to demand the end of the corrupt Mubarak regime that had ruled Egypt for thirty years.[1] January 28, 2011 was the Friday of Rage (Gum'at al-ghadab); hundreds of marches took place nationwide in protest of the violent confrontations between the Central Security Forces and peaceful demonstrators. Those clashes, which occurred during the first couple days of the uprising, led to the fall of the first martyrs in the city of Suez on January 26, 2011 as well as the arrest and detention of hundreds of protesters and activists.[2] The Friday of Rage came the morning after the former Mubarak regime had interrupted Internet and cell-phone service nationwide. Prior to the blackout, Egyptians were able to view and compare news reports broadcast by state-sponsored media and dozens of other regional and international satellite channels that had been covering the violent confrontations between protesters and Central Security Forces in more than one major Egyptian city. Through such comparisons many Egyptians became dissatisfied with the state-sponsored media and when faced with the blackout, more people took to the street to remain informed.

In Cairo, as in all major cities whose demonstrators congregated in and tried to cordon off major public squares and spaces, protesters came from various areas and neighborhoods with one focal point as their destination: Midan al-Tahrir, the well-guarded navel of the capital whose seizure from armed Central Security Forces was to become one of the revolution's epic battles. The entire world has watched, over and over again, the legendary day-long scenes of valor, perseverance, and courage that took place on Qasr al-Nil Bridge and several other vital entry points to the *midan*—such as Abdel Moneim Riyad Square, Talaat Harb Street, Qasr al-Aini Street, Muhammad Mahmud Street, and Sheikh Rihan Street, among others—as thousands of Egyptians of all ages and from all walks of life won a dramatic and costly battle, in terms of the number of lives lost, against the Central Security Forces and took over Tahrir.[3]

Exhausted and outnumbered, the embattled Central Security Forces received orders to retreat, leaving the well-protected bastion, and prize of the Cairo uprising, empty to be reclaimed by the people who would, from this moment onward, make it their own. This moment marked the beginning of a new historic and symbolic life for Midan al-Tahrir, which became the site for the initial eighteen days of unprecedented revolutionary energy that continues to inspire the successive massive sit-ins and demonstrations in Tahrir. Friday, January 28, 2011 marked the crossing of the bridge of fear, of oppression, of class and social hierarchies, of gender divide and religious affiliation, of ideological orientations and political sympathies and agendas. A crossing over to the agency and empowerment of the people *(al-sha'b)* and their will *(irada)*, which was articulated and

The Battle of Qasr al-Nil Bridge, January 28, 2011. Photograph by Islam Azzazy (*Messages from Tahrir*, pp. 18–19)

immediately engraved on one of the largest permanent banners present throughout the historic eighteen days in Tahrir for the entire world to see: "*al-Sha'b yurid isqat al-nizam*" ('The people demand the removal of the regime'). This slogan and chant was inspired by the Tunisian Revolution and it continues to resound in all the Arab uprisings.

It is precisely this will of a whole people to bring down the regime and to bring about the basic demands of the revolution—change, freedom, and social justice *(taghyir, Huriya, 'adala igtima'iya)*—that needed to be sustained, protected, nourished, and enabled during and beyond the historic day of January 28, when Midan al-Tahrir was reclaimed and became the barometer for a nationwide uprising. This challenge was met

The People Demand the Removal of the Regime. Photograph by Ahmad Saad Bahig (*Messages from Tahrir,* p. 61)

through concerted organizational planning and strategizing on the part of a growing spectrum of civic and political groups and other actors, which included youth activist groups and coalitions, syndicates, NGOs, political parties, and popular movements. Despite their competing ideological differences, they came together to sustain the unique energy in Tahrir—which was both unifying and edifying—for the first eighteen days of the uprising. The *midan* was thereby transformed into what came to be called "The Independent Republic of Tahrir."[4] Together, protesters set up the new boundaries surrounding Tahrir: checkpoints that ensured the safety of those within the square, forms of political and cultural expression and mobilization that animated it, and the sustenance of daily life for the massive sit-in of thousands of protesters camped in the *midan*.[5] These arrangements included speaker podiums, 'Tahrir radio' broadcasts of patriotic songs and important announcements, makeshift clinics for the injured, the construction of restrooms for the protesters, a nursery for the children who accompanied their parents, a lost and found area, a prison set up inside the entrance to metro stations in Tahrir for the 'thugs' who tried to enter the *midan* to attack the protesters, an artist and caricature corner, a reading wall for media updates, a map of the *midan* to facilitate a daily head count of protesters, food and drinks to be delivered to protesters, and much more.

Since deposed president Hosni Mubarak finally stepped down on February 11, 2011, Midan al-Tahrir has continued to embrace demonstrations every Friday as well as the sustained and perseverant sit-ins, which finally led to his public trial on August 3, 2011.[6] Over the past several months, millions of Egyptians have responded to political activists and coalition groups' calls for protest and have flocked to the *midan* to press on with the demands of the revolution and to keep the spirits high whenever problems occurred, and they have been many. Despite repeated violent confrontations with the Military Police, Central Security Forces, and 'thugs' who have on more than one occasion attempted to disband the protesters and clear the *midan*, Tahrir has acquired a symbolic life of its own that has become the sign and language of an ongoing revolution. Tahrir continued to breathe that new symbolic life even after August 1, 2011, when protesters endured the more recent of such violent attacks to disband the longest sit-in, which started on July 8, 2011, when the State Security Forces and Military Police destroyed the 'tent city' in the *midan*. That sit-in was made up of the families of the martyrs along with activists joined in solidarity and demanded a public trial of police officers involved in the killings of the protesters who had been camping out.[7]

In fact, the inversion of the politics of space in Tahrir since the August 1, 2011 attack further confirmed the revolutionary connotations and significations of the *midan*, where the central garden of the roundabout, the stronghold of the protesters, became the contested icon of the revolution itself. The Central Security Forces and Military Police occupied the garden in what looked like a drawn-out sit-in throughout the month of August and beyond while protesters, who had been beaten and chased out of their tents, besieged them from the side streets leading into Tahrir. Official discourse from both the ruling Supreme Council of the Armed Forces (SCAF) and the interim government over the past several months had accused protesters in Tahrir of "obstructing the wheel of production," hence the need, according to the SCAF, to clear the square of the sit-ins—even if this was done violently. In the aftermath of the August 1, 2011 attack, after witnessing the ironic inverted 'sit-in' by the Central Security Forces and the Military Police in the roundabout, the

Tent city in Tahrir during the July 8–August 1 sit-in. Photograph by Samia Mehrez

Military and police forces occupy Tahrir's central garden, August 2, 2011. Photograph by Huda Lutfi

going joke among Egyptians was that the people demand the removal of the Central Security Forces from the *midan* because they are "obstructing the wheel of the revolution!"

But despite the ongoing violence, Tahrir has become a familiar space of pilgrimage with its own rituals and its own signs and language(s). Anyone who has been in Tahrir during the initial memorable eighteen days and later throughout the following months will no doubt have noted the festive, creative, uplifting ambience that has dominated the *midan*. They will also have noted how the general dispositions of the actors in the *midan* bore many traces of the *mulid* celebration, a popular form of carnivalesque festivities that has been celebrated in Egypt for hundreds of years and whose rituals, enacted by multitudes of demonstrators, were marshaled, politicized, and revolutionized during the massive protests and sit-ins to sustain and transform the impetus and impact of revolt.

This chapter will argue that one of the vital inspirational and organizational sources for the tactics and strategies of life in Midan al-Tahrir during the initial days of the revolution, and well beyond, was precisely this historic familiarity of the millions of people who came to the *midan* with the extended and elaborate rituals and festivities of the popular *mulid* celebrations. We are by no means claiming that this is the only way to read and *translate* what happened and continues to take place in Tahrir. Nor do we wish to diminish the complex political convergences of events, forces, leaders, and movements which led to this historic uprising, including regional and global factors external to Egypt, all of which continue to partake in the performativity of Egypt's revolution (see chapters 2 and 3).[8] On the contrary, once the protesters achieved a critical point of strength and mass density and support within the reclaimed *midan*, it needed to be sustained over an extended period of time; the experience and legacy of the *mulid* in Egyptian culture and history became a very salient and useful one.

In fact, one could argue that the *mulid*-like festivities in Tahrir were instrumental in attracting thousands of entire families with children and elderly relatives for whom the *mulid* spectacle in the Independent Republic of Tahrir became not just a mobilizing factor but also a radicalizing one. Indeed, as scholarship on the relationship between ritual and politics has shown, traditional rituals and symbolic practices are the potential 'lifeblood of revolution' that can provide an impetus for change and a powerful tool for delegitimation.[9] Despite initial resistance from various activist groups against the presence of peddlers and street vendors—who are normally an integral part of *mulid* celebrations—it quickly became clear that the celebratory *mulid*-like energy that installed itself in the *midan* would become one of the most effective didactic experiences for millions of Egyptians alongside a whole spectrum of creative tactics of mass protest, all of which effectively transformed traditional ritual into an inciting mode of revolt. There is no doubt that the element of time (a stretch of more than two weeks of waiting in the *midan* for Mubarak to finally concede to the will of the people) as well as the predominantly nonviolent circumstances that surrounded the first eighteen days, in comparison to other uprisings in the Arab world, allowed for the complex and intricate rituals of the *mulid* to settle in and animate Tahrir.

This chapter then will offer a semiotic translation of the processes and rituals of the *mulid* that developed in the *midan* and will try to understand and translate how Egyptians have marshaled and deployed a myriad of specifically familiar cultural rituals, symbols, and performative aspects of the *mulid* to nurture and maintain the utopian space that they gradually constructed in the *midan*, the symbolic site of the birth of their freedom *(tahrir)*. This is not an attempt at the fetishization of the *midan* itself or the Egyptian Revolution at large, for demonstrations and sit-ins were taking place all over Egypt. However, the claim of *al-sha'b* on Tahrir in particular that became a magnet for millions of Egyptians was and continues to be the test of the birth of liberation *(mawlid al-tahrir)*. Hence, the importance of the continuing Friday demonstrations that protect, celebrate, and commemorate that birth. A comparative study of the dynamics that dominated the respective *midan*(s) (Arabic plural: *mayadin*) of *tahrir* nationwide—indeed region-wide, if not worldwide—is in order; however, such an endeavor lies beyond the parameters of this particular project.

Translating the *Mulid* of Tahrir

One of the important developments in the field of translation studies during the 1970s was the acknowledgment that "although translation has a central core of linguistic activity, it belongs most properly to semiotics, the science that studies sign systems or structures, sign processes and sign functions."[10] Here, translation is made to encompass a whole set of extra-linguistic criteria that go beyond "the narrowly linguistic approach, that translation involves the transfer of 'meaning' contained in one set of language signs into another set of language signs through the competent use of the dictionary and grammar."[11] Moreover, semiotics does not just involve the study of what we refer to as 'signs' in everyday speech, but of anything that 'stands for' something else. The development and diversification of the field of semiotics during the twentieth century signifies an increase in awareness of the communicative powers of our entire environment. Indeed, semiotics is not only concerned with (intentional) communication but also with our ascription of significance to anything in the world. Once we are able to reach the level of abstraction in which a word is a sign, we can then readily perceive gestures and objects as signs with semiotic structures. The expansion of the communicative universe through the research and articulations of semiotics opens to semiotic analysis the entire field of our experience, in which any and all stimuli become potential meaning bearers. It is thus no wonder that semiotics has become an approach in several disciplines and fields of knowledge.[12] Translation, therefore, is not merely the simple and transparent transfer of one source text into a target text, for "no language can exist unless it is steeped in the context of culture; and no culture can exist which does not have at its center, the structure of natural language."[13]

This understanding of extra-linguistic translation and transfer of meaning is precisely what challenges the notion of equivalence for, as Edward Sapir argued:

> No two languages are ever sufficiently similar to be considered as representing the same social reality. The worlds in which societies live are distinct worlds, not merely the same world with different labels attached.[14]

The title of this chapter—"Mulid al-Tahrir"—in and of itself encapsulates multiple connotations that are not necessarily translatable into an equivalent sign system, for more than one linguistic and cultural referent is already embedded within the word '*mulid*.' At the linguistic, semantic level, the word '*mulid*' in spoken Egyptian (*'ammiya*), '*mawlid*' in classical Arabic (*fusHa*), is the verbal noun derived from the root '*walada*,' which means 'to give birth, to beget, to generate, to bring forth.' At the cultural level, when the word *mulid* is used to refer to the popular religious festivities that are known all over Egypt, it simultaneously means—in both *'ammiya* and *fusHa*—the birth of the revered person or 'saint' and the celebration of that revered person's birth. For example, '*mulid/mawlid al-nabi*' refers to the Prophet Muhammad's birthday as well as the celebration of that event (in this sense, not unlike 'birthday' in English, which refers to the day on which someone is born and the celebration of its anniversary in subsequent years, though in the case of *mulid*, the reference is always to the celebration of the birthday of a religious figure). Given the sheer number of participants in these celebrations and the potential violence that may erupt, the word *mulid* also connotes, at a more idiomatic level, 'disorder' if not chaos. The chaotic aspect of these celebratory festivities is captured in the Egyptian popular saying "*mulid wi saHbu ghayib*" ('a *mulid* whose master is absent'), at once a reference to the absent celebrated spiritual figure and the absence of a figure who could control, regulate, and marshal the order of this potentially chaotic setting. It is the absence of an authority figure or authority in general that injects the word *mulid* with its subversive connotations. Indeed, the word *mulid* has acquired a proverbial status to the extent that it is used to describe chaotic situations in general. For example, in Egyptian slang, a traffic jam or a day spent in the labyrinths of the unregulated Egyptian bureaucracy may also be referred to as a *mulid*.

The title of this chapter therefore tries to capture and *translate* these multiple references. *Mulid al-Tahrir* is at once the birth of *tahrir* (liberation) and the celebration of its birth, and the subsequent anniversary of the birth of that liberation in the potentially hazardous reclaimed public space of Tahrir (the *midan* itself) through the mobilization, at one level, of the rituals of *mulid* celebrations that within this revolutionary context, acquire new politicized signification. The decision to maintain the first half of the title in Arabic *(Mulid al-Tahrir)* is therefore deliberate and doubly significant: for in the source language and culture (Arabic) it harnesses both a linguistic and cultural signification that problematizes its translation to another language (in this instance English) that does not necessarily have an equivalent that would *translate* the same levels of signification from the source to the target culture. Hence, as postcolonial theorists of translation studies have pointed out:

> [T]he word translation seems to have come full circle and reverted from its figurative literary meaning of interlingual transaction to its etymological physical meaning of locational disrupture; translation itself seems to have been translated back to its origins.[15]

To recognize "locational disrupture" in translation is to understand the complexities of cross-cultural translation that attempts to reconcile cultures that may be linguistically and culturally not just different from each other but also unequal to each other. This basically means, as James Clifford has argued, that cross-cultural translation is never neutral; it is enmeshed in relations of power.[16] How does the translator negotiate such relations of power at a time when globalization has intensified cultural contrasts as well as the focus on the representation of the 'Other' in postcolonial theory, where the terms of geographical, linguistic, and cultural 'foreignness' have been highly emphasized? It is precisely for this reason that Susan Basnett and Harish Trivedi insist on the centrality of an increasing awareness of the unequal power relations and difference inherent in the transfer of texts across cultures, as it involves political and ethical dimensions.[17] Translation emerges as "an active reconstitution of the foreign text mediated by the irreducible linguistic, discursive, and ideological differences of the target-language culture."[18] Seen as such, difference becomes, not an element to overwrite for the sake of 'transparency' and 'homogeneity,' but the locus upon which we may construct enabling theoretical, textual, and practical means of cross-cultural communication. Difference, as translation theorists have rightly insisted, is to be read as a gain. Hence our strategy in maintaining the Arabic title Mulid al-Tahrir that lies at the core of our reading and translation of Egypt's revolution in this chapter.

Codes of Conduct between the *Mulid* and the Revolution

The estimated number of *mulid*s celebrated in Egypt every year ranges from two hundred to upward of two thousand, including Muslim, Christian, and (one) Jewish celebrations, which are attended by members of these religious communities and cut across class, religious, and gender divides.[19] Indeed, the tradition of celebrating the Prophet's birthday that began during the Fatimid period in the eleventh century, as well as those of many other venerated figures in Islam, is one that punctuates the Muslim calendar in Egypt. This fact in and of itself attests to the wide familiarity of millions of Egyptians with the codes of conduct in such massive popular gatherings, which can witness the presence of hundreds of thousands who flock to these venerated sites with their families and children to partake in the celebrations. Despite state strategies and efforts to contain and constrain these popular festivities, *mulid*s have survived and continue to shape the popular imagination and to inspire aesthetic and creative production.[20] Even though these celebrations are meant to remember and commemorate the legacy of prominent religious figures and their saintly/spiritual qualities and attributes, most of the manifestations of these festivities are intricately tied to the worldly, firmly anchoring them in the social, the economic, and the political, and not just the spiritual.

These general manifestations of the dynamics of the *mulid* informed the way demonstrations proceeded in Midan al-Tahrir during the revolution as well. We want to suggest that the enactment of the popular and familiar *mulid* festivities and symbolic rituals in the reconstructed public space of the *midan* was a familiar communal dynamic force that nourished what began to be referred to as the "Independent Republic of Tahrir." Even those demonstrators who may have never attended a *mulid* would have been familiar with its festive symbolic rituals through multiple literary and visual representations, the most prominent of which is poet Salah Jahin's classic puppet show operetta *al-Layla al-kabira* (The Great Night), which was produced during the 1950s and continues to be performed live and broadcast nationwide during all major *mulid* celebrations. The new semiotics of Tahrir succeeded in drawing millions of people because at one level they represented familiar orientations for the actors/demonstrators themselves. People came in families because they understood the codes and enacted them accordingly. There was no stampeding, no harassment, no violence, and no strife. In our translation of this historic moment, the ability to instantly adopt such harmonious behavior had to do, to a great extent, with the déjà vu of *mulid* festivities and celebrations during which very similar codes are adopted over an extended period of time. Midan al-Tahrir had become a "festival of the oppressed" regardless of gender, religion, age, or class as it began to acquire its new signs that, over the days, drew more and more on familiar rituals of *mulid* celebrations.[21] Indeed, one may further argue that the initial unconscious past participation of the multitudes of demonstrators in *mulid* congregations later more consciously informed the way they adapted the new political and revolutionary congregation to that familiar form (the *mulid*), which sustained both the revolutionary animus of demonstrators and the need to persevere and remain steadfast in the face of the intransigence of the regime and its repressive response on multiple occasions.

The re-signified use of public space during *mulid* celebrations is central to these celebratory festivities.[22] *Mulid*s are normally celebrated around the site of the venerated person's body, relic, or shrine and can last for a whole week, drawing thousands of pilgrims from villages and towns and culminating in the frenzy and excitement of the "Great Night" (*al-layla al-kabira*), the very last night of a *mulid* celebration, which is the climax of festivities. The popular *mulid* then is thoroughly grounded in a particular symbolic and significant space and place that becomes the focal point for its energy. During the January 25 Revolution Midan al-Tahrir became that re-signified space. As with popular *mulid*s and designated shrine areas, the public space of the *midan* that had for long been reduced to being a traffic roundabout in the heart of the congested city was symbolically reconstructed and acquired new signification. The *mulid* (birth) of Tahrir (liberation) therefore became a *translation* of the profound social, political, and cultural transformations the country was undergoing. But it was simultaneously clear that for this 'birth' to be sustained, for the sit-ins to continue en masse, for revolutionary demands to be met, and for millions to be mobilized daily, Tahrir would have to be a *mulid*, an ongoing platform for celebration, commemoration, protest, solidarity, and festivity.

In her description of *mulid*s, Anna Madoeuf emphasizes that these celebratory *mulid* spaces are "characterized not only through dialog and contact, but also through the remixing of categories, social types, spatial codes, and norms."[23] And indeed, such was the case in the *midan*: the unique diversity in the *midan* was one of the most vital pillars of the rising sense of national identity and the unified concept of citizenship.[24] Perhaps for the first time in Egyptian history, all classes, and sectors of Egyptians joined together around the same goal, the same demands, and the same aspirations. This newfound sense of national belonging that rendered concrete the otherwise discursive 'national unity' *(wiHda wataniya)* slogan often trumpeted by the former Mubarak regime in moments of sectarian crisis undoubtedly reinforced the sense of civic responsibility and cohesion of *al-sha'b* (the people)—another concept that had been reduced to a discursive trope and emptied of its real signification. When instances of 'sectarian strife' staged by state thugs and cronies of the former regime manifested themselves in the attack on Coptic churches and homes, the *midan* continued to provide the space for reconciliation to which people returned to confirm a newfound sense of national belonging and unity in diversity. Even on July 29, 2011, when the Muslim Brotherhood and Salafi groups dominated the *midan* and seemed to hijack the secular demands of the revolution with Islamic chants, Saudi flags, calls for an Islamic state, and demands for the application of shari'a, this rather alarming show of force for the secular/liberal activists and political forces was still deemed a success of the revolution at large, for it reconfirmed the symbolic status of Tahrir as a re-signified space of liberation.[25] Similarly, throughout the sit-ins and demonstrations, and until the time of writing, the *midan* provided the space for solidarities with neighboring Arab revolutions and uprisings, which also worked as unifying poles for the demonstrators and reinforced a sense of imagined community beyond the immediate and limited Egyptian one.

Semiotics of a *Midan*

Midan al-Tahrir lies at the very heart of modern Cairo and its map of protest and uprising. It was formerly known as Midan al-Ismailiya after Khedive Ismail, who directed the construction of modern Cairo during the second half of the nineteenth century. Since its existence, it has commanded the main arteries of the city and has been the site of some of its most symbolic structures and histories.

It became, and remains, "the navel of the city" and is the site of the most important services whether they be government, companies, banks or commercial stores. The reorganization of Ismailiya Square under the July 23 Revolution, that turned it into Tahrir (Liberation) Square, also had obvious political connotations, not only in the new name of the square but also in many of the buildings that were to border it: the Arab League, built in 1964, the Mugamma', the image of an over-bloated bureaucracy, and the Nile Hilton, the first international hotel to become functional in Nasser's Egypt. . . . Just north of the hotel lies the salmon-colored Egyptian Museum and, behind it, the headquarters for Mubarak's National Democratic Party, with its monotonous Modernist facade left charred by a fire set during this the revolution.[26]

As early as 1919, Midan al-Ismailiya/Tahrir emerged as the epicenter of uprisings and *the* space that epitomizes protest par excellence during both colonial and national histories. It is repeatedly represented in both prose and poetry and has become an integral part of a collective national imagination and history of protest and liberation. The battle for Tahrir that we all witnessed on January 28, 2011 was not new, for the *midan* has forever represented the focal point during various uprisings and demonstrations throughout modern Egyptian history. It witnessed and symbolized many chapters of Egyptian resistance. The late student leader and activist Ahmed Abdalla recounts one of the *midan's* most dramatic encounters with political demonstrations against continued British presence in Egypt in 1946, as follows, when massive demonstrations were organized, and included students marching from Giza to the center of Cairo:

> When the demonstrators reached Ismailiya Square, they were confronted by the British garrison and began to burn the barracks and fences. In response, four British army vehicles moved towards them and a barrage of machine-gun fire opened up. According to the most reliable estimate, twenty-three demonstrators were killed and some one hundred and twenty injured. . . . The government disclaimed all responsibility and blamed students for allowing their "peaceful demonstrations" to degenerate into violence "because of infiltration by the mob of riffraff . . . in which students and educated people simply disappeared from view." . . . The 4th of March was proclaimed Martyrs' Day in memory of the students killed in February.[27]

Hence, history, geography, and architecture have joined together to locate Tahrir in the very heart of Egypt's revolutionary narrative in both colonial and post-colonial times, making it the symbolic space it has become. No wonder, then, that the decisive battle of the revolution on January 28, 2011 was valiantly fought and won to reclaim this symbolic space. Indeed, anyone reading Abdalla's description of the 1946 demonstrations cannot but be struck by the almost identical repetition not just of the same violent confrontations between protesters and the state in 1946 and on January 28, 2011 but more ironically the very same claims made by the state against the demonstrators then and now. Abdalla's description was to be repeated time and again in different moments of modern Egyptian history with Midan al-Tahrir always at the center of the contest.

Over the past thirty years Midan al-Tahrir had become increasingly inaccessible to public protest under Mubarak's Emergency Law, which continues to be enforced by the SCAF even after the January 25 uprising. One of the exceptional moments when demonstrators succeeded in overtaking Tahrir, the Mubarak regime's most well-guarded bastion, is represented in Palestinian poet Mourid Barghouti's autobiographical narrative *I was Born There, I was Born Here*, published in 2011, where the privileged students of the American University, led by Barghouti's own son, Tamim (now a leading poet in his own right), broke all the stereotypes that had long framed them and spearheaded Cairo's largest demonstration against the American invasion of Iraq and successfully seized Tahrir.

They set off spontaneously for Tahrir Square and occupied it before the government could put its fortifications in place. A little later, the Cairo University students and waves of local citizens poured in. The government had lost control of the situation.

The Egyptian government spends millions of pounds to protect this particular square and only very rarely in recent history have the students of Cairo University been able to get to it because the Security Forces close the university's gates on demonstrators and imprison them inside the campus, making it impossible for them to get out.

The government found that the square had fallen early and to a threat from an unexpected direction. The students of the American University in Cairo are mostly the children of the ruling class or of the social elite that can pay its fees and in the estimation of the security apparatus nothing is to be feared from these people. The state went crazy.[28]

Overview of Midan al-Tahrir during the January–February sit-in. Photograph by Samia Mehrez

The important difference of course between the January 25 uprising and the above historical and literary representations of protest in Tahrir, by Abdalla and Al-Barghouti respectively, is that on January 28, 2011 the people *(al-sha'b)* succeeded in making Tahrir their own and through this new ownership rewrote its very history. The battle of January 28, 2011 was the marker that transformed Midan al-Tahrir in the collective imagination from a place of strife to a space of harmony, from a temporary site of protest to a permanent symbol of the people's will, from a war zone to a liberation zone, from a physical space to a symbolic one.

Demonstrators effectively transformed the *midan* into a re-signified space: a sanctuary *(Haram)*, as cultural historian and visual artist Huda Lutfi described it in a lecture at AUC in February 2011.[29] Almost immediately, this reclaimed symbolic space acquired boundaries that designated the limits between outside and inside Tahrir. Protesters surrounded it with whatever they could get their hands on: corrugated iron slabs and

Memorial for the martyrs of the revolution. Photograph by Mia Gröndahl (*Tahrir Square*, pp. 132–33)

barbed wire from neighboring construction sites, broken traffic lights and signs, chunks of rock from broken pavements, bodies of charred police vehicles, security barriers left behind by the soldiers, and so on.[30] Demonstrators joining the activists in Tahrir were body-searched, or 'cleansed,' at the borders of the *Haram*—stripped of potential tools that might disrupt or threaten the utopian harmony of the Tahrir sanctuary. Once in the square to stay, demonstrators and activists organized a national campaign to clean the *midan*. This act, in and of itself, may be read on a symbolic level. True the *midan* needed to be cleaned from debris of rocks and signs of destruction after the brutal confrontations with the Central Security Forces, but it also needed to be *cleansed* of strife, of destructive energy, before a harmonious space could be envisioned. We all saw hundreds of Egyptians, young and old, almost obsessively engaged in sweeping the *midan*. Anyone familiar with Egyptian popular practices will not have failed to see small brooms suspended at doors and entrances as a symbol for cleansing domestic and public spaces of evil spirits and the evil eye. The act of sweeping *(kans)*, therefore, is itself a symbolic cleansing act that is actually understood at the level of the popular imagination

Martyr installation: photographs, garlands, and Quran. Photograph by Mia Grond-hal (*Tahrir Square*, p. 122)

as an act of exorcism, of sweeping and chasing away evil spirits—in this instance, those of the former Mubarak regime. Indeed, the ritual of *kans* had already been mobilized by activists during demonstrations against the former regime during 2005.[31] Equally quickly, demonstrators set up a temporary memorial for the martyrs of the revolution, a shrine for those who gave their lives for *tahrir* (liberation) in the *midan* itself and elsewhere in the city and the country at large.

The symbolic sanctuary of Tahrir was transformed into a *mazar* (a revered symbolic space to visit, a site of pilgrimage and homage to commemorate and collectively remember and preserve). Even after the Military Police raided the *midan* and destroyed the temporary memorial, the families of the martyrs, whose numbers were increasing by the day, continued to bring framed photographs and posters of those who lost their lives, congregating together in what looked like installations of martyrdom with flowers, copies of the Qur'an, memorabilia, and so on.

These martyrdom sites also became pilgrimage sites for thousands of Egyptians in solidarity with the families of the martyrs. Indeed, the longest sit-in (July 8–August 1) was in support of these families' demands for retribution and the public trial of those responsible for the death of hundreds and the injury of thousands of others.

Violation and Protection of the Sanctuary of Tahrir

As we have already mentioned, *mulid*s are not simply exotic festive celebrations. On the contrary, *mulid*s are potentially dangerous and threatening mass mobilizations and have historically been understood and treated us such by the authorities who have consistently tried to police and control them, but also use them to legitimate and enforce their power.[32] Indeed, *mulid*s are occasions that disrupt and redefine not just public space but public order as well. Even though the core site of the *mulid* is the revered person's shrine or mosque, the various activities that constitute the *mulid*—processions, parades, Sufi *dhikr* circles (trance incantations), *inshad* (religious chanting) and *madiH* sessions (songs in praise of the Prophet Muhammad and his family), artistic performances, traditional folk songs, games, swing boats, shooting stands and food stands, and so on—take place in the more fluid space of the neighborhood, village, or town, thus creating an atmosphere of chaos and disorder. Acknowledging the power and importance of these mass popular festivities and the impossible mission to get rid of them, successive governments have decided to take advantage of them for their own political purposes. It is widely known that the state used to propagate itself in the *mulid*s, through posters, pro-regime imams, and so forth. During the most popular *mulid*s, where more than a million people might attend, the government would post pictures of the president, exhibit military displays and fireworks, but would also send official representatives and Central Security Forces to monitor and control the potentially disruptive nature of the occasion.

During the January 25 Revolution, similar attempts at control, indeed, violation, occurred in Midan al-Tahrir. Several vicious attempts were made initially by the former regime and later by the ruling SCAF to violate the *mazar* and *Haram* of Tahrir. The first dramatic instance was on the day that has come to be known as 'The Battle of the Camel' *(mawqi'at al-gamal)* immediately following Mubarak's second speech on February 2, 2011, during which former National Democratic Party (NDP) cronies tried to disperse the demonstrators and violate the sanctity of the *midan* by attacking protesters with swords and sticks on horse and camel back, as well as hurling rocks and Molotov cocktail bottles from off the nearby October 6 flyover and other side streets downtown. On that day another

Battle of the Camel, February 2, 2011. Photograph by Omar Attia (*The Road to Tahrir*, pp. 62–63)

valiant battle was fought and won at the borders of Tahrir with many protesters courageously paying with their lives to safeguard the symbolic space that witnessed the birth of liberation. These scenes of violation have reoccurred over several months at the hands of both the Military Police and the security forces; however, even when they succeeded in suspending the physical presence of protesters in the *midan* and the *mulid* within it they have failed to strip it of its new re-signified symbolic meaning for Egyptians.

Mulid al-Tahrir and the Subversive Carnivalesque

The *mulid*, like Bakhtin's description of the carnival, represents a moment of utopian freedom, the brevity of which increases its fantastic and subversive nature.[33] *Mulids* momentarily undo established social, gender, and class boundaries, allowing villagers and town folks, poor and rich, young and old, men and women to share the same public sphere. In so doing, they also allow for the mixing of languages and dialects that *mulid* participants use to perform, to speak, to sing, and to interact. Moreover, *mulids* are occasions that permit the suspension of order across the gender divide. Men and women dance, stroll, and physically interact in ways that would be deemed totally unacceptable in normal everyday settings. Most of all, *mulid*s are fun: performances, spectacles, and parades are meant to entertain and bring about laughter. They are normally exaggerated and sometimes obscene, frequently resorting to sarcasm and mockery to mimic, critique, or contest established order and authoritative figures. *Mulid*s are therefore potentially dangerous and defy authority and accepted forms of pious and public conduct.

In fact, *mulid*s reinvent and invert the game of power: rogue and sultan trade roles in these performative festivities. The downtrodden and the dispossessed seize control of public space, unsettling, even if momentarily, hegemonic religious practices and discourses as well as oppressive political power and structures. In any given *mulid*, participants will mix freely between the spiritual and the worldly, simultaneously partaking in religious processions, Sufi *dhikr* circles, *inshad* and *madiH* sessions, supplications for *baraka*, and prayers to the venerated figure with café hopping, pop and folk music, dancing and singing, eating, smoking, and having fun.

So also did the millions of Tahrir demonstrators mix the religious and revolutionary, the spiritual and the mundane, the political, the commercial, and the recreational. The ambiance of the demonstrations combined revolutionary edge with festive elements and scathing political humor (chapter 5). Public performances, sketches, street art, graffiti, poetry, and chanting all sprang up in and around the *midan* in a manner that redefined the very role and place of cultural production that is the subject and focus of several other chapters in this volume. This was the culture of the people for the people, all inspired by Tahrir. It was in the aftermath of this jubilant creativity that Egypt witnessed its new public art festivals that are significantly called "al-Fann Midan" ('Art is a Midan') in more than one reclaimed public space in Egypt. The first of these was held in Midan Abdin, across from Abdin Palace, which had always been a state-guarded space.[34] The re-signified space of Tahrir therefore also led to a re-signified relationship to public space(s) in general, not to mention the kind of performers (predominantly from Tahrir), the nature of performances, and the audiences that overwhelmingly came from the neighborhood itself—many of whom had been denied such cultural participation under the elitist and commoditized cultural practices, policies, and politics of the former regime.

Similarly, traditional *mulid*-specific performative rituals were also re-signified, politicized, and adapted to the revolutionary context in Tahrir. A resourceful kind of creative energy erupted in the *midan*, making use of familiar popular cultural practices like the *zaffa* (procession) and the *zar* (exorcism) that are characteristic of *mulid* celebrations. In calling upon such popular practices within a revolutionary context, Egyptians invested them with newly invigorated meaning. It is a well-established tradition that almost every *mulid* is preceded by a *zaffa*, a procession leading through the area where the *mulid* takes place. The processions comprise members of the Sufi *tariqa*s (mystical schools) wearing colorful costumes and playing tambourines, cymbals, and drums. Likewise, Mulid al-Tahrir has witnessed several kinds of *zaffa*s: there was the daily *zaffa* for the incoming and departing demonstrators where they would be received by a group of protesters as they entered the boundaries of the *midan* with welcoming chants such as "*Ahlan, ahlan, bi-l-thuwwar*" ('Welcome, welcome, to revolutionaries') and greeted again upon departure with other chants like "*Muslim masiHi id waHda*" ('Muslim and Christian, one hand') or "*Ma'adna bukra maninsash*" ('Don't forget, come tomorrow');[35] there were also the multiple *zaffa*s of newly married couples who came to the *midan* to celebrate their wedding among the demonstrators and army tanks;[36] there were other *zaffa*s especially devoted to Mubarak after his resignation.[37] It is important to point out the significance of the

Tents during the first sit-in in Tahrir. Photograph by Nermine Hammam

zaffa in the Arab and Islamic tradition because the main reason for the *zaffa* is *al-ishhar*, or the public announcement of the event. The *zaffas* of Tahrir performed the same function within a radically different context, specifically those that publicly announced the end of the relationship between Mubarak and the people *(al-sha'b)*. Similarly, *dhikr*, one of the most important performative aspects in a traditional *mulid*, was also part of the Tahrir energy. *Dhikr* is a performative ritual of chanting religious lyrics and praises to the Prophet Muhammad or saintly figures by Sufis as they move their bodies rhythmically, swinging their heads from side to side while chanting "Allah," or any one of the other ninety-nine names of God in Islam, or by simply chanting "*huwa*" ('He'). *Dhikr* is a social event as well as a religious dance, a ritual to open the mind to God's influence and to lead to increased spiritual awareness and oneness with the creator. *Dhikr* is closely related to the *zar*, the more popular ritual of exorcism of evil spirits. The *zar* was given a comic twist in Mulid al-Tahrir as dervish-like circles of people performed the ritualistic dance typical of the *zar* tradition and recited incantations tailored to the occasion, calling on Mubarak to leave: "*IrHal, irHal*" ('Leave, leave') and to chase away the evil spirits haunting the revolution.[38]

People sleeping at the foot of an army tank. Photograph by Nermine Hammam

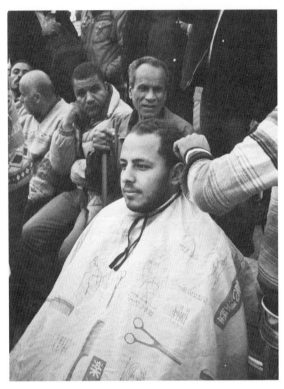

Barber of the Revolution. Photograph by Nermine Hammam

Managing the Political Economy of Mulid al-Tahrir

Despite the proverbial connotations of the word *mulid* that likens its festive celebrations to chaos, the organization and realization of such festivities demand rather strict organizational procedures: streets, facades, and mosques are decorated with colored light bulbs, tents have to be set up, stages and amplifiers get fixed, food stalls are installed, overnight places have to be found—a lot of neighborhood residents offer their building entrances, rooftops, and vacant rooms for those coming to attend the *mulid*. One of the most challenging aspects of the *mulid* is the management of enormous crowds that include families and small children. Human shields and human corridors are spontaneously created to protect participants and a sense of togetherness, camaraderie, and closeness is the hallmark of a collective mood of merriment. All such rigorous organizational procedures became a daily affair in Mulid al-Tahrir as the sit-ins extended over time and the management of the political economy of the symbolic space of Tahrir became one of the most spectacular aspects of

Peddlers at the Mulid: chickpea vendor. Photograph by Nermine Hammam

Peddlers at the Mulid: lupine-bean vendor. Photograph by Nermine Hammam

Memorabilia of the revolution 1. Photograph by Samia Mehrez

Memorabilia of the revolution 2. Photograph by Samia Mehrez

50   Sahar Keraitim and Samia Mehrez

Memorabilia of the revolution 3. Photograph by Samia Mehrez

the revolution. These codes of communal solidarity and cohesion were crucial for sustaining and multiplying the crowds for they offered not just a sense of security in the *midan* but, more importantly, a new consciousness of what a *mulid* really meant within a revolutionary context. The collective sense of responsibility and public safety among all the protesters was the rule of the day, with hundreds sleeping at the foot of the army tanks surrounding the *midan* to safeguard the boundaries of 'The Independent Republic of Tahrir' and to make sure that these 'neutral' military vehicles did not close in on protesters during the night. Food, water, and safety measures were carefully provided.

The *midan*, which initially resisted the commercial aspect of the *mulid*, gradually came to accommodate the increasing number of vendors, selling food and memorabilia, who constituted the informal political economy of Tahrir. The festive features of the *mulid*s were all rallied to the cause of the revolution, including peddlers of all kinds whose carts were adorned with flags and revolutionary slogans as well as photographs of the martyrs.

The colorfulness of the *mulid* reflected the colors of Arab flags from Egypt, Palestine, Libya, Syria, Yemen, and Bahrain, which fluttered in every size and were reproduced on all kinds of memorabilia of the revolution: tag necklaces, head bands, T-shirts, paper whistles, cone-shaped hats, and tiny purses, among other souvenirs.

Mawlid: Translating Re-signified Subjectivities

Tahrir was not just about re-signified public space and public order; it was equally about re-signified subjectivities at both the collective and individual levels. One of the remarkable energies in Tahrir during the initial eighteen-day sit-in, and much beyond, was the active participation of Egyptian soccer 'Ultras,' the committed fans of various Egyptian soccer clubs known for their exceptional organization and performative cheering and mobilizational activities in soccer stadiums. During the past few years these fans, following in the footsteps of the Italian fan clubs, have organized themselves into Ultras movements. It is worth noting that the establishment of the Egyptian soccer clubs was related to developments in the political situation in Egypt.[39] Political observers have frequently stated that the former Mubarak regime deployed a set of strategies to exploit the Egyptians' obsession with soccer for its own benefit.[40] Stifled political life in Egypt was therefore displaced onto the soccer stadium, which offered a rare venue for mass mobilization—another kind of *mulid* in and of itself—and confrontation with the authorities. As an al-Ahly (National Team) Ultra member put it, "there is no competition in politics, so competition moved to the soccer pitch. We do what we have to do against the rules and regulations when we think they are wrong."[41] It is no wonder, then, that the Ultras had a significant role to play throughout the eighteen days of the Egyptian Revolution, especially in Tahrir. Indeed, so much so that Alaa Abd El Fattah,[42] a prominent Egyptian blogger and activist, said in an interview with Al Jazeera satellite channel, "The Ultras have played a more significant role than any political group on the ground at this moment."[43] The Ultras, who are predominantly constituted of lower- to lower-middle-class fans, are normally perceived as excessive, subversive, and potentially violent during soccer matches and have had multiple confrontations and run-ins with the Central Security Forces. Throughout the demonstrations and sit-ins, the rival Ultras groups put their differences aside and came together to mobilize the thousands of protesters in Tahrir. The basic soccer stadium chant, known to all Egyptians—"Masr" (Egypt)—accompanied by four consecutive drum beats after each mention of 'Masr,' animated Tahrir on a daily basis as the January sit-in was still amassing support. Given that members of the Ultras have long experience in dealing with tear gas, street clashes, and police violence, they were at the front lines of the January protests. Moreover, the Ultras' skills in banner writing, chanting, and the use of fireworks have been very valuable throughout, especially on February 11, 2011, the day Mubarak stepped down. The mobilizational and organizational energy provided by the soccer team Ultras eventually led to the birth (*mawlid*) of Ultras Thawra (Ultras of the Revolution), a group of young activists that used the Ultras' populist model to rally for the demands of the revolution on the streets of the city.[44] Furthermore, the Ultras' front-line contribution in Tahrir has transformed their mobilization in the soccer stadium itself, which has become the site for revolutionary confrontational chants against the former regime and its machinery of oppression, leading to unprecedented brutal violence against them by the Central Security Forces.[45]

On February 1, 2012 the Ultras Ahly, fans of the national soccer team Al-Ahly, were made to pay dearly for their support of the revolution inside the stadium and at the front line of demonstrations throughout the successive waves of Egypt's uprising in what has come to be known as "Black Wednesday." Trapped inside the stadium, where the exit gate was bolted, they were attacked by 'thugs' at the end of a soccer match against Port Said's team al-Masry, an orchestrated tragic incident that left 74 dead (according to most estimates) and hundreds wounded, after which a three-day national mourning period was declared. Eyewitnesses and observers held the Central Security Forces at the soccer game responsible for this massacre, where testimonies and footage from the incident show that they stood by and watched after they allowed the armed 'thugs' to attack.[46] This vengeful attack on Ultras Ahly led to nationwide demonstrations against the Central Security Forces and the SCAF, as well as attempts by angry demonstrators to storm police headquarters in several governorates, including the premises of the Ministry of Interior in Cairo near Tahrir, leaving at least seven dead and thousands injured among the protesters as of the time of writing.

As with all other Arab uprisings, Egyptian children became an integral part of the revolution and iconic heralds of a new era and a new generation of *tahrir*. Not just children with their families, but, more significantly, street children on their own who had forever been abused by the Mubarak regime and were among the first to be shot and injured during the early days of the uprising.[47] The *Haram* or sanctuary of Tahrir suddenly presented a home and a community for this extremely poor and marginalized group: they could get a free meal, a sense of togetherness, social interaction, and protection by the protesters. One of the street children said in an interview, "I have been out in the streets for many years. I am used to being awake the whole night and sleeping a few hours after sunrise to avoid sexual harassment, but not here in al-Tahrir."[48] In Tahrir, street children became an integrated part of the whole picture, a living condemnation of the former regime. Children lifted banners, took part in the chanting, and even had their own marches around the *midan* with people saluting and cheering them on.

The most popular children's chants were normally the shortest, simplest, and the most repeated in the *midan*, such as "*Yasqut, yasqut Hosni Mubarak*" ('Down, down with Hosni Mubarak'), and "*Mish Hanimshi, huwwa yimshi*" ('We will not leave, he will leave'). Moreover, several children's songs were used in the chants. The rhythm of Muhammad Fawzi's "Dhahaba al-laylu wa tala'a al-fagru" ('Night Is Gone and the Day Has Come'), one of the most famous children's songs in Egypt since the 1960s, was used in different politicized versions in the chants.[49]

Street children in Tahrir. Photograph by Samia Mehrez

Child in military outfit. Photograph by Nermine Hammam

The commercial economic aspect related to children in the *midan* was also visibly similar to that of the *mulid*, and provided a significant part of the political economy of the revolution focused on children's gadgets, T-shirts, and face-painting with the colors of the flag. Moreover, as a symbolic gesture of the positive perception of the army's role during the initial days of the uprising, children were brought to the *midan* in military outfits and took pictures with the military officers on tanks. A tailor interviewed during the initial days of the uprising reported that he had received three hundred orders from customers requesting military outfits for children.[50]

Children's experience in Tahrir is particularly parallel to their participation in *mulid* celebrations. In both instances they find themselves implicated in rituals and ceremonial activities that they do not fully comprehend. However, in both cases—the *mulid* and the Tahrir sit-ins—their participation is a kind of initiation rite that reinforces the symbolism of the word '*mawlid*' (birth). This symbolic birth for children was also one of rebirth for the elderly who came to Tahrir on wheelchairs or folding chairs, holding banners and flags, rejuvenated and determined to be part of the *mulid*.

Six-month-old baby in Tahrir for the length of the January sit-in. Photograph by Samia Mehrez

Laila Doss, age 92, during the January sit-in. Photograph by Madiha Doss

Child with revolution memorabilia. Photograph by Nermine Hammam

Elderly activists in Tahrir. Photograph by Samia Mehrez

"Watching" Mulid al-Tahrir: Revolutionary Translations of Spectacle

For a while after January 25, 2011, people were worried that Midan al-Tahrir, which had witnessed the sacrifices of the martyrs—the struggle to topple Mubarak in February and bring him to a public trial in August resulted in hundreds of deaths and injuries—would become a spectacle, a mere display of itself, a tourist site, like the Berlin Wall, that would replace the traditional Egyptian historic sites. Amr Shalakany, an AUC professor and a regular participant in the *midan*, articulated these concerns during the initial eighteen days of the January uprising in the following terms:

> Tahrir is a place where you go to recharge, to plug in, to seek and give energy, to collectively remember what this is all about. More disturbingly, though, Tahrir has also become a place where you can go and "watch" the revolution, take a look at it, have some of its taste, and then go home to another time zone altogether.
>
> "I'll meet you at the revolution" is something that we now tell each other in full seriousness, and to my mind that's a serious problem.[51]

True, people did come to "watch the revolution" in Midan al-Tahrir and many more continue to do so. But through this very process of "watching" (whether in the *midan* or even in front of their Facebook accounts and TV sets at home) many have become implicated as active participants and have transformed that "watching," that "spectacle," into an understanding of the multiple significations and translations of Mulid al-Tahrir. For example, during the July 8–August 1, 2011 sit-in in Tahrir, a group of activists that included filmmakers, writers, and photographers came together to create Cinema al-Tahrir—a spectacle within the spectacle—in the public space of the *midan*, an initiative that would have been unthinkable prior to the January uprising given the regime's restrictions on the use of public spaces. The idea revolved around a participatory principle that recreated 'spectacles' of the revolution as they had been unfolding over the past several months through video clips and YouTube material, which were selected each night by one of the 'spectators,' to share with the multitude of demonstrators who came daily in solidarity with the families of the martyrs camping in the *midan*. Cinema al-Tahrir effectively created a double and inverted 'spectacle' of the revolution in which the whole notion of spectacle was revolutionized and re-signified.[52]

Cinema al-Tahrir, July 2011. Photograph by Lara Baladi

People who came to the *midan* to 'watch' the revolution were implicated in 'watching' the revolution through the lens of Cinema al-Tahrir, which documented and effectively *translated* for many, who have no access to social media, the revolution's significant and, in many instances silenced, moments (testimonies by families of the martyrs, by the injured, by those detained, tortured, and tried in military courts, and, in the case of women, subjected to virginity tests). It was an amazing experience to witness people at Cinema al-Tahrir in late July, more than six months after the January 25 uprising, applauding activist Asmaa Mahfouz's January 18, 2011 video blog (vlog) post, in which she had called on Egyptians to demonstrate on January 25, 2011 (chapter 2) because they were watching it for the very first time.

On another level, the 'spectacle' of the January 25 Revolution, in which thousands of Sufis participated, equally re-signified and radicalized that of the traditional *mulid* itself and the ways in which *mulid* festivities were mobilized not just to support the January uprising but also to redefine the function of *mulid* celebrations within a revolutionary context. On March 29, 2011 during celebrations of Mulid al-Husayn (the Prophet Muhammad's nephew, whose *mulid* draws the largest congregation in Cairo after that of the Prophet himself), a *milyuniya* (a one-million-person march, the very language used by Tahrir activists) was organized to protest the destruction of several shrines by fundamentalist Salafi groups who deem them prohibited by Islam.[53] And again, on June 26, 2011 as the heated debate surrounding parliamentary elections and the draft of Egypt's constitution mounted, members of the Sufi *tariqa*s (schools) planned another *milyuniya* during the final night—*al-layla al-kabira*—of Mulid al-Sayyida Zaynab (the Prophet Muhammad's granddaughter), another immense *mulid* celebration in Cairo, to support proponents of a new constitution before parliamentary elections and ensure a wider representation of the political spectrum.[54]

Finally, one of the most radical outcomes of "watching" the revolution has been the thorough understanding that Tahrir/*tahrir* is not just a physical place but a *collective state and consciousness* through which the basic demands of Egypt's revolution—*"Huriya, karama insaniya"* ('freedom, human dignity')—continue to amass signification and translations. The massive demonstrations of May 15, 2011—the "Day of the Nakba"[55]—and the subsequent sit-in in front of the Israeli embassy in late August 2011, to protest the killing of five Egyptian security personnel by Israeli forces in the Sinai, are eloquent *translations* of this collective *state of tahrir* (liberation) that continues to be misunderstood, and therefore mistranslated, by the ruling SCAF. As the Military Police joined the Central Security Forces to deny demonstrators access to their *physical* site of liberation in the *midan*, in a prolonged and symbolic showdown of the occupation of Tahrir, demonstrators had already relocated and *retranslated Tahrir* by besieging the Israeli Embassy. This decisive moment of re-signification and translation produced one of the most liberating 'spectacles' of the revolution, which witnessed the emergence of "flagman" Ahmad al-Shahat. Dubbed the Egyptian Spiderman, al-Shahat, a twenty-three-year-old construction worker from Sharqiya, scaled the high-rise building that houses the Israeli Embassy in Giza to bring down the Israeli flag, which was hung at the twenty-first floor, while thousands of Egyptians at the foot of the building were cheering him on and praying for his safety.[56] Mona Anis has contextualized the "sensationalism" of this spectacular moment within a history of popular anger at, resentment of, and protest against normalization with Israel since the Camp David Accords of 1978.[57] But beyond the power of this spectacular act that was "watched" around the globe, it was edifying to know that "flagman" was not a "young activist"—tech savvy and part of a youth movement—but a construction worker who had first been spotted in the *midan* in the July 2011 sit-in and not in January 2011. Al-Shahat's own *translation* of the significance of his 'spectacle' is instructive insofar as it re-signifies the spectacle itself. Al-Shahat stated in a press conference that he was motivated by the basic demands of the revolution that represented a collective will ("*Haga Hati-friH al-sha'b kullu*") because it was done for "our dignity" ("*karamitna*").[58] Al-Shahat's spectacular intervention in this revolutionary *mulid* of *tahrir* is one that was brought about through "watching" Mulid al-Tahrir, which was in and of itself the act that brought about *mawild al-tahrir* (the birth of liberation) not just in Egypt and the region, but most significantly in multiple globalized and globalizing *translations* of the *mulid/mawlid* of Tahrir in the world (chapter 8) all resounding, across different languages: The people demand the downfall of the regime.

Notes

1   For one of the detailed descriptions of how the marches and demonstrations started all over Cairo see Yasmine El Rashidi, "Hosni Mubarak, the Plane is Waiting," *The New York Review of Books Blog*, January 26, 2011, http://www.nybooks.com/blogs/nyrblog/2011/jan/26/hosni-mubarak-plane-waiting/; for a more general contextual background see Max Rodenbeck, "Volcano of Rage," *The New York Review of Books*, March 24, 2011, http://www.nybooks.com/articles/archives/2011/mar/24/volcano-rage/

2   See 3arabawy.org vlog on Suez martyrs, January 26, 2011, http://www.arabawy.org/2011/01/26/suez-2/

3   To view episodes from the Qasr al-Nil Bridge battle watch YouTube, June 4, 2011, http://www.youtube.com/watch?v=2ExW3vxFMig&feature=player_embedded#at=123; for photographs of Suez demonstrations see *The Guardian*, January 27, 2011, http://www.guardian.co.uk/world/gallery/2011/jan/27/egyptian-protests-suez-in-pictures

4   For the organization of the space within the 'Independent Republic of Tahrir,' see *BBC News*, February 11, 2011, http://www.bbc.co.uk/news/world-12434787. Even as the sit-in was drastically reduced with the advent of the holy month of Ramadan, which coincided in that year with the beginning of August, protesters were determined to press on with the demands of the revolution and the rights of the families of martyrs and organized a collective *iftar* (breakfast). See Hugo Massa, "Tahrir Protestors Say Ramadan Won't Faze Them," *al-Masry al-Youm*, July 31, 2011, http://www.almasryalyoum.com/en/node/482145. Also

see Rana Khazbak, "Tahrir Sit-in Draws Down, but Martyrs' Families to Persevere," *al-Masry al-Youm*, July 31, 2011, http://www.almasryaly oum.com/en/node/482139

5   On the role of "people power" and the April 6 Youth Movement to mobilize demonstrators see *Yes Magazine*, February 18, 2011, http:// www.yesmagazine.org/people-power/egypts-revolution-behind-the-scenes; on the role of social media and citizen journalism see, for example, Sahar Khamis and Katherine Vaughn, "Cyberactivism in the Egyptian Revolution: How Civic Engagement and Citizen Journalism Tilted the Balance," *Arab Media and Society*, Summer 2011, no. 13, http:// arabmediasociety.sqgd.co.uk/articles/downloads/20110603105609_ Khamis.pdf; on the organization of Midan al-Tahrir itself see the BBC interactive map at *BBC News*, February 11, 2011, http://www.bbc. co.uk/news/world-12434787

6   The Tahrir sit-in, which began in July, lasted for nearly a month. It was violently disbanded by the Central Security Forces and the Military Police on August 1, 2011, coinciding with the beginning of Ramadan. See *al-Shorouk*, August 2, 2011, http://www.shorouknews.com/Con-tentData.aspx?id=516328

7   In a decision that defied military and security presence in the *midan*, activists and protesters staged a symbolic funeral for twenty-three-year-old Muhammad Mohsen, who had been fatally injured during the Abbasiya battle on July 23, 2011; see *al-Masry al-Youm*, July 26, 2011, http://therealnews.com/t2/index.php?option=com_content&task=view &id=31&Itemid=74&jumival=7094. The funeral was followed by an *iftar* in Tahrir on the first Friday of the holy month of Ramadan. Unfortunately, the protesters were again attacked, beaten, and chased out of the *midan* into the nearby metro stations; see "Tahrir Iftar" on YouTube, August 5, 2011, http://www.youtube.com/watch?v=KRvkqX YKZS8&feature=player_embedded#at=12. Despite the fact that, from August 1, 2011 to the time of writing, the Military Police and the Cen-tral Security Forces have surrounded the central garden of Tahrir to deny access to the revolution's sit-in and encampment space, thousands of protesters performed Eid prayers in the *midan*, thereby besieging the army and the police from all angles. See the photograph of Tahrir on August 30, 2011, the first day of the Eid, at *AhramOnline*, August 31, 2011, http://english.ahram.org.eg/

8   See Jeffrey C. Alexander, *Performative Revolution in Egypt: An Essay in Cultural Power* (London: Bloomsbury, 2011), throughout which the Egyptian Revolution is read as a living drama "whose political success

depended on its cultural power: its ability to project powerful symbols and real-time performances, plot-compelling protagonists and despicable antagonists; to stimulate and circulate powerful emotions; to organize exemplary solidarity; to create suspense; and finally to minister ignominious defeat to dark and polluted adversaries while purifying the nation through a stunning victory that lifted citizens to new hope and glory," p. 10.

9   On the power of ritual in political mobilization see David I. Kertzer, *Ritual, Politics, and Power* (New Haven and London: Yale University Press, 1988).

10 Susan Bassnett, *Translation Studies* (London: Routledge, 2002), p. 21.

11 Bassnett, *Translation Studies*, p. 21.

12 Daniel Chandler, *Semiotics* (London: Routledge, 2001), p. 2.

13 Juri Lotman and B.A. Uspensky, "On the Semiotic Mechanism of Culture," *New Literary History* 9, no. 2 (1978): 211–32.

14 Edward Sapir, *Culture, Language, and Personality* (Berkeley and Los Angeles: University of California Press, 1956), p. 69.

15 Susan Bassnett and Harish Trivedi, *Post-Colonial Translation: Theory and Practice* (London: Routledge, 1999), p. 13.

16 James Clifford, *Travel and Translation in the Late Twentieth Century* (Cambridge, MA: Harvard University Press, 1997), p. 182.

17 Bassnett and Trivedi, *Post-Colonial Translation*, p. 17.

18 Lawrence Venuti, "Introduction," *Rethinking Translation Discourse, Subjectivity, Ideology*, ed. L. Venuti (London: Routledge, 1992), p. 10.

19 For general readings on *mulid* celebrations see Faruq Ahmad Mustafa, *al-Mawalid: dirasa li-l-'adat wa-l-taqalid al-Sha'biya fi Misr*, 2nd ed. (Alexandria: GEBO, 1981) and George Stauth and Samuli Schielke, *Muslim Saints: Their Space and Place* (New Brunswick, NJ: Transaction Publishers, 2008).

20 Samuli Schielke, "Policing Moulids and Their Meaning," in *Cairo Contested: Governance, Urban Space, and Global Modernity*, ed. Diane Singerman (Cairo: American University in Cairo Press, 2009), pp. 83–110; see also Anna Madoeuf, "Moulids of Cairo: Sufi Guilds, Popular Celebrations, and the 'Roller-Coaster Landscape' of the Resignified City," in *Cairo Cosmopolitan: Politics, Culture, and Urban Space in the New Globalized Middle East*, ed. Diane Singerman and Paul Amar (Cairo: American University in Cairo Press, 2006), pp. 465–88.

21 Laura Gribbon, "Popular Participation 25th January: Egyptian Revolution of the Streets: A Study of the Capability of the Individual to Effect Change" (MA thesis, American University in Cairo, 2011), p. 27.

22 Madoeuf, "Moulids of Cairo," pp. 465–88.

23 Madoeuf, "Moulids of Cairo," p. 466.

24 Anthony Shadid, "Uncharted Ground after End of Egypt's Regime," *The New York Times*, February 11, 2011, http://www.nytimes. com/2011/02/12/world/middleeast/12revolution.html

25 See Ibrahim Eissa's article in *al-Dustur*, July 7, 2011, http://www. dostor.org/editorial/11/july/30/49867

26 For a brief history of Midan al-Tahrir and for good archival images see Fatemah Farag, "Centre of the Centre," *Al-Ahram Weekly*, September 2–8 1999, http://weekly.ahram.org.eg/1999/445/feature. htm; see also Nasser Rabbat's article on Midan al-Tahrir, "Midan al-Tahrir: itar al-thawra," *Le Monde Diplomatique*, Arabic edition, March 2011, http://www.mondiploar.com/article3400.html?PHPS ESSID=be0fd6b3ce371292da20e7f7f11df326, and Nezar Alsayyad, "Cairo's Roundabout Revolution," *The New York Times*, April 13, 2011, http://www.nytimes.com/2011/04/14/opinion/14alsayyad. html?_r=1&pagewanted=all

27 Ahmed Abdalla, *The Student Movement and National Politics in Egypt* (Cairo: American University in Cairo Press, 2009), p. 67.

28 Mourid Barghouti, *I Was Born There, I Was Born Here*, trans. Humphrey Davies (Cairo: American University in Cairo Press, 2011).

29 Huda Lutfi, "Translating Masculinities: Between Text and Image," public lecture at the Center for Translation Studies, American University in Cairo, February 2011.

30 Watch photographer Islam Azzazy's footage "Friday of Rage" on *Vimeo*, January 28, 2011, http://vimeo.com/25246213

31 See, for example, the use of *kans* by activist and blogger Alaa Abd El Fattah in June 2005 during a vigil in front of the Saad Zaghlul Memorial, where he reminds activists that in moments of crisis, Egyptians will call upon their spiritual beliefs, one of which is to sweep away evil and injustice. He invites activists to join in sweeping the entrance to the Sayyida Zaynab Mosque as a symbolic gesture to sweep away the injustices of the Mubarak regime; see Wa7damasrya.blogspot.com, June 11, 2005, http://wa7damasrya.blogspot.com/2005_06_01_archive.html

32 See Schielke, "Policing Moulids and their Meaning," pp. 83–110.

33 For a comprehensive reading of the theory of carnival in Bakhtin's work see Mikhail Bakhtin, *Rabelais and His World*, trans. Hélène Iswolsky (Bloomington and Indianapolis: Indiana University Press, 1984) and Mikhail Bakhtin, *Problems of Dostoevsky's Poetics*, ed. and trans. Caryl Emerson (Manchester: Manchester University Press, 1984).

34 See the initial April 2011 schedule of "al-Fann Midan" in Cairo, Alexandria, and other cities in Egypt, http://beta.filbalad.com/events/ el-fann-midan-a-cultural-celebration-in-the-squares-and-streets-of-egypt. These public space festivals were repeated during the month of Ramadan in 2011.

35 For one of the *zaffa*s of incoming protesters to the *midan* see YouTube, February 15, 2011, http://www.youtube.com/watch?v=ZyouIlm08Z4

36 For a wedding *zaffa* in Tahrir see http://www.youtube.com/ watch?v=mB4VUr66DR8.

37 For examples of Mubarak *zaffa*s in Tahrir see YouTube, February 14, 2011, http://www.youtube.com/watch?v=O136kiSpPVk&feature= related; also see YouTube, February 11, 2011, http://www.youtube. com/watch?v=SXjJUc-QUa8&feature=related

38 For examples of Mubarak *zar*s in Tahrir see YouTube, February 6, 2011, http://www.youtube.com/watch?v=vmui6OFgZh8&NR=1; also see YouTube, February 6, 2011, http://www.youtube.com/ watch?v=QeDmcuh0cyo

39 See Dave Zirin, "Soccer Clubs Central to Ending Egypt's 'Dictatorship of Fear,'" SI.com, January 31, 2011, http://sportsillustrated.cnn. com/2011/writers/dave_zirin/01/31/egypt.soccer/index.html. Some soccer clubs have been more politicized than others and have allowed their players to become politically involved. A clear example of this can be found in the case of Muhammad Abu Trika, Al-Ahly's star player, who in 2008 famously raised his jersey revealing his T-shirt, which read "Sympathize with Gaza."

40 Under the former regime, there has been a notable official sponsorship of the national soccer team through several means: economic incentives for the players, the coaches, and the technical team, as well as presidential family presence at all vital matches. In Egypt, mass mobilization has only been allowed to take place in soccer stadiums or game-related celebrations. As a result, allowing millions of people to celebrate in the streets over three consecutive years after Egypt's team won the African Cup three times in a row was considered by many analysts as a venting valve provided by the regime to divert the people's attention away from the country's severe economic and political problems.

41 James M. Dorsey, "Soccer Fans Play Key Role in Egyptian Protests," *Bleacher Report: World Football*, January 26, 2011, http://bleacherreport. com/articles/585682-soccer-fans-play-key-role-in-egyptian-protests; see also Debbie Randle, "Rival Football 'Ultras' United in Egyptian Protests," *BBC*, March 31, 2011, http://www.bbc.co.uk/newsbeat/12914113.

42 Alaa Abdel Fattah is an activist and blogger who has become one of *the* icons of the January 25 uprising after he refused to stand military trial as a civilian on alleged charges of incitement to violence during the "Maspero Massacre," October 2011. See Zeinab El Gundy, "Portrait of a Revolutionary," *AhramOnline*, October 31, 2011, http://english. ahram.org.eg/News/25533.aspx

43 Zirin, "Soccer Clubs."

44 See "Ultras Thawra" Facebook page, http://www.facebook.com/ Ultrasthawra25

45 See the confrontation at the Cairo stadium between the Ultras Ahly and the Central Security Forces on September 3, 2011, during which the Ultras were attacked and beaten by the police inside the stadium for chanting slogans against them, Mubarak, and former minister of interior Habib al-Adli. The official report from the Ministry of Health estimated 130 people were injured, including sixty-seven police officers and soldiers. YouTube, September 6, 2011, http://www.youtube.com/ watch?v=lrBAMAZBdac

46 See Mai Shams El Din, "Port Said Massacre a Conspiracy by Security, Say Ultras Witnesses," February 2, 2012, http://thedailynewsegypt. com/people/port-said-massacre-a-conspiracy-by-security-say-ultras- eyewitnesses.html; see also http://www.youtube.com/watch?v=Sw9ektv AIo4&feature=player_embedded#

47 Nathan Diebenow, "Mubarak Regime Abused 50,000 Homeless Chil- dren in Cairo," *The Raw Story*, February 14, 2011, http://www.rawstory. com/rs/2011/02/14/mubarak-regime-abused-50000-homeless-children- in-cairo-reporter-says/

48 Robert Fisk, "Cairo's 50,000 Street Children Were Abused by This Regime," *The Independent*, February 13, 2011, http://www.independent. co.uk/opinion/commentators/fisk/robert-fisk-cairos-50000-street- children-were-abused-by-this-regime-2213295.html

49 To listen to the revolutionary lyrics of "Dhahaba al-laylu," see YouTube, January 22, 2011, http://www.youtube.com/watch?v=m-5kRHViqx0

50 Ahmad Al Sharif, "The Military Outfit is the New 2011 Fashion for Egyptian Kids," *Masrawy*, February 14, 2011, http://www.masrawy. com/News/Writers/General/2011/February/14/baby.aspx

51 Amr Shalakany, "Meet You at the Revolution," *The New York Times*, February 9, 2011, http://opinionator.blogs.nytimes.com/author/amr- shalakany/

52 In *The Society of the Spectacle*, Guy Debord's seminal text of the 1960s, the spectacle is defined as the inverted image of society in which

"relations between commodities have supplanted relations between people" and in which "passive identification with the spectacle supplants genuine activity." However, in the case of the January 2011 uprising—indeed, regional uprisings in general—it was the spectacle itself that motivated rather than supplanted political activity and mobilization. See Guy Debord, *The Society of the Spectacle* (Cambridge: Zone Books, 1995).

53 See article in *al-Yawm al-Sabi'*, March 30, 2011, http://www.youm7.com/News.asp?NewsID=380019&; see also Hoqook.com, June 28, 2011, http://www.hoqook.com/index.php/news/2011-04-12-11-07-59/12122-2011-06-28-11-37-51

54 *al-Masry al-Youm*, Sunday June 26, 2011, http://www.almasryalyoum.com/node/471747

55 May 15 is the annual day of commemoration of the displacement of Palestinians that followed the establishment of the state of Israel in 1948.

56 Video of Ahmad al-Shahat removing the Israeli flag, YouTube, August 20, 2011, http://www.youtube.com/watch?v=Bq8kcKz5eZ8&feature=player_embedded#

57 Mona Anis, "The Power of the Spectacle," *Al-Ahram Weekly*, August 25–31, 2011, p. 17.

58 Selections from Ahmad al-Shahat's press conference in *al-Safir*, August 21, 2001, http://www.assafir.com/Article.aspx?EditionId=1927&articleId=2625&ChannelId=4548; see also *Cairo Today*, August 21, 2011, http://www.youtube.com/watch?v=4v2bPHg02vw&feature=related; and al-Shahat's interview with Al Jazeera, August 21, 2011, http://www.youtube.com/watch?v=cEEKIvdHRz0&feature=related

2

Of Drama and Performance: Transformative Discourses of the Revolution

Amira Taha and Christopher Combs

Since early January 2011, many Egyptian activists had been using social networking and video streaming websites to call for mass protests on January 25, Egypt's Police Day. Renaming it 'Egypt's Day of Rage' (not to be confused with the 'Friday of Rage,' which was several days later), Internet activists used all available tools, such as intensely passionate interviews on international satellite news networks and emotionally charged video blogs (vlogs), to mobilize Egyptians to demonstrate that day. And their persistent efforts showed in the numbers of Egyptians that joined the call and remained determined not to leave the streets until their demands were answered. The Egyptian government aggressively countered those efforts through the use of violence against protesters, and the deployment of state-owned media to spread misinformation about activists and protesters and regain support. However, eighteen days after that date the people's efforts were paid off with the resignation of former President Hosni Mubarak.

Over those eighteen intense days in Tahrir, numerous public appearances, including videos, interviews, speeches, and communiqués by several key actors on the Egyptian political scene, played transformative roles in the course of the revolution. This chapter will translate selections of these appearances and point to reasons why these particular moments played a significant role in shaping the reaction of the Egyptian public. Selections translated and discussed include videos and interviews by activists Asmaa Mahfouz and Wael Ghoneim, and speeches by former President Hosni Mubarak, former Vice President Omar Suleiman, and Major General Mohsen al-Fangary of the Supreme Council of the Armed Forces (SCAF). Choosing these selections was based on several factors, including the rich semiotic details, the impact on the audience, and how representative each performance was of a specific discourse. Throughout the translation project, it was necessary to translate these public appearances on two levels, namely on the level of language and discourse, and on the level of semiotic signs, including the gestures, intonation, and appearance of the actors.

Using analysis from the fields of translation, performance, and gender studies, and from social movement theory, this chapter argues that these selections need to be seen as performances to understand why and how they molded the audience and helped gain public support over the different phases of the revolution and counterrevolution. Additionally, the chapter aims to show through theory that the use of the term "performance" does not necessarily indicate a lack of authenticity; rather, here it refers to the multiple levels of semiotic sign language in these selections, which enhanced their impact on the course of events. Translating and analyzing the selections as performances then allows the reader to gain a better understanding of the Egyptian Revolution through comprehending both the discourse and the semiotic sign language in the selected public appearances. As the chapter concludes, it aims to shed light on later stages of the Egyptian Revolution and on counterrevolutionary efforts that present the reader with a wider perspective to experience these rich events from the eyes of informed audience, actors, and directors.

Prologue: Translating Performance in Theory

In framing the multilayered translation project undertaken in this chapter and to shed light on how the selected public appearances helped mobilize the Egyptian Revolution at its different stages, insights from the fields of translation, performance, and gender studies, as well as social movement theory, will provide a useful framework for a dynamic analysis of the events. In this sense, a theoretical introduction is necessary to contextualize the analysis and translation we undertook for this chapter as it will help us understand the elements involved in the process.

Developments in the field of translation studies have shown that translations vary in the way they highlight or conceal foreign and unfamiliar elements of the source language text.[1] According to the translation studies scholar Lawrence Venuti, the fact that translators always have to negotiate the differences in language and culture of the source language "by reducing them and supplying another set of differences, basically domestic, drawn from the receiving language and culture to enable the foreign to be received there," means that translation always communicates in a troubled manner.[2] Foregrounding this foreignness by way of maintaining cultural and linguistic differences in the translation may be experienced as disruptive to the cultural or moral sensibilities of the target language reader. For Venuti, such foregrounding can be seen as an act of "resistance against ethnocentrism and racism, cultural narcissism and imperialism;" he regards the absence of such foregrounding in translations as a form of ethnocentrism.[3] A smoother and less disruptive translation may preserve the illusion of equivalence between the source language text and the target text, but the reality is that translation always results in something different and this difference should be accepted as a cultural fact with various levels of meaning rather than as a flaw in the translation.[4] This insight from modern translation studies informs both the analysis and the style of translation presented in this chapter; the authors of this chapter made a conscious effort to maintain certain indigenous aspects of the Arabic performances in the English translation, thereby avoiding the westernization or, in certain cases, secularization, of the original Arabic communication.

With the emergence in the 1970s of modern theater studies as a field independent from literary studies, the dramatic text was increasingly viewed as only one among several important aspects of theater. And in the 1980s, the emergence of the related field of performance studies expanded the concept of performance beyond the realm of aesthetics and into the realm of social sciences, which permits the application of the theory of theater studies to the analysis of, for example, religious or political 'performances.'[5] Hence, our use of the term 'performance' in translating selections from transformative political discourses of the Egyptian Revolution is justified by several theorists. According to Diana Taylor, a professor of Performance Studies and Spanish at New York University, performance

> is the object of analysis of performance studies, that is, the many practices and events . . . that involve theatrical, rehearsed, or conventional behaviors. . . . performance also functions as the methodological lens that enables scholars to analyze events as performance.[6]

However, one might ask about the implications of the use of 'performance' and other 'theatrical' terminology in terms of the authenticity of the actors and actions translated and analyzed in the chapter. Taylor points out several understandings of the term 'performance' that put to rest this concern about authenticity. First, performances reveal "culture's deepest, truest and most individual character"; second is the idea of the "constructedness of performance" in which the constructed is read as being synonymous with the real; third is the idea found in a series of authors from Aristotle, Shakespeare, and Calderón de la Barca down to the present that "performance distills a truer truth than life."[7]

In the field of linguistics, a discourse is primarily an oral phenomenon that occurs between a speaker and a listener; however, it can exist in writing as a reproduction of spoken discourse or writing that uses the style and function of the same. For example, a theater script is not itself discourse; rather, it is a representation of spoken discourse in written form.

> In accordance with this usage . . . discourse means "the specifically theatrical use of language in the broadest sense, from verbal utterance to nonverbal uses comprising the visual elements, including gesture, facial expression, movement, costume, players' bodies, properties and décor."[8]

Also worth noting is the related concept of performativity, which lies at the heart of philosopher Judith Butler's work and provides a useful theoretical framework for the translations undertaken in this chapter. Her conception of the term, especially as it relates to gender roles, is highly influential in today's gender and linguistics studies and is especially applicable to the performances of the two revolutionary activists translated and discussed in this chapter, namely Wael Ghoneim and Asmaa Mahfouz, as they defied traditional gender roles in ways that likely furthered the effectiveness of their message. In this sense, Butler defines performativity as a repeated and "citational practice by which discourse produces the effects that it names,"[9] rather than a single or intentional "act." She describes it as

> a reiteration of a norm or a set of norms, and to the extent that it acquires an act like status in the present, it conceals or dissimulates the conventions of which it is a repetition. Moreover, this act is not primarily theatrical; indeed its apparent theatricality is produced to the extent that its historicity remains dissimulated (and, conversely,

its theatricality gains a certain inevitability given the impossibility of a full disclosure of its historicity).[10]

Finally, insights from social movement theory can also enrich our understanding of the influence of the performances discussed in this chapter, especially those given by the social activists who drove the protests. One key concept in social movement theory is the process of framing, which renders "events or occurrences meaningful and thereby function[s] to organize experience and guide action." "Collective action frames" interpret and summarize reality in a way that is intended to mobilize supporters and demobilize opponents; that is, they are "action-oriented sets of beliefs and meanings that inspire and legitimate the activities and campaigns of a social movement."[11] The Egyptian activists' framing of grievances against the regime played an important role in mobilizing the revolution. Former President Mubarak and, more recently, the transitional military regime also engaged in framing but with a counter-revolutionary aim, namely to hinder the mobilization of protesters. In other words, activists, government, and media are all engaged in an intellectual and propaganda battle over the hearts and minds of the people. It is important to keep in mind that the acts of framing (and counter framing) executed by the personalities discussed below is distinct from the different levels of translation of these performances carried out by the authors of this chapter.

Since the 1990s there has been a greater focus on the role of emotions in social movement scholarship, which has been incorporated in this chapter. Prior to the 1990s, the role of emotions had been largely ignored or was dealt with in a pejorative manner that regarded emotional behavior as irrational and primitive. One contemporary social movement scholar observed that

"moral shocks" are often the first step toward recruitment into social movements: when an unexpected event or piece of information raises such a sense of outrage in a person that she becomes inclined toward political action.[12]

In addition, pride has been shown to play an important role in eliciting action, while shame often has the opposite effect. Both of these emotions have been cultivated in the performances described in the chapter for the sake of mobilizing or demobilizing the public. For example, the first activist discussed in this chapter, Asmaa Mahfouz, besides cultivating feelings of moral outrage, takes advantage of culturally specific attitudes regarding gender to create a sense of shame that demobilizes inaction. Resignation and depression also hinder action while "anger, outrage, indignation, and pride, on the other hand, encourage action."[13] Effective framing depends on the emotional aspect: "Gamson . . . argued that 'injustice frames,' essential to protest, depend on 'the righteous anger that puts fire in the belly and iron in the soul.'"[14]

Egyptian Revolution, Act I

The events described throughout this chapter shall be seen as theatrical performances that molded the audience and helped gain much support over the different phases of the revolution, not only because of the deployed discourse, but because of the multiple levels of semiotic signs used in them. Although there is no one definitive way to classify the different components of signs in performance, the Polish semiotician Tadeusz Kowzan came up with a systematization of categories including language, tone, facial signs, gestural signs, movement, makeup, hairstyle, costume, props, décor, lighting, music, and sound effects (including 'noises off').[15] In this chapter, translated performances will be contextualized and placed in chronological order to give the reader a better understanding of how the events unfolded.

January 18: The Call for Action

The Tunisian Revolution, which brought an end to the longtime tyrannical rule of Zine El Abidine Ben Ali on January 14, 2011, played on the emotions of opposition youth in Egypt. Having fought against the corruption and suppression of their own government, young members of opposition movements were inspired to call for mass protests beginning in mid-January, 2011. Among these was the April 6 Youth Movement, which was founded in 2008 in support of industrial workers planning a strike in al-Mahalla al-Kubra, a major industrial city in the Nile Delta. The movement has since organized public rallies, and used new social media tools to report on strikes, alert their networks about police activity, organize legal protection, and draw attention to their efforts.

Asmaa Mahfouz, an activist and one of the founders of the April 6 Youth Movement, was particularly important in setting the stage for the Egyptian Revolution. From sharing energizing videos and notes against Mubarak's regime online, to organizing public rallies against it, Mahfouz has played a significant role in mobilizing Egyptians onto the streets. Recorded on January 18, 2011 to call for mass protests on January 25, 2011, the vlog translated and discussed below was initially shared by Mahfouz on her Facebook account, and then spread swiftly. At the time this chapter was written, one version of Mahfouz's vlog had reached about two hundred thousand viewers on YouTube. In the vlog, she calls upon Egyptians to join her in protest on January 25, 2011 against the corrupt Egyptian regime and to demand fundamental human rights for the Egyptian people.

Recent developments in performance studies show that the linguistic system is only one optional component in a set of interrelated semiotic systems, which creates challenges for the translation process. As introduced earlier, performance semiotics concerns itself with how the meaning is produced by means of visual and auditive signs that are either actor-related or space-related.[16] In this sense, Mahfouz's performance presents us, as translators, with very rich semiotic material, such as her intensely high-pitched tone, her conscious gestural signs, her challenging facial expressions, and the use of props.

After setting the stage for her message and preparing her audience for her call, she enters a dramatic part of her vlog, where she raises the pitch of her voice and delivers her message in a faster, more urgent manner. She also plays on the emotions of her target audience and manages finally to provoke many into joining her by enhancing her message with dramatic intonation and choice of words. This performance includes major transformative themes that challenged gender roles and perceptions and used religious references to lead her audience directly into the streets.

The location of the vlog was particularly important in gaining sympathy for her and her call. Set in a plain-walled, white-painted, office-like room, this scene is one that many middle-class Egyptians can relate to, since it resembles the plainness and sparseness of their own abodes, thus making the speaker one of them. Mahfouz introduces her message by referring to recent cases of self-immolation undertaken by disenfranchised and marginalized Egyptians and by referring to the Tunisian Revolution. Her shocking introduction, in which she talks about four Egyptians who set themselves on fire, establishes an intensely emotional mood for the rest of the video. As she continues, the emotions build up and the intensity of events drives her out of the methodical manner in which she started.

In her provocative introductory report-like sentences, she uses the term "animals" to describe how Egyptians are treated by their government and to refer to their dire and inhumane living conditions. This helped evoke sympathy among her target audience for the cause that she and the self-immolators represent, and the call she is about to present.

> Four Egyptians set themselves on fire out of the humiliation, hunger, and poverty they have been living through for thirty years. Four Egyptians set themselves on fire hoping the Tunisian revolution could be replicated; hoping Egypt would be a free country, where they could live in justice, have dignity, and be treated as human beings, not like animals.[17]

In the vlog, Mahfouz's clothing and appearance present her audience with the image of an average middle-class Egyptian girl whom they could easily relate to. However, by speaking out publicly and calling for civil disobedience, Mahfouz is not only breaking some norms and shattering stereotypes about young Egyptian women in a male-dominated society, but she is also shaming and pressuring her viewers, especially men, to follow the example of their bold female fellow Egyptian. In posting her video, she was disillusioned by Egyptians' apathy and fear of authority. She had called for a protest in Tahrir one week earlier but was only joined by a few young men.

In the vlog she was directly addressing a male-dominated viewership to join her on January 25, 2011 in Tahrir by provoking the society's perception of manhood and honor, which are both very sensitive taboos in the Egyptian society. According to Judith Butler's conception of gender performativity, one's gender is an act that constitutes the identity it is professed to be, which is asserted through repeated bodily gestures, movements, and styles.[18] In this sense, Mahfouz's constant challenging eye contact, assertive body posture, and cynical language not only shamed and provoked her audience into action, but also constructed her gender as a woman in a way that opposes the usual social construction of a victimized or weak female. The societal opposition to her bold and unusual stance could be easily noticed in the viewers' comments following her video.[19]

She keeps emphasizing that she is not afraid to take to the streets alone to protest, while alluding to her young age and her gender. Additionally, not only has she taken to the streets, but she also posted her phone number, hoping that others would contact her and be motivated to join in. However, this in itself is also an act frowned upon by Egyptian society and perceived as a sign of immodesty.

> I posted that I am a girl, yet I will go to Tahrir alone and carry a sign hoping that people would follow suit. I even posted my number to encourage others to join in.
>
> Only three young men showed up! Three young men, but were faced by three trucks full of central security soldiers, officers, and tens of thugs. Yet, they were all frightened! They may have shoved us roughly away from the crowds, but once far, they told us we are all one and pleaded with us to end the protest.

Furthermore, addressing the predominantly religious and conservative society in Egypt, Mahfouz also tackles concerns related to the widespread negative societal perception of female participation based on cultural grounds and strict religious interpretations. By doing so, she intelligently confronts a large segment of her audience, who reject her public appearance in the first place. She counters objections to female participation in the public domain by calling upon those young men to join the protests to assert their manhood and spare females the hassle and potential public disapproval.

> Anyone who thinks of himself as a real man should join in. Anyone who whines about how inappropriate and *Haram* it is for girls to join demonstrations because they get harassed should protect their honor by joining the protests on the twenty-fifth.
>
> If you are a man with dignity, join us to protect me and protect any other girl.

The decision to retain the religiously loaded word *Haram* as it is in the target language in the many instances it is used throughout the interview was driven by several factors. First, this word holds many layers of meaning and significance in the Arabic language that relate to shameful, religiously unlawful, and excessively negative actions, which have no equivalent in the target language. Second, the significance and widespread use of this word in the Arabic language justifies inserting it in other texts to help acquaint the audience with its importance. Finally, the term is already used in spoken English by members of the Muslim community in countries such as the United States and the United Kingdom.

Additionally, in order to relate to a large segment of her target audience who view such calls for public protest as secular with a 'western' agenda, Mahfouz further asserts her message based on religious grounds. In addition to her veil, she deploys religious language and Qur'anic verses that portray the Egyptians' fight against a corrupt regime not just as religiously acceptable but even as a religious duty. She repeats her message in a very clear and consistent manner using a firm tone and ends her argument with a Qur'anic verse, which helped her reach the audience in a way that made them remember and contemplate her message once the video ended.

> Never say there is no hope! As long as you say there is no hope, hope will be lost. As long as you come out and take a stand, hope endures. Never fear the government, fear God. God says: "Indeed Allah will not change the condition of a people until they change what is in themselves. (13:11)" Why? Definitely not so you remain compliant and avoid seeking radical change!

As Mahfouz ends her vlog, she says the following sentence while maintaining challenging eye contact with her audience: "I'm going out on the twenty-fifth to say no to the corruption and no to the regime!"

Finally, and in a very dramatic move, she raises her arms, which she had maintained below the table in front of her up until this point, carrying a banner that says: "I'm going out on the twenty-fifth to protect my dignity as an Egyptian!"

Following Mahfouz's and other activists' call for demonstrations on January 25, 2011 tens of thousands of Egyptians took to the streets in a very bold move against their cruel government. The brutal tactics of the Central Security Forces against demonstrators, including the excessive use of rubber and live bullets, water cannons, and tear gas, led to the deaths and injuries of many Egyptians. By the time the regime cut off Internet services throughout Egypt on the evening of January 27,

Asmaa Mahfouz ending her video blog, January 18, 2011

the protest movement clearly had the momentum it needed to continue without this medium of communication; the following day the protesters were able to take over Tahrir.

February 1: Counterrevolutionary Tirade[20]

The performance of Hosni Mubarak and his government in the early days of the revolution did little to inspire the confidence and sympathy of the people. Mubarak's first speech early in the morning on Saturday, January 29, 2011 was a continuation of this poor performance.[21] His fleeting, matter-of-fact expression of regret for the loss of life in the demonstrations and the weak case he made regarding his support of the people's aspirations including democracy and a better standard of living, diluted by his preference for security, stability, and the preservation of public order, did little to boost his credibility. Furthermore, his announcement of the resignation of the government was perceived as too little too late; the revolutionary movement had by that point raised the bar to the point where nothing less than the fall of the Mubarak regime was acceptable. All this was exacerbated by the regime's strategy to sow fear among the population to undermine support for the revolution by removing the Central Security Forces from the streets and allowing the release of prisoners onto the streets of Cairo.

Hosni Mubarak delivering his first speech, January 29, 2011

Very late in the evening on Tuesday, February 1, 2011 President Hosni Mubarak delivered his most effective performance of the revolutionary period. Before this speech, the number of people protesting in Cairo and in other important Egyptian cities had increased substantially since the start of the protests one week earlier. Previous attempts made by elements associated with the regime to discourage the protesters through intimidation, including the withdrawal of the Central Security Forces from the streets and the unleashing of thugs to create a sense of vulnerability among the populace, had failed to undermine the protest movement's momentum. The president begins framing the stance of the regime with his take on the recent events:

> The homeland is exposed to difficult events and harsh trials that began with honest youth and citizens exercising their right to demonstrate peacefully to express their grievances and aspirations . . . . Those who sought to sow chaos and resort to violence and confrontation to violate and attack the constitutional legitimacy quickly took advantage of the situation. These demonstrations changed from an elevated and civilized manifestation of freedom of opinion and expression into regrettable confrontations that were driven and controlled by political powers that sought to add fuel to the fire and targeted the security and stability of the country with provocative acts, incitement, looting, stealing and lighting fires, highway robbery, violating state facilities

and public and private property, and infringing upon diplomatic delegations on Egyptian soil.[22]

Mubarak then describes the revolutionary events as a burden on the Egyptian people, which can only be removed by his government. He makes strategic use of the first person plural, "we," followed by "our" and "us," as a deliberate strategy to persuade the listeners that his interests and their interests are one and the same.

> Together *we* are living distressing days. What weighs most heavily on *our* hearts is the fear felt by the overwhelming majority of the Egyptians. What overwhelms them most is the annoyance, preoccupation, and suspicions over what the future has in store for them, their friends and families, and the future and destiny of their country. The events of the last few days impose on all of *us*, both people and leaders, the choice between chaos and stability. [emphasis by the translator]

As he frames the situation as a dilemma threatening the interests of the people, actually *his* people, Mubarak speaks in the firm and steady tone that Egyptians have grown familiar with from watching him speak and perform in public for many years. Here he plays the role of a patriarchal authority poised to impose discipline on his younger subjects while cultivating a sense of fear of the consequences of defying his authority, the authority of the father. A degree of arrogance can be detected in the way he disparages the behavior of the protesters with a discernible look of scorn on his face. His performance is much less dynamic than that of Asmaa Mahfouz in terms of emotional range, nevertheless the discourse of Mubarak's second speech combined with more subtle changes in tone and emotion result in a sense of drama in this performance: unshaken, responsible, and commanding but deservingly so. For example, in the following quotation Mubarak speaks with a softer tone and, after alluding to his age, he appeals to the Egyptian people to allow him to finish his term in order to fulfill his responsibility as the father of the nation.

> My primary responsibility now is to recover the security and stability of the homeland to achieve the peaceful transition of power in an atmosphere that protects Egypt and the Egyptians and grants the transfer of responsibility to whomever the people choose in the next

presidential elections. I say in all honesty, despite the present situation, that I have never intended to run for another term because I have spent enough of my life in the service of Egypt and its people. But now I am very keen on concluding my work for the sake of the nation to ensure the transmission of its trusteeship and banner. As I carry this out our beloved Egypt will remain safe and stable, and its legality and constitution will be preserved and respected.

The high-stakes tension at this point, the fact that the protesters were now aiming for nothing less than Mubarak's departure and that nothing short of that would end their confrontation with the regime, enhanced the sense of drama surrounding this speech.

In dramatic performances there is a strong connection between the dialogue and the overall situation. One way of explaining this is to refer to speech act theory, a branch of modern linguistics and the philosophy of language, which addresses how actions are performed by language or how discourse enacts events of a drama. For example, Oxford philosopher John Austin, focusing on the "pragmatic status of speech as an interpersonal force in the real world," maintained that "in issuing utterances we are not only or always producing certain propositional content but are, above all, *doing* such things as asking, commanding, attempting to influence or convince our interlocutors, etc."[23] Also worth noting here is the idea of the Prague School of linguists and literary critics reiterated by Kowzan that "everything is a sign in a theatrical presentation."[24] Seen in this light, Mubarak's crisp, professional appearance and his calm, steady tone throughout the speech—despite his apparent frail and beseeching demeanor—may be viewed as a signal on the part of the president that he is still in control of the situation in Egypt. On the other hand, the apparent absence of an audience or members of the press in the same room during the speech may be seen as a sign of his isolation from the Egyptian street.

After reviewing some of the practical measures of his government to respond to the protesters, Mubarak ends his speech on a more emotional and personal note:

My fellow citizens, Egypt will emerge from the current difficult conditions stronger than it was before they were felt; and its people will emerge more confident, cohesive, and stable while being more conscientious about their interests and keener to avoid forsaking their destiny and future. The Hosni Mubarak who is speaking to you today is honored by the long years he spent in the service of Egypt and its people. This dear country is my homeland as it is the homeland of every individual Egyptian. I have lived and fought for its sake and defended its land, sovereignty, and interests. I will die on this land and history will judge me and others for the good we did and for our misdeeds.

Here Mubarak appeals to Egyptians' patriotism by making optimistic predictions about Egypt's future, highlighting his service to the homeland, and alluding to the sacred nature of this service. He again fails to conceal his arrogant stance toward the protesters as he implies that their challenge to his rule is tantamount to "forsaking their future and destiny." As he raises his hand and finger in a series of subtly defiant gestures, Mubarak highlights his lengthy efforts to defend and serve his homeland while insisting that he will die on that same land, as if this somehow legitimizes holding on to power for over three decades. In mentioning that he fought for his country, this section refers to his role as commander of the Egyptian Air Force during the October 1973 War, which eventually led to Egypt's recovery of the Sinai territories lost to Israel in the 1967 War. The reference to his own death by the visibly aged leader may have come as striking for some listeners, given that the Egyptian media always depicted Mubarak as a healthy man while downplaying concerns about his serious health issues.

One lesson that can be derived from the discussion above about speech act theory is that the various discursive events described in this chapter can be thought of as a dialogue characterized by actions and reactions that shape the plot of this political drama. Mubarak's second speech, as an element of the 'dialogue' between the regime and the Egyptian people, had such a transformative impact, polarizing the Egyptian public. Mubarak's emotional appeals created a real sense of sympathy for Egypt's aging leader and this provided the pro-Mubarak camp with the momentum to maintain a strong counterrevolutionary movement for approximately one week after the speech. Many Egyptian celebrities publicly expressed their support for Mubarak after his second speech on state- and privately-owned media, which had negative repercussions for many after his resignation.[25] The anti-Mubarak camp remained in Tahrir, for the most part, while the pro-regime group held counter-demonstrations in front of the Mustafa Mahmud Mosque in Cairo's upscale Mohandiseen neighborhood.

Days into the revolution, a general sense of fear for the future was spreading among Egyptians, which was expressed in the growing pessimism and thinning of crowds in Tahrir. Mubarak seemed to be clinging to power and using all maneuvers possible to maintain his rule until September, such as appointing a new cabinet, and a vice president and promising more political reforms. This had energized the pro-Mubarak camp and led to the "Battle of the Camel," when thugs hired by the aged president's partisans entered Tahrir on their camels and horses wielding swords and injuring demonstrators in a scene reminiscent of medieval battles. This fed into the frustration of the anti-Mubarak camp and created empathy for the Tahrir demonstrators among nonaligned Egyptians.

February 7: Re-energizing Tahrir[26]

Two weeks into the revolution, Egyptian state-sponsored and affiliated private media were also engaged in counterrevolutionary framing by working to undermine the credibility of international satellite news networks like Al Jazeera while portraying the people protesting on the streets as immature, reckless, irrational, poor, and homeless youths. Many of those who had never taken to the streets truly believed it. These efforts sapped the momentum of the uprising and nothing was happening to reverse this situation.

Like other important activist bloggers, Wael Ghoneim was one of the masterminds behind the protests on January 25, 2011. The only major difference was that before he was abducted from Tahrir Square on January 26, 2011 at 2:00 AM by the State Security apparatus, the Egyptian public had not known who he was. Acting in anonymity for almost a year, Ghoneim had created the "Kullina Khaled Sa'id" ('We Are All Khaled Sa'id') Facebook group, named after the twenty-eight-year-old man who was arrested, tortured, and killed by the police after posting online evidence of police officers dividing up confiscated narcotics. The Facebook group played an important role in framing grievances against the regime by exposing the police's use of torture and repeatedly called for protests against them, while persistently attempting to maintain the anonymity of its administrators. By early 2012, the number of its fans had reached over 1,885,000.

As one of the organizers of the January 25 revolt, Ghoneim was incarcerated for twelve consecutive days after his arrest on January 26, 2011, during which time he was unaware of the turmoil taking place all over

Egypt. International and local calls to former prime minister Ahmed Shafik's interim cabinet pushed for his release. By the time Ghoneim was released on the evening of February 7, 2011 people were losing hope and dividing into two opposing camps, one calling for the overthrow of the Mubarak regime and the other calling for an end to the revolutionary movement. The heartbreaking and dramatic forty-five-minute interview with Ghoneim by TV host Mona al-Shazli on February 7, 2011 presents another clear example of how a persuasive message coupled with tactical performance played a crucial role in re-energizing the revolution at a critical moment when crowds were thinning in Tahrir. The translated examples from Ghoneim's performance illustrate two ways in which he achieved this, namely by presenting a positive image of himself and the protesters in general through his discourse, and by connecting on an emotional level with his audience in a way that gained sympathy for the cause of the protesters through semiotic emotional gestural and facial signs.

Ghoneim's emotional public appearance right after his release effectively managed to undermine negative public perception of the protesters and revive the struggle against the regime. His moving performance throughout the interview effectively challenged the impact of Mubarak's performance during his latest speech. Consequently, Tuesday, February 8 witnessed a significant increase in the number of protesters in Tahrir, and

Wael Ghoneim during his first interview upon his release from state security detention, February 7, 2011

all across Egypt, demanding Mubarak's immediate removal. Ghoneim's appearance, body language, use of formal Arabic expressions, including religious language, and his frequent sobbing broke stereotypes and made his audience relate to him on an emotional level.

In contrast to the image of the protesters shown by the state-sponsored media, Ghoneim was a well-educated Egyptian professional. He graduated from Cairo University's Faculty of Engineering, received his MBA from the American University in Cairo, then worked as Google's marketing manager for the MENA region, and up until 2010 had no history of political activism. He was well-spoken, bilingual, affluent, and had a very reputable job. The image he presented caused more Egyptians to view him and the demonstrators much more favorably and to begin to respect and appreciate their efforts.

Despite having been released only a couple of hours earlier, Ghoneim seemed to be well aware of the negative societal perception of demonstrators and emphasized aspects throughout his interview on Dream TV to break widely held stereotypes. He kept stressing the protesters' good social standing, their courageous opposition to the tyrannical regime, and the fact that they are definitely not traitors to their country.

> Some of us are rich, live in fancy houses, and drive the best cars. I don't need anything from anyone. And I've never needed anything from anyone. Everything that was done put all of our lives in danger.[27]

Moreover, to further address the negative stereotypes about the demonstrators and to connect with the audience on an emotional level, Ghoneim started off his interview in a very serious deep tone to pay condolences to the families of the martyrs. His facial expressions showed how he was deeply moved by the issue and how he somehow felt responsible for it. Avoiding eye contact with the camera, looking down, and keeping his arms to his sides were all signs of his deep grief and complete respect for the role played by revolting Egyptians. By smoothly inserting a *fusHa* expression of condolences in a tearful reference to the martyrs of the revolution in the middle of his *'ammiya* discourse, Wael was signaling his above-average educational, cultural, and professional standing. His occasional use of English terminology further reinforced this image and acted as a sign of belonging to a middle to high social class.

First I would like to say something to everyone, to the mothers and fathers who lost their children: I'd like to convey my deep condolences and may God accept their children as martyrs whether civilians, police officers, or soldiers. Anyone who died is a martyr.

By the way, if I had been a traitor, I would have stayed by the pool at my villa in the Emirates, having a good time. My salary keeps increasing and I had no problems.

Among the formal terms used by Ghoneim was the word *Hadritik*, which is a respectful way to address one's interlocutor. He uses this term to address al-Shazli, the presenter of the talk show, which again shows his elevated class background and good knowledge of social address codes in the Arabic language: "*Hadritik*, we no longer listen to each other carefully. I just want to say that it is a trend now to call each other traitors."

Additionally, Ghoneim often also used the religious and culturally loaded word *Haram*, which we maintained as it is in Arabic in order to avoid indigenizing the concept as it was expressed in the source language (see discussion of Venuti in the introduction). The term was used to convey Ghoneim's sense of injustice regarding the fact that, after he was detained, his parents spent days without knowing anything about his whereabouts and well-being. As his emotions built up, he spoke much faster and used hand gestures, including banging on the table, to express his fury. Ghoneim's sobbing and emotional state while he used the term *Haram* amplified the impact of the message related to his family, again a very important value in the Egyptian culture. His reference to his visually impaired father generates more sympathy from his audience, as well as improving the image of protesters that have been largely viewed as family-less and insolent for protesting against the aged figure, Mubarak.

Haram, Haram, Haram that my father who is half blind and could totally lose his sight would spend twelve days not knowing his son's whereabouts. Why [sobbing]?!

In another dramatic tactic, Ghoneim directly addressed his audience by using the expression '*ya gama'a*,' which we decided to also maintain in Arabic. Some English-speaking readers may already be familiar with the latter term from references to political Islamist groups like *al-Jama'a al-Islamiya*. In order to reflect the harder pronunciation of the Arabic letter '*jim*' in the Egyptian dialect, it was spelled with a 'g' instead of a 'j,' to read '*gama'a*' instead of '*jama'a*.' We decided to maintain the use of this term in English to introduce it in a context devoid of any political/religious connotation; and to offer the common use of the expression, which is to address a group of people with whom one is acquainted.

> *Ya gama'a*, please! There are no heroes. The heroes are the ones on the streets. The heroes are each and every one of us. The time when one hero would ride his horse to lead the masses is long gone. So, please don't let anyone fool you! This is the Internet youth revolution. This is the Internet youth revolution, which became the young people's revolution, and later became the Egyptian nation's revolution. It has no single hero that dominates the scene. We have all been heroes.

Ghoneim's reference to the Egyptian Internet youth generation manages to impress his viewers, 75 percent of whom are Internet-illiterate.[28] And relating these young people's fight to the rest of the nation very smartly attracted viewers to it and led them into joining it. Ghoneim, however, acts humbled throughout the interview by the situation he was put in. His consistent emphasis in the quote above and the one below that he was not a hero, but rather only a member of this movement, played a role in winning over the audience to his cause. This repetition was maintained in the English language translation to better convey the message and intense emotions he was stressing.

> In Egypt we like to create heroes but I'm not a hero. I've been away sleeping for twelve days. The heroes are the ones who took to the streets, the heroes are the ones who joined the demonstrations, the heroes are the ones who sacrificed their lives, the heroes are the ones who were beaten, the heroes are the ones who were arrested and exposed to real dangers. I was not a hero.

This position is in stark contrast to Mubarak's emphasis on the heroic nature of his service to Egypt throughout his military and political career as illustrated in the following quote from his third speech on February 10, 2011, the last speech he would make as president.

When I was young, like the Egyptian youth of today, I learned Egyptian military honor, loyalty to the nation, and sacrifice for its sake. I have dedicated my whole life to defending its land and sovereignty. I have witnessed the nation's defeats and victories in war. I have lived the days of defeat and occupation as well as the days of the crossing, of victory and liberation. The happiest days of my life were when I raised the flag of Egypt over Sinai. I faced death many times as a pilot, in Addis Ababa, and much else besides this. Not one day have I given in to foreign pressures or dictates. I have preserved peace and worked for the sake of the security and stability of Egypt. I have struggled for the sake of its renaissance and its people. I have never sought power or empty fame. I am confident that the overwhelming majority of the people know who Hosni Mubarak is, and I am saddened by what I see today among some of the people of my nation.

Besides making opposite claims to those of Mubarak regarding his own personal status as a hero, Ghoneim emphasizes the heroic nature of all Egyptians who took to the streets against the regime. While Mubarak seems to imply that their behavior is the antithesis of his own heroic and patriotic service, Ghoneim transforms the nation's rebellious youth into heroes.

Finally, Ghoneim's apologetic discourse and sobbing at different points of the interview also set a contrasting image to that of Mahfouz's firm and challenging appearance in her vlog. Just as Mahfouz challenged stereotypes about Egyptian women, Ghoneim broke stereotypes surrounding Egyptian notions of masculinity. Butler's idea of constructing gender through language and gestures is also useful in analyzing Ghoneim's interview from the perspective of the Egyptian societal norms and perceptions. His apologetic discourse, hunched body posture, and tearful eyes cast him in a rather feminine light.

In general, Ghoneim did not hide his intensely vulnerable emotions, which culminated in sobbing at several instances throughout the interview. This was further accentuated by the last seconds of the show, when he was shown photographs of Egyptians who were killed during the revolution. The clip displayed on the screen was accompanied by very melancholy music, which led him to break into tears and rush out of the studio. He left with the following words, bringing his performance to a dramatic close and causing a surprised and confused al-Shazli to follow him off-camera:

I'm sorry, but this is not our fault. I swear to God we are not to blame. This is the fault of each and every one who so persistently wouldn't let go of power. I want to leave.

Ghoneim's engaging emotional performance, coupled with al-Shazli's compassionate remarks and empathetic facial gestures, surpassed Mubarak's relatively colder and blander presentation. However, it was this abrupt finale of the interview that came across to the audience as completely genuine, which further added to the positive impact of the performance on the millions of Egyptians who took to the streets for the following four days.

February 11: Act I, Final Scene—The Victory[29]

The video, speech, and interview translated in this chapter presented two levels of analysis, namely the level of linguistic discourse and the level of non-verbal semiotic performance. Both levels contributed to molding the public reaction and directing action on the Egyptian streets. What we have translated led to the final scene of Act I of the eighteen days of political drama. From February 8 until February 11, 2011, a rising sense of drama and suspense took place in Tahrir, which was affected by actions and performances taking place outside it. Mubarak's third, incoherent speech on February 10, 2011 was poorly structured and delivered; it neither sent a strong message, nor had a mobilizing impact comparable to his second speech.[30] This disillusioned millions of Egyptians, thousands of whom were camped in Tahrir anticipating that his third speech would be his resignation statement. That night, many demonstrators announced they would march to the Presidential Palace the following morning. The sense of drama was heightened by the vague military communiqué issued on the morning of February 11, 2011 and led to much confusion all across Egypt and elsewhere. Average people, as well as political analysts, could not determine whether the message was that the SCAF was taking power, or if it was just sending an alarming message to Mubarak. As the afternoon drew to an end, TV and radio channels started broadcasting that vice president and chief of intelligence Omar Suleiman was about to deliver an important speech.

Delivered at 6:00 PM, the thirty-seven-second statement signified an unprecedented victory for the Egyptian street. Suleiman, who had assumed the post of vice president only two weeks earlier, dramatically

Omar Suleiman delivering Mubarak's resignation statement, February 11, 2011

announced the resignation of Hosni Mubarak, in a message that was displayed on large screens in Tahrir Square as it was being broadcast.

From the first second he looked frustrated and depressed; the demonstrators on the street picked up on this right away and started cheering before he even finished his statement. This epic moment was met with celebration all over the streets of Egypt, not just because it showed Egyptians that their efforts paid off, but most importantly because the defeated look on Suleiman's face allowed Egyptians to finally feel stronger than their oppressive regime.

> In the name of God, the most Gracious, the most Merciful. Fellow citizens, in light of the difficult circumstances the country is experiencing, President Muhammad Hosni Mubarak has decided to step down and hand his powers to the Supreme Council of the Armed Forces to run the country. May God help us and grant us success.[31]

In the terminology of theater, this episode can be described as a peripeteia: "a sudden and unforeseen change, turning point or reversal in the action."[32] Indeed this was the major turning point in the revolutionary period. Both the fact that the announcement was delivered by Suleiman and the very short length of the statement came as a surprise to many. Perhaps their expectations were shaped by the precedent set by Gamal

Abdel Nasser's moving *naksa* ('setback') speech on June 9, 1967, follow-ing the military defeat in the war with Israel, in which he announced his resignation from his position as president. Unlike Mubarak, who throughout the days of the revolution continued insisting that he retain his position at least until power was transferred following elections in September, Nasser accepted responsibility for the military defeat and stated his intention to leave politics for good, even if it was just a tactic he used to regain support after a humiliating defeat.[33] Furthermore, Nasser acknowledged that the goal he was working for, Arab unity, did not depend on him alone, while Mubarak seemed to cling to the idea that Egypt needed his leadership up until the end of the revolution. Finally, following the examples of Nasser's longer resignation speech and Mubarak's last three speeches (ranging from ten to seventeen minutes) which all contained various levels of sentimentality, Suleiman's unsenti-mental thirty-seven second announcement of the end of Mubarak's three decades of rule was clearly unanticipated, if not astonishing.

In classic works of drama, the peripeteia is typically followed by the dénouement, "when the contradictions are resolved and the threads of the plot unraveled . . . the episode of the comedy or tragedy that finally eliminates the conflicts and obstacles."[34] However, at the time of writing, and as this analysis demonstrates, the plot of the 2011 Egyptian Revolu-tion—with all its contradictions, conflicts, and obstacles—has yet to be resolved. This is best explained by the concerns raised by the thousands of Egyptians who have returned to Tahrir week after week since the *ayyam al-thawra* (days of the revolution). A few examples of these many concerns include the perception that there has never been a clean break with the policies and people of the former regime, the predominance of military over civil authority, and the timing of elections vis-à-vis the implementa-tion of a new constitution (for more examples, see the section "Egyptian Revolution Act II" below).

February 11: New Beginnings[35]
Ever since 1882, when Ahmad 'Urabi led a military campaign against British intervention in Egypt, the Egyptian military has been, in general, highly respected by the Egyptian public for the role it played in resisting colonialism and autocratic rule (chapter 7). The tradition of mandatory military conscription has also generated popular support for the military. Furthermore, the military establishment has for years played the role of

service provider to the Egyptian people, especially at times of social and economic distress. This was exemplified on several occasions in the past three decades, including riots, food shortages, and times when the military had to step in to make up for the lack of infrastructure. For example, during the bread shortage in 2008, the military was ordered by Mubarak to intervene by increasing production and ensuring fair distribution.

Since Egypt's Friday of Rage on January 28, 2011, the Egyptian military has assumed posts across major cities, while police forces retreated after bloody battles with protesters. This shift in authority was seen as a victory for protesters, and thus, the military forces were very well received and tanks were immediately sprayed with slogans, such as "The army and people are one" (al-sha'b wa-l-gish id waHda). Many protesters and their children posed for photographs with soldiers and much affection was displayed for the military over the following two weeks and spread in the private- and publicly-owned media. This was also intensified after the release of the military's first two communiqués, in which they promised not to harm protesters and to pursue demonstrators' demands.

On the evening of February 11, 2011 after Mubarak relinquished his power, Major General Mohsen al-Fangary of the SCAF read out the third military communiqué to the Egyptian people. The communiqué reinforced the Egyptians' widespread sympathy for the military, which had already assumed the powers of the presidency. Major General al-Fangary's performance that evening included transformative moments that shaped the audience reaction and reinforced support for handing over the president's power to the military.

In the third military communiqué al-Fangary first addressed the Egyptian people as peers by referring to them as "fellow citizens." However, despite this gesture, the tone and language he used in the rest of the communiqué represented his restraint and his strict military background. Forsaking one's leader is neither an easy nor a common act in the military institution, and in this communiqué, the SCAF was not only accepting the responsibility to lead the country, but was also recognizing the ouster of the general commander of the army, Hosni Mubarak, who had occupied this post for thirty years. It was unconstitutional for Mubarak to cede his power to the military; in such cases the head of parliament or the head of the Constitutional Court—if the former is indisposed—assumes presidential authority. Yet, the SCAF accepted the responsibilities and the Egyptian masses did not wish to reject that temporary settlement.

In an awkward use of the Arabic language, Hosni Mubarak was referred to in the communiqué as "president," not "former president." In similar cases, the words "deceased" or "former" are used to describe a president who is no longer in power. This word choice somehow implied the military's long-term loyalty to their lifelong ruler. Yet, followed by a dramatic gesture that gained the military much support, the masses chose to overlook these subtle messages. Average Egyptians put complete faith in the military institution, so as to overcome an entrenched fear of the future and a sense of despair due to an unconventional power vacuum.

In a remarkable gesture, the major general stopped for four seconds in the middle of the statement and gave the martyrs of the revolution a military salute. In contrast to Mubarak's brief reference to the deceased in his second speech, in which he portrayed their death as an accidental loss, this display of appreciation and respect managed to gain mass popular respect for the military, stressed by the demonstrators' slogan "The army and the people are one." Soon after that, still shots of the salute were displayed as profile pictures by thousands of Egyptians on their Facebook pages as a sign of support and affection for the military.

> Fellow citizens, at this decisive moment in Egypt's history, marked by President Muhammad Hosni Mubarak's decision to resign from the position of president of the republic and to hand over to the Supreme Council of the Armed Forces the management of the affairs of the country; the Supreme Council of the Armed Forces salutes, with high esteem and respect, the souls of the martyrs [stops to give a military salute for the martyrs] who sacrificed their lives for the freedom and security of their country; and all the members of its great people. May God help us and grant us peace and success.[36]

Egyptian Revolution, Act II

Only a few months after al-Fangary's dramatic gesture, hundreds of thousands of Egyptians remarkably took to the streets again, but this time in opposition to policies set forth by the SCAF and the Egyptian interim governments. Protesters rose up against the SCAF's policies—including military trials for civilians, the slow pace of trials for members of the former regime, and inadequate security measures. The positive impact of the military's performance described above lasted with some Egyptians, but definitely not for all and not for long.

عاجل

المجلس الأعلى للقوات المسلحة يصدر بيانه الثالث

Major General Mohsen al-Fangary, member of the Supreme Council of the Armed Forces, delivering the third military communiqué, February 11, 2011

Since March 2011, Egyptians have been joining weekly protests against the SCAF's policies, which have often ended in bloody confrontations with the Central Security Forces. Following a controversial sit-in that started on July 8, 2011, Major General Mohsen al-Fangary delivered a statement on July 12, 2011 using aggressively threatening hand gestures, facial expressions, and tone. He insisted that the SCAF would remain in power throughout the transitional period and sternly warned the protesters against interfering with everyday activities and acting against the interests of the nation.[37] Raising his eyebrows and waving with his pointing finger, al-Fangary warned against the continuation of protests and described them as subversive, selfish acts that were creating obstacles in the transition to a democratically elected civilian leadership.

In contrast to the first communiqué described earlier in this chapter, this statement—which referred to the protesters as thugs and disregarded their demands—was poorly received by many and, consequently, degraded the mass popular support for the military leadership. Jokes and caricatures immediately started circulating following the speech, which was considered offensive by many. One of these caricatures was a cartoon by Carlos Latuff, a popular Brazilian political cartoonist who has drawn cartoons in support of the Egyptian people since the start of the January 25 Revolution. Latuff has been consistent in rapidly picking up on themes from the Egyptian street and drawing cartoons that the Egyptian public,

Major General Mohsen al-Fangary addressing the public, July 12, 2011

who often feel he is living among them rather than in Brazil, can relate to. Some fans have even created pages for him on Facebook, which display his work and news about him. Picking up the widespread discontent with al-Fangary's speech, Latuff depicted him as a tiny figure nervously pointing his finger at a young oversized Egyptian revolutionary. In that image, Latuff shows only the Egyptian revolutionary's sneaker-clad feet, which creates a stark contrast between him and the military figure in uniform.

Additionally, later in July, the SCAF attacked the April 6 Youth Movement and accused them of spreading false rumors about the SCAF, receiving foreign support, and creating unnecessary turmoil, thus hindering a smooth transitional period. This stance against young revolutionaries involved mass arrests of young opposition figures, who were to be tried before military courts. The public, Internet activists, and political cartoonists protested against the SCAF crackdown. Here again, Carlos Latuff proved to be synchronized with the Egyptian Revolution when he produced another empathetic cartoon; this one depicted the SCAF as an oversized prehistoric man carrying a stick, pointing his finger at a young revolutionary, and calling him "thug."

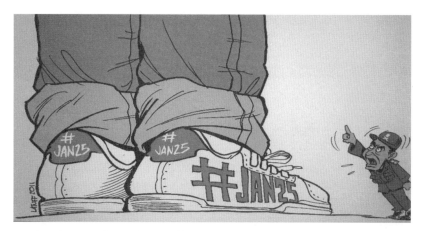

A political cartoon by Carlos Latuff following al-Fangary's provocative speech on July 12, 2011. Credit, Carlos Latuff

A political cartoon by Carlos Latuff following SCAF's accusations of activists and civil-society movements. Credit, Carlos Latuff

Asmaa Mahfouz was among those arrested; she was charged with defamation of the military establishment and inciting violent acts through her Twitter account. The charges were dropped following public disapproval and alleged foreign pressure on the SCAF. However, before the charges were officially dropped, Mahfouz appeared in a televised interview on a private Egyptian network (ON TV) on August 14, 2011, where she

A tearful Asmaa Mahfouz in a TV interview, August 14, 2011

and her lawyer, Hossam Eissa, seemed apologetic for the language she had used against members of the SCAF.[38] Mahfouz's tearful performance during the interview stood in contrast to the challenging and firm stance she took in her earlier vlog and managed to win some hearts of the audience as she reminded them of the early revolutionary days in January and the role that young men and women had played in it. She also tried hard to distinguish between insulting the SCAF as a political leader of the country, and insulting the military establishment, which she insists she did not do.

On August 3, 2011 Hosni Mubarak, along with his two sons Gamal and Alaa, the former interior minister Habib al-Adli, and six senior police officers appeared in court inside a metal cage to face murder charges for the killings that took place during the revolution. The Mubaraks' performance that day was rather remarkable and certainly a climactic moment among the performances discussed in this chapter. Hosni Mubarak appeared on a hospital stretcher as a tactic to gain sympathy and to appear senile or oblivious to his surroundings, and Alaa Mubarak held a copy of the Qur'an.

That same day, the Al Arabiya network aired an interview with Egyptian film director Magdi Ahmad Ali. The director discussed the theatrical aspects of the former president's trial, which was broadcast on TV—a

Hosni Mubarak in trial on a hospital stretcher, August 3, 2011

rare event in contemporary times. Ahmad Ali observed what he viewed as artificial behavior on the part of the accused in order to gain sympathy from viewers. The atypical atmosphere for a courtroom scene was at times characteristic of a comedy, including the chaotic moments when the crowd of lawyers, who were packing the front rows of the courtroom, was shouting at the judge. As the defendants departed from the courtroom, former Minister of Interior Habib al-Adli was saluted by officers as if he were still in power rather than a defendant accused of serious crimes. Ahmad Ali remarked that this salute gave him the urge to shout "Stop!," remind the participants of their proper roles, and reshoot the scene.[39] With the trial of members of the former regime underway and constant maneuvers to undermine the protesters undertaken by the SCAF, the Egyptian Revolution is well into the second act of its political drama. Additional events and performances continue to unfold and the future seems more uncertain than ever.

Conclusion

The eighteen revolutionary days in Tahrir were shaped by intensely dramatic discursive moments, which included speeches, interviews, and communiqués by several key players that have had a crucial impact on both public opinion and the course of action throughout this historic event. This chapter translated selections from transformative discourses by actors as diverse as activists Asmaa Mahfouz and Wael Ghoneim, former president Hosni Mubarak, former vice president Omar Suleiman, and Major General Mohsen al-Fangary of the SCAF. Our decision to translate these selections was based on several factors, including the rich semiotic details, the impact on the audience, and how representative each performance was of a specific discourse. Other performances not presented in this chapter but which also had a major impact on the Egyptian street included activist/journalist Nawara Negm's sarcastic interview on Al Jazeera TV on January 25, 2011,[40] and former prime minister Ahmed Shafik's heated interview with journalists Alaa Al Aswany, Yosri Fouda, and Hamdi Qandil on March 2, 2011, one day before Shafik's resignation from his post.[41]

We analyzed the translated selections from the standpoint of theatrical performance with multiple levels of discourse and sign language used by each speaker/actor to mold the reaction of her/his target audience. As demonstrated above, theoretical insights from theatre, performance, and translation studies can shed light on matters normally covered by the social sciences. This is consistent with the idea that, "in its broadest sense, performance is a norm of all human activity."[42] As the early stages of Mubarak's trial and the current strife over the first post-revolutionary elections indicate, the political drama of Egypt's latest revolution has yet to reach its dénouement.

Notes

1   Carol Bardenstein, *Translation and Transformation in Modern Arabic Literature: The Indigenous Assertions of Muhammad 'Uthman Jalal* (Wiesbaden: Harrassowitz Verlag, 2005), p. 2.
2   Lawrence Venuti, *Translation Studies Reader* (London: Routledge, 1999), p. 468.
3   Bardenstein, *Translation and Transformation*, pp. 18–19.
4   Bardenstein, *Translation and Transformation*, p. 5.
5   Christopher B. Balme, *The Cambridge Introduction to Theatre Studies* (Cambridge: Cambridge University Press, 2008), pp. 11–12.
6   Diana Taylor, "Translating Performance," in *Profession* (Modern Language Association) 1–2 (2002): 45.
7   Taylor, "Translating Performance," pp. 45–46.

8 Patrice Pavis, *Dictionary of the Theatre: Terms, Concepts and Analysis* (Toronto: University of Toronto Press, 1998), pp. 105–106.

9 Judith Butler, *Bodies That Matter* (London: Routledge, 1993), p. 2.

10 Butler, *Bodies That Matter*, pp. 12–13.

11 Robert D. Benford and David A. Snow, "Framing Processes and Social Movements: An Overview and Assessment," in *Annual Review of Sociology*, August 2000, p. 614.

12 James M. Jasper, *The Art of Moral Protest: Culture, Biography, and Creativity in Social Movements* (Chicago: University of Chicago Press, 2008), p. 106.

13 Jeff Goodwin and James M. Jasper, "Emotions and Social Movements," in *Handbook of the Sociology of Emotions* (New York: Springer, 2006), p. 619.

14 Goodwin and Jasper, "Emotions and Social Movements," p. 617.

15 Keir Elam, *The Semiotics of Theatre and Drama* (London: Methuen, 1980), pp. 50–51.

16 Balme, *Cambridge Introduction to Theatre Studies*, p. 78.

17 See Appendix 1 for the original Arabic of Mahfouz's remarks.

18 Judith Butler, "Gender Trouble, Feminist Theory, and Psychoanalytic Discourse," in *Feminism/Postmodernism*, ed. Linda Nicholson (London: Routledge, 1990), pp. 324–40.

19 See Asmaa Mahfouz's vlog that mobilized thousands of Egyptians to demonstrate on January 25, 2011 on YouTube, January 18, 2011, http://www.youtube.com/watch?v=ZhbKN9q319g

20 Mubarak's speech on February 1, 2011, *Nilenews*, February 2, 2011, http://www.youtube.com/watch?v=2q0j9F-wtEg.

21 See former President Hosni Mubarak's second speech, which resulted in divisions on the Egyptian street, on YouTube, February 1, 2011, http://www.mashahd.net/video/f986c7f1f2e60b6511a

22 See Appendix 1 for the original Arabic of Mubarak's remarks.

23 Elam, *Semiotics of Theatre and Drama*, p. 157.

24 Elam, *Semiotics of Theatre and Drama*, p. 20.

25 Ali Abdel Mohsen, "The Blacklist: Pro-Mubarak Celebrities in the Doghouse," *al-Masry al-Youm English Edition*, July 3, 2011, http://www.almasryalyoum.com/en/node/342400

26 See Wael Ghoneim's interview with Mona al-Shazli on *al-Ashira Misa'an* on YouTube, February 8, 2011, http://www.youtube.com/watch?v=VlBAzvX9Xw4&feature=related

27 See Appendix 1 for the original Arabic of Ghoneim's remarks.

28 Africa Internet Usage and Populations Statistics, Internet World Stats, http://www.internetworldstats.com/stats1.htm

29 See Omar Suleiman's statement announcing President Hosni Mubarak's decision to step down, YouTube, February 11, 2011, http://www.youtube.com/watch?v=ph8e11KR8mk

30 See Hosni Mubarak's final speech delivered on February 10, 2011 on YouTube, February 10, 2011, http://www.youtube.com/watch?v=XOiXKqPiPVw

31 See Appendix 1 for the original Arabic of Suleiman's remarks.

32 Pavis, *Dictionary of the Theatre*, p. 262.

33 See Gamal Abdel Nasser's abdication speech on YouTube, February 17 2010, http://www.youtube.com/watch?v=JshfnSfHL28&NR=1

34 Pavis, *Dictionary of the Theatre*, p. 93.

35 See first military communiqué delivered by General Mohsin al-Fangary, in which he saluted the martyrs of the revolution, on YouTube, February 11, 2011, http://www.youtube.com/watch?v=ayeU6XebjTg&feature=related

36 See Appendix 1 for the original Arabic of al-Fangary's remarks.

37 See General al-Fangary's speech on YouTube, July 11, 2011, http://www.youtube.com/watch?v=pHx3Q_ihd1A

38 See Yosri Fouda's interview with Asmaa Mahfouz on *Akhir kalam*, ON TV, August 14, 2011, http://www.youtube.com/user/ONtveg#p/search/0/tjxHwctIis4

39 Interview with Egyptian director Magdi Ahmad Ali on Al Arabiya, August 4, 2011, http://www.alarabiya.net/articles/2011/08/04/160828.html

40 http://www.youtube.com/watch?v=eE2itEB__v8&feature=results_main&playnext=1&list=PLF011179DB12BEB09

41 http://www.youtube.com/watch?v=GgWLVbceOKY

42 Balme, *Cambridge Introduction to Theatre Studies*, p. 91.

3

Signs and Signifiers:
Visual Translations of Revolt

Laura Gribbon and Sarah Hawas

Beginning on January 25, 2011, thousands of ordinary Egyptians occupied Tahrir Square, in downtown Cairo, marking the beginning of the initial eighteen-day countrywide revolt that resulted in the successful removal of former President Hosni Mubarak. They have returned to Tahrir on several occasions since, demanding an end to injustice and corruption, and an opportunity to participate in the rebuilding of a democratic nation. The uprising unleashed a seemingly endless array of banners and signs, many of which were long, elaborate, and constantly changing. This awakening of individual and collective spirit—a rebirth of public consciousness—was reflected on countless banners. Egyptians articulated in written form extended expressions of what could only previously be spoken, thought, or felt. This was notably conducted in a distinctly visual and visible manner, as protesters proudly presented themselves to photographers—journalists and others alike—to be recorded. The signs featured and translated in this chapter are mainly from Midan al-Tahrir. This is not to suggest that the *midan* was wholly representative of the revolution; rather, Tahrir became a magnet for creative expression due to its occupation by protesters over extended periods of time. Furthermore, our selection of images is by no means an attempt to outline a chronology of the revolution, which, at the time this chapter is being written, is still ongoing.

International media, such as the UK *Telegraph*'s feature,[1] have focused on signs in English, and there are now several books and websites that have translated signs for the English reader.[2] We are not seeking to merely add to this body of work, but to engage the material on a deeper level. Given that the signs historicize events in such a unique way, our translation of these banners, and their respective referential worlds, engages and excavates the discursive significations of the uprising within its social context. The banners were themselves a *translation* of the demands and desires of revolution, in that they constructed a narrative of resistance that drew on various signs and symbols to articulate the story of a people in revolt: their history, their present, and their will to change the future.

Generally, the role of the protest sign is to articulate the demands of the individual holding it. However, the ways in which Egyptians also used these tools as a means of responding to and challenging dominant narratives, relating to one another and galvanizing support, reflected conscious participation in a specific culture of resistance.[3] Many signs functioned as organizational tools. They enabled protesters to communicate with one another, and made the aims of the revolution an ever-present, explicit call to action. This played a role in preserving the internal coherence of the uprising, as well as allowing for diverse, individual interests to be expressed. The dualism was complementary. On the one hand, the signs were wholly about self-expression and an outpouring of emotion: rage, hope, pride, desire, and grief. On the other hand, they functioned as a communication tool within Egypt and to the outside world, as well as a means of organization and motivation within the mass of voices.

Tahrir was not only a stronghold for those that occupied it throughout the uprising; it became a home for those who would return daily to take part in protests. The sense of collective energy in the *midan* was incredible. There was no hierarchy among protesters, and lateral connections between people required a significant degree of organization. On several occasions a contribution box was passed around for people to give donations. Those needing money for food, blankets, medicines, or even cigarettes were encouraged to take from it. A free clinic, school, hospital, open-air kitchen, and other services were set up and run cooperatively in a remarkable display of burgeoning participatory democracy. This is not to suggest that Tahrir was a new or shocking spectacle of nonviolent resistance and mutual aid; rather, it was the natural expansion of decades of survival through a culture of cooperative resistance, akin to the subversive appropriation of the outskirts of districts by rural migrant communities. The outworking of this concept in Tahrir enabled many protesters to return daily, or to remain in the *midan*, for the duration of the eighteen days, providing them with the space to create these unique displays of visual civil resistance.

Translation as Revolution

For many around the world who followed the Egyptian Revolution on TV or online, visual images and signs enabled them to 'watch' events as they unfolded. Protesters seemed to possess a conscious understanding they were on display to a wider audience. This is especially true in the case of signs in multiple languages, as well as the urging of foreigners to "tell people what you've seen." However, this newfound 'permission to speak' was no simple task. Who was the readership targeted by these banners: the state, the media? And if so, which media, and why? Which banners spoke to an international audience, and what did they have to say? Which ones focused on protesters, or other Egyptians? In short, how did these banners function to render the Tahrir uprising intelligible in multiple contexts and to various demographics?

As tweets capture a thought or demand in 140 characters or less, so signs were used to put out a concise message, which spread and was often repeated in chants and refrains or on other banners. The signs evolved over time, becoming more elaborate, more demanding, and more humorous in the weeks and months that followed. Initially they seemed to be about individual expression and were addressed to fellow Egyptians and the regime, but as time passed and there was a growing sense of the world's eyes on Tahrir, they increasingly communicated a globally conscious message.

The self-translating nature of this decentralized, spontaneous uprising, networked by social media and televised across the world, naturally implicates its readers. We have therefore consciously situated ourselves as committed political subjects, not as divorced observers or scribes. Our task as translators is to grapple not just with the concrete developments that prompted the daily occurrence of new and diverse banners, but also with the referential world that guided these increasingly creative responses, giving them their own specific character and energy. This requires an honest and comprehensive engagement with everything from the religious and national imagination, to popular culture and patterns of humor. Engaging culture and cultural references is never an easy task, but the complexity of the question is taken ever more seriously by the translator. In post-colonial translation, especially into a dominant language (in this case English), the translator is required to be continually self-critical, in order to avoid a native valorization of the source language.[4] Maria Tymoczko developed this concept through her studies of early

Irish texts in English. In *Post-colonial Translation*, edited by Susan Bassnett and Harish Trivedi, Tymoczko focuses on texts emerging from colonized or oppressed peoples. She speaks of missing or "silenced" voices and the need to cite translation within specific sociopolitical situations, where several parties have a vested interest in the production of texts. She warns about the temptation to search for an equivalent, or similar phrase in the target language, in order to stress universality and enable the reader to rapidly understand the embedded meaning. She concludes that sometimes it is necessary to maintain the "foreignness" of the source language and highlight differences, in order to more effectively convey layers of cultural, political, religious, and even economic meaning.[5] Consequently, in this chapter we have sought to expose and expound upon the referential within the source language, so that these narratives might present to the English-language reader a glimpse into the contemporary moment, within its deeper historical and cultural context.

Between Sign and Signification:
Narratives and Counter-narratives

Encountering these texts and translating them, moving between language and discourse, and locating the contours of signification allows us to reflect on both the stakes and possibilities that lie in translation. At a moment when global powers appear willing to absorb resistance, if not through armed intervention as in Libya then through a politics of the intelligible, translation appears inevitable and necessary. This is evident in the global consciousness—both of imperial alliances and global solidarities, addressed later in this chapter—displayed by the revolutionaries themselves, as well as international reactions to the uprising. The revolution was therefore, from the beginning, not just about Egypt, but also about regional geopolitics, the United States, the Muslim world and the western, and multiple similar constructs. As the months following Mubarak's departure have shown, there is nothing stable or universally intelligible about the notions of 'revolution,' 'freedom,' 'democracy,' 'change,' and so on. The experience of translating banners and signs from Midan al-Tahrir is instructive in this regard; by laboring to establish both autonomy and visibility, protesters actively took over the process of translation while simultaneously rendering themselves vulnerable to mis- or dis-translation. This tension, between the necessity for localized cultural and emotional economies that draw on codified behavior and the desire for global solidarity that trespasses the borders of states, constitutes our very contemporary moment. Our task—both as translators, but also as *beings in translation*—is to navigate just this space.

Translation has frequently been marginalized as an arbitrary, mechanized action that takes place between two seemingly cohesive languages with clearly demarcated borders. Through the professionalization of translation, categorical distinctions are made between a creative author with perceived monopoly on meaning, and a translator whose task is to find equivalence in the target language.[6] In actuality, both writer and reader are involved in their respective modes of translation. Language is not necessarily stable, and texts signify different things *in different ways* to their writers and readers. It is therefore crucial to note the inherently political act of translation: at the level of selection, contextualization, and commitment. In this way, our subtitle to this section alludes to the multiple layers of signification occasioned by the banners and signs of revolution. They need to be unpacked at multiple levels in order to effectively convey meaning to various audiences.

While images supposedly denote a situation, they are often used to connote a narrative or discourse of events. Roland Barthes, a critical figure in modern semiotics, studied cultural signs and systems from an outsiders' perspective. His work drew on the theory and practice of intertextuality, using discursive practices to challenge established norms. He noted that the way in which signs and pictures persuade their viewers to believe in a concept is through the "rhetoric of the image," being an ideal medium for ideologies to appear normalized.[7] Barthes argues that these "codes of connotation" are culturally understood by people with a shared history and culture, slowing down the process of interpreting the meaning of certain symbolic references to a non-native audience. As Barthes also suggests, the act of photographing and compiling certain images from any event decontextualizes the subject, reinscribing a further narrative of events.[8] By individuating these subjects (the protesters) and removing them from the wider context of the *midan*, they go from being part of collective revolt, to becoming bearers of specific historical narratives, each distinct in its own way. Our attempt to translate these signs and to engage their signification is an attempt to reconstruct a broader narrative, while remaining distinctly loyal to its various subjects.

Taking Back the Sign: Censorship and the Egyptian Street

So what did it mean to overcome the fear of speaking, indeed, of writing? And how did this experience transform subjects such that they sensed a rebirth of their collective belonging? Indeed, what was specifically 'Egyptian' about breaking the fear barrier? Over the last few decades, Egypt has not only been regularly characterized by alleged mass cultural illiteracy but also by heavy-handed, and occasionally arbitrary, state and street censorship. Richard Jacquemond has written at length about "the very heavy symbolic power attached to the written word, completely blown out of proportion in comparison with its actual social diffusion and erected as the showcase and yardstick of society's 'fundamental values.'"[9] Debates around art were rooted in what Jacquemond describes as a "realist-reformist" paradigm, which denied art any sense of autonomy. Readers were treated as minors in need of cultural gatekeeping, a task attended to by everyone from professors, teachers, journalists, critics, publishers, and official censors to university students, their parents, religious institutions, and workers distributing the material. In its unique instance of biopower,[10] the cultural field variously policed itself into the regeneration and protection of a social and moral order in which an entire people were converted into accomplices, informers, and censors. Some writers have sought to radically transform the parameters of their work, doing away with social-realist notions of aesthetic conformity and responsibility, the most notable example of which is Sonallah Ibrahim.[11] Such individuals have been regularly adopted as symbolic capital for the state's liberalization, in an attempt to neuter dissidence and hijack autonomy. The state therefore relied partly on the moral economy of a narrow elite and their cultural patronage to delimit what is permissible or not for the written word. The specific position of cultural players vis-à-vis the state was increasingly compromised by both selective state patronage and the arbitrary liberalization of public discourse, as well as a tightening grip on the limits of what could be written, both in literature and in the media. The state cultivated an ever-growing fear of the written word, effected in a myriad of ways: Ibrahim Eissa,[12] prominent journalist and political pundit, was repeatedly targeted for actions as minor as commenting on or inquiring about Hosni Mubarak's state of health, while both public and private university professors were regularly intimidated into censoring course content.[13]

A palpable sense of guilt, responsibility, and complicity underwrote many of these banners, drawing on a collective memory of censorship and participation in silence, and paving the way for a new moral economy: that of revolt. Signs pleading "Forgive me" addressed the nation, and later, God. In this way, the written word would go from being the social lab of officials and cultural elites, to becoming a national, even a religious duty. Indeed, it would become the distinct marker of national belonging to have the courage to write: "I used to be afraid. Now I'm Egyptian." The *silence*, imposed by the outgoing regime and upheld by society, became reinscribed in a revolutionary narrative as sacrilege, as sin itself.

The signs themselves were a translation of the political environment as it unfolded, and we must remember that we are translating that translation. For example, the banner above, "I used to be afraid. Now I'm Egyptian," embodies a history of oppression that needs further explanation for the reader, which is precisely what we attempted to provide through our translation of this history, which lay behind the visible inscribed lines. Indeed, the banner below—"Silence is complicity," urged fellow Egyptians to do the right thing, maintaining it is a 'sin' not to support those who dare to stand against injustice. It stood out because it was written in classical Arabic, and is a common saying used to emphasize the importance of having the courage to tell the truth. In the case of this banner, and considering the elevated language register, the literal translation—'He who is silent about the truth is a speechless devil,' maintains the characteristics of the proverbial, and is more in keeping with the notion of equivalence in translation.[14] However, this gives the indication of religious overtones. Although the word 'shaytan,' or devil, is a word loaded with religious connotations in Islamic culture, this saying is more proverbial than overtly religious. In this case then, and in the context described by Jacquemond as a social diffusion of self-censorship, the translation "Silence is complicity" seems more appropriate.

"I used to be afraid. Now I'm Egyptian." Photograph by Karima Khalil

"Silence is complicity." Photograph by Laura Gribbon

Egyptians displayed a remarkable recognition of the absolute *necessity* to speak out, to labor, and to risk their lives in doing so. The image below acknowledges the price of freedom that Egyptians were now willing to play: the price of human life and blood.

Along similar lines, the following picture depicts a young man wrapped in a *kafan* (shroud), signifying his willingness to die for freedom. The lines on the banner are actually the lyrics of a song about the martyrs who had already given their lives to the revolution. This public display of more bodies prepared in their *kafan*, and willing to follow in the footsteps of those killed, confirms the demonstrators' genuine understanding that freedom comes at great cost.

Several banners challenged the dominant narratives of Mubarak, the regime, state television, and the international community in a dynamic expression of hope, fear, anger, complaint, celebration, and mourning. Some were subversively humorous, affording protesters the endurance they needed to remain; others posited political positions, or provided

"We're not tired, we're not tired, freedom is not for free." Photograph by Huda Lutfi

commentary or satire. They were not all celebratory; many acknowledged the past and a sense of loss through martyrdom. We have split the banners and signs into categories to enable the process of discursive translation. The sections that follow cover the demands of the revolution, a history of empire and international relations, solidarity among protesters, and humor and tragedy.

Demands: The Regime and the New Statesmen

The following selection of signs details the claims made to and regarding the state. These were the actual political demands of the revolution. They are perhaps the most obvious and explicit. Many were simple claims that were repeated and became refrains or chants that were taken up by the masses; others were longer and more complex. Here, the state is the addressee, and the protesters are no longer just subjects, but citizen leaders—the 'new statesmen.' So, who are the 'new statesmen and -women'? The subjects of this revolution are a generation of Egyptians responsible for tearing down the wall of fear, protecting their families and homes, and demanding effective citizenship. Most were born under Mubarak's rule,

"If I die, O mother, do not weep; I will die so my country may live." Photograph by Huda Lutfi

experiencing a collapsing public education system and rising inequalities, as well as witnessing regional and international events, such as the war in Iraq and U.S. support of Israel. As a result, they are more courageous and intolerant of injustice. They have challenged the very notion of the 'state' and what it means to be a citizen and to call for government accountability.

When protesters first took to the streets on January 25, the select banners visible called for 'bread, liberty, and human dignity' ("*'ish, Huriya, karama insaniya*"), already making a distinct and categorical connection between the police state and their decades-long economic dispossession. Bread, a staple food in the Egyptian diet, has long been a source of contention. Used within the context of the revolution it symbolized neoliberal policies and rising inflation, as the Egyptian state has attempted to remove bread subsidies several times in favor of market-based efficiency under international pressure to liberalize the economy, provoking the Bread Riots of 1977. However, the word for bread in the Egyptian colloquial dialect is the same as the word for 'life' in classical Arabic, giving

"This is a revolution, not politics; gooooooo." Photograph by Samia Mehrez

it a double meaning when viewed in this way. Protesters also demanded 'liberty,' or freedom, as in: freedom of speech, the right to vote and elect a government or leader, freedom of movement, and freedom of assembly. Heavy restrictions on political discourse had been imposed by the regime; even the mention of Mubarak or his family in publications was heavily monitored, and the president appointed the editors of the three main newspapers—*al-Ahram*, *al-Akhbar*, and *al-Gumhuriya*. All political opposition groups had been banned from official activity, and those whom the state considered to be subversive were heavily monitored and subject to arbitrary detention and routine torture. Demands for 'justice' and 'dignity' were therefore central to the revolution. The emergency law, extended every three years since 1981, has allowed constitutional rights to be suspended and censorship to be legalized. Under this law, police powers have included regular interrogation, and civilians were denied the right to a fair trial. This hasn't ceased since Mubarak's ousting either. More than ten thousand civilians have been tried in military courts since February 2011, and in August 2011, several prominent activists, including Asmaa Mahfouz and Nawara Negm, were detained, interrogated, and released on bail on charges of 'defamatory insults against the military.' Presidential candidate Mohamed ElBaradei tweeted, "Military trials for young activists, while Mubarak & Co. stand before civilian courts, is a legal farce. Don't abort the revolution."[15]

By January 28, 2011 ('Friday of Rage'), demands had evolved to categorically call, at a mass level, for Mubarak's resignation and the downfall of the regime. Tahrir was now definitively occupied by tens of thousands of protesters, sitting in and securing the square in an unprecedented display of persistence. The men captured in the lower image on page 115 are standing on a burned-out vehicle on January 29. They hold a sign that reads, 'True reform is Mubarak's resignation—Signed, the Egyptian people.' This sign is a direct response to Mubarak's highly anticipated, delayed first speech, in which he only promised minor reforms and a reshuffling of cabinet ministers, further angering protesters. 'Reform' had become a buzzword of the regime, used frequently in relation to structural adjustment policies and corporate legal reform, and signifying an increase in cronyism, privatization, and dispossession. The banner reclaims the word, demanding 'true reform,' which it equates with Mubarak's departure. This obviously leads to issues of translation at a global level. What is 'true reform'? And what are the implications of such change? The international community largely supported peaceful moves toward 'reform,' but most foreign governments stopped short of demanding Mubarak's immediate resignation for fear of a power vacuum threatening economic interests and the security of Israel's presence in the region. At the time of writing there have been six months of growing frustration at the pace of reform by Egypt's military junta, accompanied by the harsh realization that the rhetoric of 'reform' has been used by the interim government and international community without any substantive changes. It is unlikely that true reform will be initiated by Egypt's comfortable political elites; rather, such change has to come from the street. Clashes with Central Security Forces on June 28 and 29 revealed interim rulers were willing to use the same repressive tactics as Mubarak: state violence, tear gas, intimidation, and bullets, and they predictably blamed the resultant disorder on 'criminal thugs.'

The Arab world has been undergoing change to varying extents. Amr Moussa, former secretary general of the Arab League, said in an interview on January 30, 2011, "This is the motto now, reform, change, modernization."[16] Yet these changes have meant little for the vast majority of Egyptians and other Arabs, who have experienced growing inequality and

Top: "Bread, liberty, human dignity." Bottom: "True reform is Mubarak's resignation—signed, the Egyptian people." Photographs by Laura Gribbon

"The people demand that you and your corrupt mafia leave" . . . "Stop passing the buck. The blood of the youth is on you." Photograph by Laura Gribbon

corruption at the expense of Sadat's so-called 'pioneering' modernity. The Egyptian steel and cotton industries have been aggressively privatized into monopolies, and natural gas exports to Israel have cost Egyptian tax-payers nine million dollars a day.[17] This surely casts such modernity as a curious myth, presenting a challenge to any translator.

As time went on and Mubarak still didn't leave, there was an increase in signs directed at him personally, imploring him to listen to the people and go. The language of these directives evolved from pleading—"If you love your country, leave"—to exasperation—"Hosni, you germ" . . . "Get out, you moron" . . . "Leave, you (bleep!) son of a (bleeeeep!)."[18] An example is pictured below; literal translation: (In his left hand) "The people simply demand: the departure of you and your corrupt party, O Abu Alaa." The other banner reads: "The price of the youth killed by your dogs is your departure, not the departure of a government. Egyptian blood is dear, O Abu Alaa." Referring to people as 'Um . . .' or 'Abu . . .' (meaning 'mother of' and 'father of') is a common colloquial manner of address. To refer to Mubarak as the 'father of Alaa' (Abu Alaa), the elder son, rather than the 'father of Gamal' (Abu Gamal), the younger 'heir-to-be,' is at once significant and deliberate. It harks back to the sudden death of Alaa Mubarak's twelve-year-old son only a few years earlier, a loss that moved all Egyptians to mourn with the Mubarak family despite their acute dissatisfaction with the regime. Calling Mubarak 'Abu Alaa' therefore serves not just to embarrass and incriminate Mubarak, but to remind him as well that all Egyptian blood spilled during the revolution by none other than Mubarak himself should be as dear to him as his own grandson's—that is, that the family of 'Abu Alaa' (Mubarak) is the Egyptian people whose lives he should have protected.[19]

The demand "*irHal*," literally translated as 'leave' or 'go' but possibly more accurately 'get out,' became indicative of the eighteen-day uprising in late January and early February 2011. This demand was frequently displayed across the *midan*, allowing individuals the freedom to embellish it with their own hand-held signs, such as: "Leave . . . my hand hurts, I have exams to take, I need to work/shave/shower/sleep/give birth." These one-line claims placed everyday life alongside the severity of the situation, and were indicative of the ways in which the president continued to intercept the mundane details of protester's lives. The reality was that Mubarak had not left, and daily protests were taking their toll on multiple levels.

This explains why millions of protesters cheered and cried tears of relief when news of Mubarak's resignation spread across Tahrir Square. The street celebrations continued for days. Other demands, however, took a little longer: Parliament was dissolved on February 13, 2011, the beginnings of the dismantling of the state security apparatus occurred on March 15, 2011, a provisional constitution was adopted by the Supreme Council of the Armed Forces (SCAF) on March 30, 2011, and the National Democratic Party was dissolved on April 16, 2011. Still to be met, at the time of writing in August 2011, are demands for the release and pardon of all political prisoners and the removal of the Emergency Law, along with the completion of Mubarak's trial and those of other key ministers and presidential aides. In the picture on page 119, which outlines these demands, the banner holder identifies himself as a 'lawyer for Egypt.' This is significant, as it posits protesters as the arbiters of justice, rather than state-appointed lawyers. Protesters have repeatedly called for the transparent trials of Mubarak and his family, as well as the fair trials of all political prisoners within civilian courts.

"Leave! Shame on you, my arms ache. Signed: Just an Egyptian." Photograph by Mariam Soliman

Of course the most famous of banners, bearing the chant that would become a popular refrain, was "*al-Sha'b yurid isqat al-nizam.*" This demand was used as a prefix in various manifestations over the initial eighteen days and beyond to demand the removal of Mubarak, the cleansing of the regime, the withdrawal of the SCAF from political process, and the removal of Field Marshal Tantawi. The phrase stands out, because it is in Modern Standard Arabic *(fusHa)*, which is uncommon on the streets in Egypt, rather than colloquial. Mirroring the Tunisian Revolution just weeks earlier, this chant would go on to form the core lexicon of uprisings throughout the region. This is significant: what is '*al-sha'b*' in a historical context of colonization, monarchies, and military coups? And why '*al-nizam*'? Egyptians have lived under martial law since the 1952 coup. Nasser's populism, as well as a sordid bureaucratic apparatus that mimics the ghost of a welfare state, have been used to legitimize an increasingly corrupt and schizophrenic neoliberal regime, which has been protected financially and militarily by the United States and its allies. The prevailing government was so far removed from

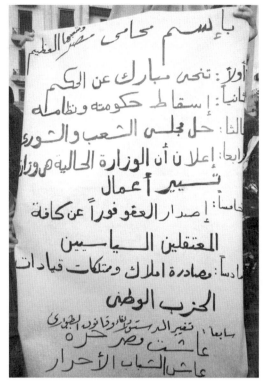

"In the name of a lawyer for Egypt and its great people: First: Mubarak's stepping down from power; Second: The downfall of his government and regime; Third: The dissolution of the Shura Council and Parliament; Fourth: A declaration that the current cabinet is a care-taker one; Fifth: The assurance of pardons for all political prisoners; Sixth: The seizure of all assets and property from the National Democratic Party; Seventh: Constitutional amendments and dissolution of the Emergency Law. Long live free Egypt. Long live the free youth!" Photograph by Samia Mehrez

the needs and aspirations of the majority of Egyptians, a thorough rebirth of the concept of popular, collective will was in order. Indeed, in the months following Hosni Mubarak's departure and institutional reforms, the protest movement has continued to deploy 'al-sha'b yurid' to fight an ongoing battle against co-optation, by counterrevolutionary forces on the one hand and partisan interests on the other. The significance of 'al-sha'b' lies also in the almost sacrosanct and natural reverence of decentralized organizing throughout the revolution. It has been of prime importance for the majority of protesters to maintain a leaderless and non-partisan, non-ideological position, that 'iradat al-sha'b' has been deployed almost as frequently as 'iradat Allah,' or the will of God. 'Al-sha'b yurid isqat al-nizam' has been resurrected as a chant and as a banner, to reclaim, indeed to emphasize, the core philosophy of this uprising. It has connotations of collective desire; 'the people "will" the removal of the regime.' As Youssef Rakhua writes, "As far as it exists at all, deprived of the right to gather, decide for itself, fight back, to say, or to be, the people, which in recent memory has only existed as an abstraction, has absolutely no will."[20] By taking back the streets, protesters—'al-sha'b'—took back their rights, and with that, reappropriated an entire lexicon that had been abused by the regime.

Confronting Empire: Mubarak, History, and Global Alliances

A detailed and critical consciousness of historical tyranny allowed protesters to situate events in Egypt within a selective narrative of historical struggle, stretching back as far as Ancient Rome. Some compared Hosni Mubarak with historical tyrants Hitler and Nero. By association with Hitler, an analogy usually reserved for Israel itself, protesters drew attention not only to Mubarak's fascism and dictatorship, but also to the blood on his hands. Just as Hitler was engaged in mass industrial genocide against the Jews, so Zionists persecuted Palestinians in 1948 and continue to do so today. During his second speech, Mubarak explicitly stated that Egyptians should choose between security under his rule or chaos without him. Indeed, for a large part of January 28, 2011, Cairo

"Al-sha'b yurid isqat al-nizam." Photograph by Laura Gribbon

Top: "Nero is burning Cairo." Bottom: Mubarak as Hitler. Photographs by Huda Lutfi

was literally on fire, as Mubarak looked on and continued to persuade the international community of his role as guardian of stability, insisting that the world must choose between him and chaos. Just as Nero burned Rome and implicated the Christians, Mubarak accused the "Islamists" and "foreign hands" when churches in Alexandria burned in December 2010 and fires were started across the city in January 2011.[21] There have also been comparisons drawn with the huge fires of 1952, which burned for more than twelve hours in the commercial heart of Cairo, destroying over seven hundred premises. On both January 25, 1952 and January 28, 2011, large demonstrations took place amid widespread arson and looting, organized prison breaks, and the notable absence of security forces. Although British forces were heavily suspected in 1952, their involvement was never proven, and the propaganda machine then, as today, was extensive. Blame was levied at organized groups of 'thugs' from the left and right, who were assumed to be under the direction of either King Farouk, the Muslim Brotherhood (who were banned from Egypt at the time), or Misr al-Fatat (the Egyptian Socialist Party).[22] By his refusal to step down, Mubarak set fire to Cairo and its people, wreaking havoc and destruction, turning people against each other, and destroying the very fabric of society.

"Down with the butcher. Leave, you pig!" Photograph by Laura Gribbon

Images of former President Nasser, whom many Egyptians still equate with liberation and freedom, were strangely absent from the discourse, as were direct references to the Egyptian revolutions of 1919 and 1952. Instead they gleaned inspiration from global events, forming a visual dialogue with the past and present, and carving out critical geographies of empire and oppression.

In reference to a more contemporary historical struggle, countless signs addressing imperial alliances between the United States, Mubarak's regime, and Israel punctuated the narrative. Both Mubarak and Omar Suleiman, representatives of a collaborating ruling class, were frequently characterized as '*umala*', or agents, for the US and Israel. The sign on page 122 reads, 'Down with the butcher. Leave, you pig,' and below the picture, 'Thirty years of injustice.' This banner operates on several symbolic levels, leading semiotic analysis to address a hierarchy of meaning. Here, Mubarak is depicted as the 'butcher' or slaughterer, and is smiling with blood dripping from his mouth. He has the Star of David, signifying Israel, and "USA" written on his face. The symbols, both the picture and text, imply that the blood Mubarak is responsible for is not just that of the martyrs of the revolution, but also the blood of Palestinians. This is particularly significant, given the Israeli plea for the United States and Europe to curb their criticism of Mubarak in a special cable on January 31, 2011, the day before this picture was taken. The history of Israel and Palestine is of course at the heart of Arab memory, but it is also tied to Sadat's initial isolation of the Egyptian people from the wider Arab region, marked by his signing of an unelected peace treaty with Israel, alongside which he declared open-door economic policies *(infitaH)*, which were aggressively pursued under Mubarak with the backing of the United States.

Translating Affect: Solidarity at Home and Abroad

Protest banners and signs are a specific kind of popular literature, typically combining elements of the written with the visual. The kind of quasi-essentialist spatial and temporal economy allotted to the written word in a banner statement is crucial to our engagement and understanding of the language used. Therefore, to read the Egyptian uprising through its visual representations is to engage with a self-translating revolutionary impulse that commands an instantly collective consciousness: a process of becoming, one in which we are all variously involved. For if a moment of revolution is one in which all people are compelled to action, today's revolutionaries continue to prove that literary voyeurism is not an option, and the political command of these texts is such that reading in itself becomes participation, foregrounding the translation process.

The immediacy and importance of the banners in Tahrir were translated in the multiple contexts, physical and cultural, that shaped the political moment. The innumerable registers and discursive trajectories that colored these banners attest to the ongoing process of translation that took place both horizontally and vertically. They reflect the constant movement—and mobilization—of the political in the creation of an arresting and universalizing process toward autonomy. The feelings and meanings generated by the banners and signs of Tahrir Square therefore cannot be reduced to the text or its bearers, but rather constitute the emotional economies that seize upon viewers and mobilize them in a performance that at once demands attention and translates itself. Both the immediate and absent intelligibility of these performances can be traced to the delicate borderlands of language and to the affects generated by the same.

Spinoza was one of the earliest philosophers to theorize the concept of affect as a categorically positive change amounting to empowerment.[23] Deleuze would go on to elaborate the nature of these impacts, which transcend and arrest both space and time to operate beyond the logical order of effective space. By divorcing subjects from their art and space, Deleuze theorized affect as the positive and uncontained change induced within a subject—that is, the adaptation of the subject by space, and not the other way around.[24] Affective labor, as identified by Hardt and Negri,[25] is that which engages affects, which are both mental and physical phenomena, in an effort to make audiences relate to products through particular effects. We argue that the temporary autonomy generated in Tahrir Square was the result of a decentralized, voluntary laboring process that sought to implicate a broad multitude of spectators as participants both locally and globally. Banners, signs, and placards of all shapes and sizes, and the extensive, round-the-clock labor involved in their creation and display, were central to this process.

In contrast to the plethora of individual signs, there were also banners drawn up collectively in the *midan* by several protesters. Many of these large banners were displayed on surrounding buildings or suspended over the *midan* (see next page).

Just as several of the individual banners shared similar messages and echoed mutual sentiments, so the collective banners expressed the overarching demands of protesters, freeing individuals to express more

Large banners.
Photographs:
top, Huda Lutfi;
bottom, Lewis
Sanders

personal desires on their hand-held banners and signs. Tahrir mobilized traditional art forms in the creation of these cooperative banners, such as calligraphy, as well as new art forms, such as graffiti (chapter 4). The suspension of collective demands on buildings within the public space, in lieu of the aforementioned regime of censorship, replaced and mimicked corporate advertisement billboards that dotted the downtown Cairo skyline. Where the advertisement industry was one of the earliest to construct affects—that is, a relationship between product and subject (producer and spectator or consumer)—through massive billboard ads, revolutionaries would deploy similar tactics in the generation of affects to fellow protesters, other Egyptians, and the world at large.

The sign below appropriates a billboard advert for a gated community owned by the Talaat Moustafa Group, Madinaty. The original campaign read, 'My new address: Madinaty.' The revolutionary banner (below) reads: 'My new address: January 25, Tahrir Square.' There have been several debates about the buying of public land from the Mubarak regime at reduced cost. In this case the land for the Madinaty estate was sold below legal value to Hisham Talaat Moustafa. The sign therefore had several layers of meaning. On the one hand it exposed the appropriation of land by Egyptian elites, as well as the dispossession of millions of Egyptians living in informal housing on the outskirts of the city, in stark contrast to their fellow compatriots living in the new gated-community complexes of New Cairo. Additionally, Tahrir became the *first* address for many Egyptians for whom the fear of eviction had been removed.

Protesters also used their bodies as canvases, along with the space surrounding them, including Central Security Forces trucks and military tanks. The tendency to resort to using one's body as a canvas for a written sign highlights not only the copious amounts of writing that took place in Tahrir Square, but also the highly personalized act of writing and participating in the protests. Tanks and burned-out military vehicles were used frequently as materials for signs and slogans, along with fabric, bandages, helmets, shoes, and walls. The defacing of these symbols of war, which protesters rode on and got married next to, somehow reduced their menace and transformed them into everyday vehicles, which people got used to seeing on the streets and in the *midan*.

Although frequently termed a 'youth revolution,' the following signs prove that protesters of all ages participated in Midan al-Tahrir. The sign on page 129 reads, "I beg you, leave." We don't know how long this man

Top: "My new address: 25th January, Tahrir Square." Photograph by Amira Taha. Bottom: "Freedom Resort." Photograph by Hossam El-Hamalawy

has been begging for change. The banner is stuck over his mouth, as several protesters did with their signs, as if saying 'We won't speak until you leave' or 'No more needs to be said.' It is interesting to contrast this older gentleman's frustration with the brash outspokenness of the 'youth' in Tahrir.

The use of children within the Egyptian Revolution was significant (chapter 1). Some were too young to understand, being deployed by their parents to sit on tanks or pose for photographers while holding banners. Others were more aware of the events evolving around them, as evidenced by YouTube videos of children leading chants.[26] The photograph of the following banner was taken on February 1, 2011, a day when

Top: "Get out, Mubarak, you agent." Bottom: "This is a revolution of the whole people."
Photographs by Laura Gribbon

"I beg you, leave." Photograph by Omnia Ibrahim Magdy

citizens all over Egypt responded en masse to the protesters' calls for a million people to take to the streets. The girl holding the sign and the woman with her—probably her mother—are representative of the new actors appearing on the streets. People from all sections of the population, especially families, began to feel safe about joining the protests, as street fights had largely ceased. For many of them, it might have been the first time they publicly voiced their demands or expressed their grievances. This young girl proudly presents her sign to the photographer, pointing at her message as if asking for it to be read. It has been printed, which shows someone else had designed it for her to hold. However, its simple wording and logic and the use of colloquial dialect match the girl's age.

Mobilizing Memory: Humor and Tragedy

As this chapter has already demonstrated, metaphorical language, historical references, and the proverbial have all been used to emphasize a communal sense of identity among opposition groups. It is in this context that we've chosen to cast the humorous and tragic banners of this section within the framework of "mobilizing memory." The evolution of collective memory has always played a critical role in interpreting the

Left: "Free Egypt." Right: "I am a child, I want my rights." Photographs by Laura Gribbon

history of conflict within communities.[27] Maurice Halbwachs suggests memories supply the individual with a way of understanding the world, and are essential to the construction of cultural, religious, ethnic, and national identities.[28] States, communities, and collectives have historically utilized societal memory to form narratives of nationhood and solidarity. However, it is essential to note that memories do not supply an objective history of the past; they are selective, and the denial of memory or recasting of events are socially constructed in order to meet the needs of the present. Daniel Bar-Tal maintains societal memories can be used to justify the outbreak and development of conflict, present a positive image of the in-group, delegitimize the opponent, and present sections of society as victims.[29] One of the ways in which Egyptians delegitimized the state and Mubarak was through their use of humor, reducing their opponents to the level of humiliation they had personally experienced at the hands of the regime. In this way, the series of banners below draws on a history of collective oppression to make a mockery of the need to 'respect' or 'honor' the president. They testify to the failure of the regime on all counts, incorporating examples of deprivation, oppression, and widening inequalities.

Egyptians are well known for their humor and wit, as has been further developed in the chapter on the jokes of the Egyptian Revolution (chapter 5). Midan al-Tahrir contained much juxtaposition, as life, death, hope, victory, humor, and injury were witnessed and experienced within the same space, blurring the lines between the public and the private. Humor is an anti-authoritarian, rebellious, ambivalent mode of communication. By nature it blurs social boundaries and subverts rules. It can be superior, derisive, hostile, or playful.[30] Considering Mubarak's estimated family fortune of US$70 billion, the following banner is obviously sarcastic. The former president had more than enough money to leave the country, but he specifically cited his love for Egypt, during his second speech to the nation, as his reason for not going:

"We demand the honoring of the president" . . . "but how?" . . . "such that he suffers like the people did" . . . "that he may live in the shanties of Duweiqa" . . . "that he may ride in bus number 678" . . . "that he may drink from the water of the gutter" . . . "and chase after a gas canister" . . . "be treated in a public hospital" . . . "eat subsidized bread." Photographs by Samia Mehrez

"Why has the President not gone yet?! Maybe he hasn't got the airfare; he wants to increase his fortune up to 100 billion; maybe he's a pain in the ass; maybe he doesn't get it; maybe he loves the people and can't bear to part with them (it's just too much!)." Photograph by Huda Lutfi

This will be the land of my living and my death. It will remain a dear land to me. I will not leave it nor depart it until I am buried in the ground. Its people will remain in my heart, and it will remain—its people will remain upright and lifting up their heads.[31]

Patrick Devine-Wright, in "A Theoretical Overview of Memory and Conflict," suggests victimization of the 'in-group' by members of the 'out-group' creates in-group cohesion, out-group dehumanization, in-group idealization, and a common sense of self.[32] An example of the use of collective memory to deepen the sense of 'them' and 'us' is the narrative around the death of Khaled Said, which sparked mass involvement in the Facebook group "We are All Khaled Said," started by Google employee and revolutionary activist Wael Ghoneim. Egyptians across the country identified with the story of his death and sympathized with his family. Indeed, Khaled Said's mother became known as the 'mother of all Egyptians.'

"The funeral of Mustafa Said al-Sawy" and "Down with Mubarak." Photograph by Laura Gribbon

In the few months between the end of January and mid-April 2011, more than eight hundred protesters died, with further deaths and casualties resulting from violent clashes with Central Security Forces on June 28 and 29, 2011.[33] Rather than instilling fear and terror, as was obviously intended, protesters' deaths reinforced a shared sense of victimization, galvanizing even greater support for opposition forces. Those who died have been commonly referred to as "martyrs." The term *shahid* (martyr) is derived from the Arabic root *shahada*, which means 'to witness.' It is often associated with death or persecution resulting from the refusal to renounce a religious belief, but has been used here to denote death for a noble cause, whether viewed in a religious or a secular realm. Just as the martyrs have been held in high esteem, so this regard has been extended to their family members. As these women, the family members of one of the martyrs, walked through Tahrir, people parted and cheered, before going back to chanting their demands. The banner itself sets mourning for the deceased alongside a demand that Mubarak leave.

As the sign on page 134 depicts, the martyrs have paid a high price for freedom, and the collective recognition of this sacrifice by the people will serve as a reminder of their communal pursuit of justice, freedom, and democracy. The sign is addressing the regime, including the armed forces

"The blood of the martyrs is not cheap." Photograph by Hossam El-Hamalawy

and Central Security Forces, who have 'cheapened' the memory of the martyrs and made a mockery of their sacrifice in their failure to wholly meet the demands of the people until absolutely pushed, as was the case with Mubarak's arrest and trial. Additionally, in an attempt by the state to suppress the collective memory of the costs of the revolution, police disrupted a memorial service by the families of the martyrs on June 28, 2011, provoking the subsequent battle on June 29, 2011 in which more than one thousand people were injured.[34]

It is essential that grief and victimhood be acknowledged and managed in Egypt as events continue to unfold. John D. Brewer writes about the role of memories in post-trauma societies:

> Nations require a sense of their past for social cohesion, memories of which are embodied in acts of public commemoration and in public memorials, in public images, texts, photographs and rituals that socialize us in what to remember. . . . A post-violence society thus needs to find pathways to healing for the society as well as for the individual.[35]

The creativity demonstrated in commemoration of the martyrs in Tahrir has been a key element of the 'affect' of the revolution. Their clothes hung from walls and lampposts, makeshift galleries of their pictures were displayed and paraded, several songs have been written, and numerous tributes have been posted on Facebook and YouTube. At the time of writing, there has been much debate among opposition groups about how to collectively honor their bravery. Suggestions for a Tahrir memorial monument and several street and station name changes from the Mubarak family to the names of the martyrs have been proposed.[36] Midan al-Tahrir has in many ways become symbolic of the struggle for freedom and victory. Egyptians from all across the country, along with international tourists, are increasingly visiting to buy a flag or other piece of revolutionary memorabilia. The same stands and individuals selling hats and flags also sell small memory cards on ribbons with the faces of the martyrs on them. Indeed, the revolution appears to be a growing tourist attraction, as illustrated by a conversation with one of the camel owners at the pyramids in May 2011, who suggested business was slow because "the only tourists visiting Egypt now were 'revolution tourists'— more interested in Tahrir than ancient Egypt."[37] Patrick Devine-Wright suggests that "commemorating the past defines the individual's location in the temporal continuity (and) . . . relates the individual participant to other group members who have existed in history."[38]

Victimhood is often politicized, and can be manipulated by various actors. The collective remembrance of tragedy through museums, events, and commemorative holidays is often the relic of a society that has enforced collective memory in order to deal with the past and establish new national identities. Examples include South Africa and Northern Ireland, as well as Israel's notorious exploitation of the memory of the Holocaust.[39] The political implications for this kind of translation work manifest themselves most clearly in the manner in which political forces and the regime itself co-opt revolutionary desire toward various ends. For example, shortly before Ramadan 2011, the Muslim Brotherhood convened a political rally in the Nile Delta town of Shibin al-Kom with a tribute to the local families of the martyrs, before moving on to business.[40]

Conclusion

To interpret the visual output of Tahrir Square during the revolution necessitates the translation of a rich cultural and emotive bricolage that was never static. Not simply because of the ebb and flow of the protests, or because the banners were created and recreated in response to unfolding events and discourses, but because they drew on cultural memory to articulate identity, values, desires, and aspirations. Our study, therefore, brings history and collective memory together with the signifying language that is used in the social construction of the present.

As this chapter has shown, the eighteen-day uprising that ousted Hosni Mubarak was inscribed within a much larger context of regional and global change, building up over the years, such that the protesters in Tahrir drew on a rich tapestry of political signifiers to express a wealth of consciousness about the political stakes—not just for Egyptians, but for other Arabs, and people around the world more generally. Apart from heralding and celebrating national unity and denouncing sectarianism, the vibrant collection of banners on display in Tahrir actively engaged imperial alliances, carving out and resisting an undemocratic network that included Mubarak's regime, Israel, and the United States. The visual aspect of Tahrir was thus in constant dialogue with the past and the present, and protesters drew inspiration for their material from global as well as local phenomena.

Like pride and humor, fear is a cultural product that only gains poignancy through collectively expressed behavior, in that it cannot be used as a political tool unless one is afraid. Therefore, the very act of writing and speaking out in such a visual manner has been instrumental in eliminating this fear and holding the state, military, and fellow revolutionaries to account. At the time of writing, August 2011, the people continue to make their demands publicly, and banners and chants calling for the trial of Mubarak have already forced the hand of the SCAF in commencing a public trial. However, on August 1, 2011 the Central Security Forces were beating and arresting the families of the martyrs and their supporters, in order to force an end to the sit-in for justice and accountability, which had begun on July 8, 2011. The level of coercion and violence witnessed that evening far surpassed anything experienced since Mubarak's departure, and it is in this context that protesters would resurrect the prefix '*al-Sha'b yurid*' ('The people wills') to demand the liberation of the *midan*, as shown in the image on page 138. The occupation of Tahrir by Central Security Forces and Military Police since August 1 has forced to the surface some of the real crises of translation that have been central to the ongoing revolution and its inscription in a wider regional context. Clearly, people have been resisting and continue to resist efforts to domesticate and adopt the Egyptian uprising and its demands for the downfall of an entire system, taken on by a ruthless counterrevolution seeking to neutralize and silence revolutionary desires. The trials that began on August 3, 2011 have since been suspended and repeatedly postponed, and at the time of writing are no longer scheduled to be broadcast publicly.

The image on page 138, which shows the state has definitively snatched the *midan* away from protesters, perfectly illustrates the larger failure of translating a politics of liberation, but also echoes its necessity. Chapter 5 in this volume, which addresses the difficulties of translating revolutionary humor, contains many of the jokes that have been circulating since January 25, 2011. Following August 1, 2011, one of the more prominent and most cynical of these, transmitted via social media and word of mouth, was the following: "The people demand: one, the right of return to the square; two, a return to the February 10 borders; and three, the recognition of the central garden in the *midan* as the everlasting capital of Tahrir." These demands are a rhetorical play on the exhaustive repetition of a few core Palestinian demands for liberation: the right of return for refugees from the 1948 Nakba, Israeli withdrawal to pre-1967 borders, and the recognition of East Jerusalem as the undisputed and eternal capital of Palestine. The chosen referential world of this biting joke effectively translates the people's consciousness of ongoing struggle, and their identification with the Palestinians in this context reiterates the corrupt imperial nature of the Egyptian regime in its continued presence and revived repression of protesters. It is a sad joke that at once insists upon the people's ownership of Tahrir, their home, but that equally laments the tragic situation in which the revolution finds itself—ultimately, untranslated, mistranslated, and deadened by an unruly, imperial machinery of violence.

The image also captures a moment in which the city of Cairo, and Egypt at large, is undergoing a crisis of translation. The alienating effects of the months following Mubarak's ouster have been created through the onslaught of a counterrevolutionary movement that has sought to terrorize the revolutionaries into submission. This has included the outlawing of strikes and protests, the alliance of the SCAF with the Muslim Brotherhood, and the utilization of an economy of morality in which 'the wheel of production' has been a recurring trope. A discourse of sovereignty has also been deployed, in which dissidence and resistance to the SCAF's unilateral political interventions have been translated as an attack on the mythical revolutionary army of 1952, and therefore on the Egyptian national imagination itself. This has discursively and explicitly rendered many of

"The people demand the liberation of Tahrir." Photograph by Huda Lutfi

the same revolutionaries that ousted Mubarak as foreign agents and traitors. In light of these moments, the demand for the liberation of Midan al-Tahrir, as illustrated in the above-pictured banner, is now, more than ever, a demand for the liberation of the city, and a demand for the right to *embody* the urban landscape as the site of revolution par excellence.

Though there is something to be said for the way in which 'Tahrir Square,' or 'Liberation Square' as many media outlets chose to translate it, was rendered and reclaimed as part of a wider narrative of urban revolt, it is important to recognize the way in which it has come to connote its own specific culture of resistance, so that not only would social movements in Greece, Spain, and Israel go on to identify their squares, boulevards, and streets with Tahrir, but uprisings throughout the rest of Egypt and the Arab world would similarly dub their squares 'Mayadin al-Tahrir.' In this regard, the image is heartening. It demonstrates the resolve of the people to continue to make demands, even in the face of the state's occupation of Tahrir. Our treatment in this chapter of the banners that adorned the eighteen-day uprising, therefore, should be read first and foremost as a translation of the right to the city, and a reading of the affective embodiment of a space that is now re-experiencing a loud and discomfiting silence in the face of a cruel and incomplete translation process, a process that is central to struggle itself.

Notes

1   "Signs of the Revolution: The Best Posters Carried by Protesters in Egypt," *The Telegraph*, Spring 2011, http://www.telegraph.co.uk/news/ picturegalleries/worldnews/8295934/Signs-of-the-revolution-the-best-posters-carried-by-protesters-in-Egypt.html
2   Mia Grondahl and Ayman Mohyeldin, *Tahrir Square: The Heart of the Egyptian Revolution* (Cairo: American University in Cairo Press, 2011); Karima Khalil, *Messages from Tahrir: Signs from Egypt's Revolution* (Cairo: American University in Cairo Press, 2011); Sherif Assaf, Omar Attia, Timothy Kaldas, Rehab Khaled, Zee Mo, and Monir Al Shazly, *The Road to Tahrir: Front Line Images by Six Young Egyptian Photographers* (Cairo: American University in Cairo Press, 2011).
3   Rayya El Zein and Alex Ortiz, "Signs of the Times: The Popular Literature of Tahrir," *ArteEast*, April 1, 2011, http://arteeast.org/pages/ literature/641/
4   Gayatri Chakravorty Spivak, "Teaching for the Times," *Death of a Discipline* (Cambridge, MA: Harvard University Press, 2003), p. 116.
5   Maria Tymoczko, "Post-colonial Writing and Literary Translation," in Susan Bassnett and Harish Trivedi, eds., *Post-Colonial Translation: Theory and Practice* (London: Routledge, 1999), pp. 19–40.
6   Susan Bassnett and Peter Bush, *The Translator as Writer* (London: Continuum International Publishing Group, 2007).
7   Graham Allen, *Roland Barthes* (London: Routledge, 2003).
8   Roland Barthes, *Camera Lucida: Reflections on Photography* (Hill & Wang, 1994).
9   Richard Jacquemond, "The Shifting Limits of the Sayable in Egyptian Fiction," *The MIT Electronic Journal of Middle East Studies*. Arab World Books, http://www.arabworldbooks.com/Readers2006/articles/ jacquemond_fiction.htm
10 Michel Foucault, *The Will to Know* (London: Penguin Books, 1998). "Biopower" was a term used by French philosopher Michel Foucault to denote the state's subjugation of the people through various techniques. He first used the phrase in *The Will to Know*, the first volume of his work *The History of Sexuality*.

11   Samia Mehrez, *Egypt's Culture Wars: Politics and Practice* (Cairo: American University in Cairo Press, 2008), pp. 72–88.

12   Mehrez, *Egypt's Culture Wars*, pp. 62–63.

13   Mehrez, *Egypt's Culture Wars*, pp. 229–50.

14   The notion of equivalence within translation has been heavily debated. See for example Roman Jakobson, "On Linguistic Aspects of Translation," *The Translation Studies Reader*, ed. Lawrence Venuti (London: Routledge, 2000), pp. 113–18; Mona Baker, *In Other Words: A Coursebook on Translation* (London: Routledge, 1992).

15   "Egypt's Activist Arrest Sparks Protest," *Press TV*, August 15, 2011, http://www.presstv.ir/detail/193995.html; Salma Shukrallah, "Military Trials of Civilians in Egypt under Strong Attack," *Al-Ahram Weekly*, August 16, 2011, http://english.ahram.org.eg/ NewsContentPrint/1/0/19025/Egypt/0/Military-trials-of-civilians-in-Egypt-under-strong.aspx

16   Reuters Africa, "Arab League Head Wants Egypt Multi-Party Democracy," January 30, 2011, http://af.reuters.com/article/egyptNews/ idAFLDE70T0B620110130?sp=true

17   Islamic Awakening, "Hosni Mubarak Sells Gas to Israel Cheaper than Egyptian Muslims," January 13, 2009, http://forums.islamicawakening. com/f18/hosni-mubarak-sells-gas-israel-cheaper-than-20640/

18   El Zein and Ortiz, "Signs of the Times."

19   It was common knowledge from 2000 onward that Gamal Mubarak was being groomed for the presidency. In 2005, President Mubarak changed article 76 in the constitution to allow multi-candidate elections. The Egyptian people showed many signs of disliking the idea of presidential inheritance and also Gamal himself. Prior to the revolution, Gamal was the deputy secretary-general of the now-dissolved National Democratic Party. On April 13, 2011 he was imprisoned on charges of corruption, abuse of power, and his role in enabling the deaths of protesters.

20   Youssef Rakhaa, "Post-mortem," *Al-Ahram Weekly Online*, February 17–23, 2011, http://weekly.ahram.org.eg/2011/1035/sc1201.htm

21   "Mubarak Blames 'Foreign Hand' for Church Attack," *Daily News Egypt*, January 2, 2011, http://thedailynewsegypt.com/crime-a-accidents/mubarak-blames-foreign-hand-for-church-attack.html

22   Fayza Hassan, "Burning Down the House," *Al-Ahram Weekly Online*, January 24–30, 2002, http://weekly.ahram.org.eg/2002/570/sc3.htm

23   Moira Gatens and Genevieve Lloyd, *Collective Imaginings: Spinoza, Past and Present* (London and New York: Routledge, 1999), p. 144.

24 Gilles Deleuze, *Expressionism in Philosophy: Spinoza* (Brooklyn: Urzone Books, 1990), pp. 255–72.

25 Michael Hardt and Antonio Negri, *Labor of Dionysus: A Critique of State-form* (Minnesota: Regents of the University of Minnesota, 1994), pp. 8–9.

26 YouTube, "Cairo Protest," http://www.youtube.com/watch?v=KHQQEcu-BBI

27 Ed Cairns and Michael D. Roe, *The Role of Memory in Ethnic Conflict* (New York: Palgrave Macmillan, 2003), pp. 3–8; James V. Wertsch, *Voices of Collective Remembering* (Cambridge: Cambridge University Press, 2002), pp. 4–9; Maurice Halbwachs, *On Collective Memory*, trans. and ed. Lewis A. Coser (Chicago: University of Chicago Press, 1992), pp. 37–40; Paul Connerton, *How Societies Remember* (Cambridge: Cambridge University Press, 1989), pp. 6–40.

28 Halbwachs, *On Collective Memory*. Halbwachs was a student of Emile Durkheim.

29 Daniel Bar-Tal, "Sociopsychological Foundations of Intractable Conflicts," *American Behavioral Scientist*, 50 (Sage Publications, 2007), pp. 1436–38, http://www.sagepub.com/Martin2Study/pdfs/Chapter%203/martinch3bartal.pdf

30 Eyal Zandberg, "Critical Laughter: Humor, Popular Culture and Israeli Holocaust Commemoration," *Media, Culture and Society* 28, no. 4 (2006): 568.

31 Hosni Mubarak, "Second Speech," translated by *The Washington Post*, February 10, 2011, online at: http://www.washingtonpost.com/wp-dyn/content/article/2011/02/10/AR2011021005290.html?sid=ST2011020703989

32 Patrick Devine-Wright, "A Theoretical Overview of Memory and Conflict," in Ed Cairns and Michael D. Roe, eds., *The Role of Memory in Ethnic Conflict* (Palgrave Macmillan, 2003), p. 15.

33 An Egyptian governmental fact-finding mission—"Fact-Finding National Commission about January 25th Revolution"—announced on April 19, 2011 that at least 846 Egyptians had died in the nearly three-week-long popular uprising: http://www.ffnc-eg.org/assets/ffnc-eg_final.pdf

34 Human Rights Watch, "Egypt: Cairo Violence Highlights Need to Reform Riot Police," July 8, 2011, http://www.hrw.org/news/2011/07/08/egypt-cairo-violence-highlights-need-reform-riot-police; Jack Shenker, "Cairo Street Clashes Leave More than 1,000 Injured," *The Guardian Online*, June 29, 2011, http://www.guardian.co.uk/world/2011/jun/29/cairo-street-clashes-demonstrators-police-egypt

35 John D. Brewer, "Memory, Truth and Victimhood in Post-trauma Societies," in Gerard Delanty and Krishan Kumar, eds., *The SAGE Handbook of Nations and Nationalism* (London: Sage Publications, 2006), pp. 214–24.

36 "A Monument for Egyptian Martyrs," *The Egyptian Gazette*, March 18, 2011, http://213.158.162.45/~egyptian/index.php?action=news&id=16219&title=A%20monument%20for%20Egyptian%20martyrs; Secrets7days.com, "Martyrs . . . Alternative Name for the Metro Station Mubarak," May 2, 2011, http://secrets7days.com/news/21/1606/Martyrs--Alternative-name-for-the-metro-station-Mubarak_en

37 Conversation on May 9, 2011 with an anonymous camel owner at the pyramids.

38 Devine-Wright, "Theoretical Overview," p. 14.

39 Halbwachs, *On Collective Memory*.

40 "Now What?" *Guardian Magazine*, August 13, 2011, pp. 26–30.

4

Reclaiming the City:
Street Art of the Revolution

Lewis Sanders IV

S treet art is an aesthetic product of resistance. It is a resistance to
the dominant narratives that have subjugated other visual and cultural narratives to a minor role, if not abolished them altogether.
It is a way of reclaiming and reappropriating space, and providing a new
understanding of the city as rightfully belonging to the people. During
the Egyptian Revolution it was used precisely for this purpose, be it the
first tags exclaiming the downfall of the regime or rock formations in
Tahrir made from chunks of broken pavement during the early days
of the uprising. Even elaborate murals memorializing the martyrs or
charging the military with infidelity showed a substantial shift in the way
people were interacting with their dwelling space, the city. The protesters began to view their surroundings as properly theirs rather than as an
extension of the government's instruments used to monopolize Egyptian
life and identity, and to homogenize their narrative. Indeed, street art
during the revolution highlights a wide transition in the accessibility of
public political expression. As Lyman G. Chaffee notes in his book *Political Protest and Street Art*,

> Street art, in essence, connotes a decentralized, democratic form in
> which there is universal access, and the real control over messages
> comes from the social producers. It is a barometer that registers the
> spectrum of thinking, especially during democratic openings.[1]

This burst of political expression in the city represents a shift in the Egyptian people's approach to aesthetic creation and communication, especially
for the artist. Tahrir had become a place in which public expression was

given the opportunity to creatively flow through several mediums, unobstructed by the dominant narrative of the Mubarak regime, the state.

On one level, street art of the revolution is, in and of itself, a *translation* of a newfound political, spatial, and aesthetic transformation of the protesters' realities—an expression of their thoughts, emotions, ambitions, dreams, and desires, and the shift in social perceptions of public space activated by the revolution. On another level, this heterogeneous and increasingly complex visual narrative, inscribed by the artists/protesters onto the city, demands *translation(s)*, that is, the active involvement of passersby, of interlocutors, to transform the signifiers of street art into signifieds, to participate in the production, assimilation, and claim of this new signification. The semiotic translation of these works is therefore critical in understanding the way street art shifted the dominant visual narrative of the regime as situated in urban space. It should be noted, before beginning the translation of these works, that this chapter offers a limited glimpse into a far more elaborate and extensive tapestry of revolutionary street art, which is circumscribed by the process of selection involved in translating the pieces of art under consideration. These will be divided into two chronological distinctions; first, the eighteen days leading to the resignation of Mubarak, and second, the immediate post-Mubarak era. By situating the pieces within these categories, we begin to map the development of the revolution's art as it took place on the streets.

Pathways of Significance, Revolutionary Guides

In a way, translating works of street art is a process of constructing narratives that have oriented and produced them. This is due, in fact, to the openness of the product of art since it does not speak of itself or for itself. Though Italian semiotician Umberto Eco's concept *opera aperta*, the open work, situates the artist as the provider–creator of openness in the work, the openness of the work is already inherent since it stands alone from the author. Eco explains, "Hence, every reception of a work of art is both an interpretation and a performance of it, because in every reception the work takes on a fresh perspective for itself."[2] The passerby, an interlocutor with the city, provides meaning to the symbols carried in these artworks, translating them into a common narrative of resistance designated by the revolution. The passerby, a spectator fixing his or her gaze on the work of art, visually consumes the remnants of signification. Thus, the piece of art, the mural or graffiti, is situated by the street artist as a guide to the various representations, the various signifieds embedded in the work. Images become placeholders of meaning in flux. This is why images experienced in the work of art are freed only to the degree that they are experienced, when gazed upon by passersby. Yet, a question that must be answered is whether the street artist is able to produce a message in a work of art that will contest the dominant visual narrative impacting the identity of the person who passes by and views the art. The potential of this question lies in two readings of street art: first, how it interrupts striated space and the politics of display, and second, in the way that images presented by the street artist are culturally designated. If not culturally designated, these images are designated by a common or shared nodal point that intersects the spectator's experience with that of the artist. The street artist paves a series of pathways that cross each other, guiding the traveler, the spectator, toward designated and undesignated destinations. Once the work of art is completed or laid to rest, it is left for the spectator to discover, appropriate, designate, and situate, constructing meaning within the infrastructure of images left behind by the artist. Yet, the artist only paves the road. This does not mean that the images constructed by the street artist restrict the road of signification. Notably, the spectator, again a traveler on the pathway of signification, may pass through the limitless panorama affording the significance of the work variant destinations off the pathway and into the surrounding landscape. However, the spectator does not construct the surrounding landscape, he experiences it. This is to say that pathways of significance may be traversed or disregarded for alternate trails, alternate paths, alternate readings. In our case, the pathway is "a site at which a discursive formation intersects with material practices[,]" an assemblage of visual narratives, which may result in *multiplicities* of effects or readings.[3] The spectator's faculty to choose and designate the avenue of potential to an infinite prescription of meaning and/or signification is activated through the work of art as situated in the street.

Interestingly enough, this paradigm is situated in the interstate of signification, where the landscape or context is unobstructed, though it shares a common nodal point: the Egyptian Revolution. The pathways of signification are not constrained by the urban scene, striated by form such as skyscrapers or low-rise housing projects that inhibit the movement of the spectator—the traveler—in its path of signification, for significance. Here it is worth discussing French philosopher Gilles Deleuze and psychoanalyst Félix Guattari's notions of striated and smooth space along with those of the nomad and the state. The interplay of these concepts is essential to understanding the context, function, and translation of street art as a performance and product of aesthetic smoothing.

Cairo: The Smooth, the Striated, and the State

Cairo is a city and, like any city, it is subjected to a series of logics. These logics can be found in such places as Tahrir. It is a roundabout (not a square), providing taxi drivers formulated guidelines to reach their anticipated destinations. There is a garden in the center, where you will find families having *iftar* at sunset during the month of Ramadan. It serves as a regulating space for moving vehicles, while doubling as a place of leisure. These logics can also be found in the police's function to regulate flows of traffic or discipline Egyptian life. These logics take many forms, such as architectural planning, cultural mannerisms, and visual discourses, to name a few. The shared narrative of these logics is the city. Though we can speak of several logics found in a notion of private space, these logics come together publicly in the people's practices as they appear on the street. In this sense, street art is an occupation of public space, prescribing an alternative to these logics by deconstructing the notions surrounding them in a space that is routinely accessed by Cairo's inhabitants. The city as space is striated by form and certain logics though there exists potential for becoming discursively unhindered. When the police left the streets on January 28, 2011—the Friday of Rage—street art in Cairo began to flourish. Though street art had existed before in a much lesser capacity, the ability to aesthetically produce on the streets was no longer regulated by the state's disciplining mechanism, the police. This opening of unregulated potential for aesthetic creation and communication gave the protesters an opportunity to lay claim to their city and reterritorialize this space by making it smooth.

In Deleuze and Guattari's *A Thousand Plateaus*, the concepts of smooth and striated space become ways of *describing*, not defining, space in terms of practice and potential. These spaces are not the same yet they never exist in pure distinction. This is to say they are not formulated in a logic of binary opposition, for, as the authors put it, "the two spaces in fact exist only in mixture: smooth space is constantly being translated, transversed into a striated space; striated space is constantly being reversed, returned to a smooth space."[4] These spaces are constantly folding in and out of each other in multiple directions. In describing smooth space, we can say it is uninhibited in its lack of form or organization as compared to striated space, which is organized and structured through and by form. Deleuze and Guattari further elucidate:

> Whereas in the striated forms organize a matter, in the smooth materials signal forces and serve as symptoms for them. . . . Perception in it is based on symptoms and evaluations rather than measures and properties. That is why smooth space is occupied by intensities, wind and noise, forces, and sonorous and tactile qualities, as in the desert, steppe, or ice.[5]

Therefore smooth space, as occupied by intensities and forces, in contrast to forms, prescribes performance while not proscribing it or limiting the potential of performance. The street artist, in the act of performing and producing art in the street, reterritorializes a territory that has been subjected and disciplined by certain logics, most of which are constructed and managed by the state. Street art of the revolution is a 'symptom' of this discursive smoothing. In a moment of creative free flows such as the revolution, the potential for intensities and forces to manifest—such as spraying political demands on a public utility or painting cultural criticisms on a government building—becomes more likely. Since smooth space is likened to open terrains such as the desert or tundra, the potential of movement, like aesthetic practice, is unhindered by form, allowing the potential of continuous variations of free action. We do not have to speak of ridding the city of buildings for it to be smooth, though it is an interesting observation that the people did deconstruct city structures like the sidewalk to protect themselves and reclaim their space. Instead, the city becomes smooth through smoothing practices and reterritorializations like street art that resist the dominant visual narrative and logics enforced by the state.

On the other hand, striated space is contradistinctive to smooth space inasmuch as it inhibits, constructs, forms, regulates, and disciplines movement. Its quality lies in its practice and potential to homogenize. As Deleuze and Guattari describe it: "Returning to the simple opposition, the striated is that which intertwines fixed and variable elements, produces an order and succession of distinct forms."[6] Thus, striated space immures and situates the subject, whether form or person. By ordering and organizing matter and phenomena, it measures and impedes movement and free flows. "The city is the striated space par excellence," organizing, measuring, and disciplining forces such as life and movement through form.[7] Cairo is a striated space like any city where movement is inhibited. It is organized in a series of logics and practices that regulate urban life via form, structure, policing, and so forth.

The state in this case operates in a capacity of creating hierarchical systems of relations thus striating space. "One of the fundamental tasks of the State is to striate the space over which it reigns. . . . If it can help itself, the State does not dissociate itself from a process of capture of flows of all kinds, populations, commodities or commerce, money or capital, etc."[8] Indeed, throughout the reign of Mubarak's regime this capture of flows was extended to the political life of the Egyptian, measuring "in detail the relative movements of subjects and objects" and repressing or impeding its flow when it felt necessary.[9] At this moment, when the state captures these flows, especially with regard to subjects, regulating and disciplining the city dweller, Deleuze and Guatarri direct us to Paul Virilio's *Speed and Politics* to define the state's existence. Virilio defines the state's political power as "the polis, the police."[10] He continues:

[S]ince the dawn of the bourgeois revolution, the political discourse has been no more than a series of more or less conscious repetitions of the old communal poliorectics, confusing social order with the control of traffic (of people, of goods), and revolution, revolt, with traffic jams, illegal parking, multiple crashes, collisions.[11]

The state must striate and control, object and subject, to the extent to which it is able to homogenize them. This was evident during the Mubarak years within the lives of the Egyptian people as well as his regime's approach to supplanting the country's modern cultural hub, downtown Cairo, to the periphery of the city. One example is the regime's plans to relocate the Egyptian Museum outside of Cairo.[12] This process was the state's strategy to striate and deterritorialize the organic growth and cultural production of modern Cairo. Egyptian sociologist Mona Abaza details three zones, in what she calls the "Dubaisation" of Cairo, where one may observe this deterritorialization of urban life and culture.

First, the rich have opted to move out of the centre of Cairo, to the outskirts, to new satellite cities on the eastern and western parts of the Egyptian desert. . . .

Second, the zone of the Nile Corniche, juxtaposing the residential island of Zamalek and nicknamed by several investors as the 'Bermuda triangle,' has witnessed a process of the 'cleaning-up' of popular life, and of the removal of informal-sector retail shops and rundown *belle époque* buildings. . . .

Thirdly, what remains then is the *belle époque*, Haussmannian Europian/colonial city centre, which has witnessed the depopulation of its residents during the past six decades.[13]

The state's willingness to accord this deterritorialization, whether through explicit or implicit consent (think of the regime's allowance for this process or the provision to investors and the rich through incentives for such a process), exemplifies this striation of urban life, culture, and form.[14] The revolution that began on January 25, 2011 disrupted not only the state's strategies of striation within the life-form of the Egyptian but also contested its space in what Abaza calls the "space wars," as Tahrir, at the heart of downtown Cairo, was the epicenter of contestation.[15]

Urban Nomads: Street Artists of Cairo

In its mode of being, the street artist is the counterpart to Deleuze and Guattari's nomad. The nomad is antithetical in essence to the existence of the state and all its efforts of striation. The authors explain:

It is in this sense that nomads have no points, paths, or land, even though they do by all appearances. If the nomad can be called the Deterritorialized par excellence, it is precisely because there is no reterritorialization afterward, as with the migrant, or upon *something else* as with the sedentary (the sedentary's relation with the earth is mediatized by something else, a property regime, a state apparatus). On the contrary, deterritorialization constitutes the nomad's relation to the earth to such a degree that the nomad reterritorializes deterritorialization itself.[16]

The nomad, like the street artist, smoothes striated space by reterritorializing it, or in other words, reclaiming it. There exists in striated urban form the potential for aesthetic and discursive smoothing. Street art is the product of this aesthetic smoothing, reclaiming and reterritorializing what is at once deterritorialized and striated. In a conversation with filmmaker Joe Lukawski,[17] who has filmed and written about urban scenes, he explained that by seeing urban space differently and by altering urban display practices, like graffiti, the striated city street becomes a "smooth" space of expressing popular will, political dissent, and so on. This act is almost always seen as symbolically violent to those whose politics it attempts to reterritorialize, as its suppression is also a form of aesthetic and symbolic violence. "War-like artistic practice in public space is always about territory. While war is about physical space, challenging dominant narratives through artistic practice in public space is about head space."[18] Hence, contesting the autoerotic nature of the Mubarak regime, as it engulfed all forms of cultural expression on the street, "is a matter of re-territorializing space, whether through physical action and or through artistic practice."[19] This is why the war of the street artist, an urban nomad,[20] is fought in the physical space, likened to Abaza's "space wars," while also being fought in Lukawski's conception of head space, which is comparable to the space of visual consumption. First, the war for territory is fought by the street artist in the physical-spatial because street art interrupts the passerby's homogenized routine of interaction with urban space. It is fought in the head space since street art reterritorializes the striated visual narrative of the urban street. For example, after the military attacked protesters on the evening of April 8, 2011 and into the early morning of April 9, 2011, Tahrir was occupied by the people again. This was one of the few times when any policing authority, military or police, was absent from Tahrir. When the military reclaimed the contested space of Tahrir a few days later, they erected immense billboards parading the greatness of the military, its siding with the people (reminiscent of the chant "The people and the army are one"; see chapter 7 for a discussion of the meaning of this phrase), and photographs of Field Marshal Muhammad Tantawi, the Head of the Supreme Council of the Armed Forces (SCAF)—the council in charge of stewarding the revolution until parliamentary elections—along with other high-ranking military personnel saluting the martyrs. Besides these billboards, soldiers stood on the high pavement of the garden in the center of the roundabout, surrounding and regulating the green empty space in the middle of Tahrir. This was the military's effort to reappropriate and showcase its domination of the visual narrative of the revolution in the epicenter of its space, Tahrir. The politics of display are played out in a war on space for space: the military attempting to resubjugate the visual narrative of the revolution and Egyptian life as it takes place on the street while the street artist resists domination by reterritorializing these contested spaces through aesthetic and discursive practices.

Head Space

A heavily contested space before and throughout the revolution is head space. In describing it, we can say that it is a metaspace. As similar to the Latin *post* or *trans*, here *meta* is understood in its Greek etymological root as both 'beyond' or 'after' as well as 'a change of place or nature.'[21] In this way, French sociologist and philosopher Henri Lefebvre describes *meta* in *La présence et l'absence* as "transgression, a going beyond, an excess, etc."[22] Head space is a metaspace insofar as it transgresses, goes beyond, and is itself an excess of both physical and mental space. In other words, it is an 'other' space. It exists as a mirror. It is at once both a potential of physical and mental space though it is neither since it reflects both spaces to themselves while juxtaposing its own existence onto them. Head space is where perceived and experienced space is rearticulated to the person. In the process of rearticulation, these spaces are encoded so they may be understood by the interlocutor, the passerby who engages and *converses* with them. Just as a mirror "transforms what I am into the sign of what I am," head space transforms the object of visual consumption into the sign of the object of visual consumption, both taking place in physical and mental space.[23]

Since head space is a smooth space that is striated by systems of logic, these systems of logic (for example, binary logic, symbolic systems, language, representations, and so on) form structures that inhibit and discipline, regulate and confine head space. These striated structures are constructed through visual consumption and interaction with phenomena in physical space as well as mental space. They are embedded, settled, and structured as signs and representations. These representations are only structured and given the illusion of concretization in head space when they are accepted as such, intertwined into the nodal point of identity. Though in flux, they are made to appear as if they are static. In assuming stasis, it is disciplined. The Egyptian Revolution inverted the state's control over identity, as situated in its projected conception of the citizen, by focusing on the people in a process of smoothing striated identities formed by the state in which several flows (political, social, cultural, spatial, and so forth) were not captured by the state but instead by the protesters. This was experienced on the street as a free flow of creative works, some of which are found in this book, as the Egyptian people smoothed the discourses of art, expression, activity, and so on. They are discourses that the Mubarak regime had long denied access to the Egyptian people through its repressive measures. This shift in power took place within head space as the Egyptian people resisted the striating attempts of the regime by altering urban form when they dismantled the sidewalk in order to protect themselves, by expressing their demands on banners and through chants, and by creating aesthetic works on the street. These smoothing approaches, all of them dismantling the structures and thus the representational structures that the state had striated in physical and mental space, which were transposed to head space, were ways of reclaiming and reterritorializing the city.

Thus, head space is a metaspace. It allows for the infinite potential of approaching, though never touching, what Deleuze calls the plane of immanence,[24] a plane of continuous smooth space. Its potential lies in its ability to infinitely approach a state of immanence in which becomings meet the minimalist structuring, and movement meets the least possible resistance. The street art of the revolution interrupted and smoothed the striation of head space by interrupting physical space, by altering urban architectural form as visually consumed, and mental space insofar as the state's control over the city's visual narrative (think of the regime's attempt to impede and decenter the organic growth of downtown Cairo, Egypt's modern cultural hub, as previously described by Abaza, in conjunction with the regime's efforts to engulf all forms of cultural expression on the street) was reterritorialized. Head space is thus a discursive space. It is a critical space since it is subject to control and thus power and domination, and a space of processing that reflects both physical and mental space while being neither. By contesting the dominant narrative of the regime, the street artist reinvigorates the smooth space of head space through its aesthetic practice.

Understanding street art within this paradigm is crucial to its translation. It allows for the context, function, and translation of street art to be understood as a radical process of reterritorialization, a process that reclaims the city from the state and offers it to the Egyptian people in its potential for smooth space. Translating these aesthetic smoothings offers a glimpse into the reality that the revolution was not only staged in the physical wars of Tahrir and elsewhere around the country, but also in the head space of the Egyptian protesters. By translating these works of protest and resistance, this chapter is as much an archive of what will one day be, or has already been, painted over, dismantled, and erased, left only in the imprint of the Egyptians' minds. As Italian poet and anarchist Angelo Quattrocchi wrote during his participation in the May 1968 uprising in Paris, "Almost all which is visible has now receded, apparently. The invisible is in people's minds. The minds of the participants."[25]

Street Dynamics Between Smoothing and Striating: The People and State
Demands, Demands, Demands!
The first object of translation represents the urgency with which the protesters sought to reclaim space and articulate their demands.

In this photograph, taken on January 25, 2011, a protester is scribbling his demand on a concrete column near Tahrir. The words state his demand: "Down with Mubarak." It is evident, as we progress to other pieces, that in the first days of the revolution, the slogans and works of art were less complex and more direct. Another concept that must be taken into consideration in this piece is *the writing on the wall*, which signifies an impeding doom. This common literary expression dates back to the biblical story of Daniel. In the story, King Belshazzar of Babylon is partaking of a drunken

Yasqut Mubarak. Photograph by Sarah Carr

feast, praising gods of gold and silver, and he orders his servants to bring "the gold vessels that had been taken from the temple of the house of God which had been in Jerusalem."[26] As they were drinking from the stolen items, an ethereal hand appeared and wrote on the wall. When the king's soothsayers and wise men could not read or understand the writing, it was suggested that Daniel, a prophet, should be summoned to interpret it. For the sake of translation, the first word is most important. Daniel explained, "This is the interpretation of each word. 'Mene': God has numbered your kingdom, and finished it."[27] Though this story in particular may be unknown to the protester, it still represents the act of writing on the wall. The people have numbered Mubarak's reign, and finished it. 'Down with Mubarak,' the people's omen for the modern pharaoh, has come true.

The second target of translation is a formation of stones taken from the pavement, which were used to protect the protesters in confrontations with the police and *baltagiya* (thugs) during the first days of the revolution. It spells out '*irHal*' ('leave').

This word reverberated in many of the chants of the protesters as well as in their banners (chapter 3). Its beauty lies in its simplicity. Though in this composition, the stones were assembled during the day to aesthetically relay the focal demand of the protesters, at night the objects that pieced together this work of art were transformed into objects of violence. At once, the stones formed the aesthetic and symbolic violence to which street art reclaims and reterritorializes the city, yet they also symbolized the spatial confrontation that was taking place with the Mubarak regime, police, and *baltagiya* alike. They even represented the symbolic violence of dismantling striated space, smoothing by deconstructing the pavement. To

IrHal. Photograph by Rania Helmy

differentiate them in their functions is to discredit them entirely of their significance in the revolution. These are the pieces of pavement that the protesters appropriated—dismantling the concrete in order to stake their claim on Tahrir as well as to protect this reterritorialization, in a physical 'space war' as well as a war over the politics of display.

In the following object of translation, the words "Down with the regime" can be read with an upside-down eagle, the centerpiece of the Egyptian flag. The words are taken from the popular slogan that became synonymous with the protesters efforts, *"al-Sha'b yurid isqat al-nizam"* ('The people demand the downfall of the regime').

It is noticeable that this piece was done with a stencil, a tool commonly used by street artists to repeat a piece in numerous places. The stencil is a way of distributing the message of the work throughout the city while being time-efficient, since street art is generally considered illegal. The upside-down eagle is an interesting inversion. Egypt's contemporary flag came into existence with the Free Officers' coup, which installed Abdel Nasser, leader of the bloodless military coup that brought down the monarchy in 1952.[28] The colors of the flag, deemed the "Arab Liberation Flag," represented various characteristics of the 1952 Revolution; red symbolized "the period prior to the coup, a time characterized by the struggle against the monarchy," the white symbolized "the bloodless nature of the coup," and the black symbolized "the end of the oppression of the Egyptian people."[29] But what about the eagle? In an online article titled "Does Egypt Need a New Flag?" Egyptian artists discuss the importance of the eagle of Saladin in the contemporary Egyptian flag. Ganzeer, an Egyptian graphics artist widely known for his revolutionary

Yasqut al-nizam.
Photograph by
Sarah Carr

"We want freedom, we want to live, we want hashish." Photograph by Sarah Carr

street art, explains, "The current 'Eagle of Saladin' emblem in the white band of the flag, however, wasn't used until 1984. Which means . . . the current eagle on our flag belongs to Mubarak's regime."[30] This connection of the 'Eagle of Saladin' with the Mubarak regime provides the key to understanding this stencil piece. The 'Eagle of Saladin,' symbolizing Mubarak's era in the work, is upside down, representing the then-future fall of his reign, made possible through the people *(al-sha'b)*. Yet, only in bringing down the existing order under Mubarak are the Egyptian people then able to reterritorialize their space and create their own order.

The fourth object of translation is a tag stating, 'We want freedom, we want to live, we want hashish' with the word 'to live' in blue and 'hashish' in gold.

In translating this demand, the invariant core, the collective signified of all the signifiers of a text or image, those symbolic elements of significance which manifest in the bricolage of the work (see chapter 6 for a longer discussion on invariant core), lies in the protester's desire to live freely, having the ability to do what he or she likes—in this case the use of hashish. What sets this phrase apart from others used during the revolution is the word 'hashish.' Though this substance is a drug, this should not be a surprising find. Hashish has cultural ties, not only to *sha'bi* dwellings but also the lives of intellectuals, as represented in the works of such celebrated Egyptian authors as Naguib Mahfouz and Khairy Shalaby. For example, in Shalaby's novel *The Hashish Waiter*,[31] a group of intellectuals gather in Hakeem's den, located in downtown Cairo, to converse and smoke hashish. Its use is also found in Mahfouz's works, such as *Midaq Alley*[32] and *Adrift on the Nile*,[33] though, notably, it is condemned for its escapist function in his works. Even Sayyed Darwish, the early-twentieth-century Egyptian singer and composer, was known for having written "compositions based on the voices of hashish addicts."[34]

In 2010, the hashish market experienced a drought due to an unprecedented government crackdown.[35] Thus, this protester's demand represents a glimpse into a particular subculture of hashish use in Egypt while juxtaposed with the well-known demands for freedom and life made during the revolution. It also serves as a demand to undo the former regime's corrupt and self-interested policies. On the night after the military attacked protesters on April 8, 2011, a longtime Egyptian activist who had demonstrated against the regime for five years preceding the revolution—when only a few people would appear surrounded by hundreds of riot police—cheekily asked, "Have we [the Egyptian people] not done this to *at least* enjoy a joint of hashish in the middle of the *midan*?"

Street Statue Mubaraaak. Photograph by Lewis Sanders IV

Representations of Mubarak

In the next photograph, the target of translation is a street statue, an effigy of Mubarak, hung from the lamppost in Tahrir on February 1, 2011.

The figure shows Mubarak in a business suit with U.S. dollars in his pocket, one of them falling down his front half. His face is downcast, his eyes lowered as if in a dismal trance. The words 'Mubarak—Mubaraaak' are written on his abdomen. The juxtaposition of his clothes with the US currency marks the social perception that, besides being the president of Egypt, he is a wealthy businessman, who has been judged by the Egyptian people. The significance of the symbol for the US dollar on the bills stresses the self-beneficial relationship that he and his regime shared with the United States, being propped up by US$2.1 billion a year in aid.[36] Also, his name written the second time with three additional *alifs* (translated into 'A's) in the middle is a play on the name of Israel's former prime minister, Ehud Barak. The cozy relationship that Mubarak kept with these two countries, namely the United States and Israel, signifies a corrupt agreement in which he is portrayed as being guilty of betraying Egypt's interests. In the image, he is hanged in order to reflect that the Egyptian people have already judged him. These symbols of Mubarak's relationship with these two countries are found in many artists' pieces during the revolution. In a conversation about this object of representation, Abdallah al-Ghoul,[37] a Palestinian filmmaker from Gaza, explained that during times of war between Gaza and Israel, he would search through the hospitals for his friends. The doctors at the hospital would write the names of the deceased in a black marker on their corpses, usually on the inner thigh or the abdomen, for identification purposes. Though this cultural context needs further examination within Egyptian society, the street statue serves as a form of identification of he who has been judged by the Egyptian people through aesthetically reterritorializing justice. By contesting the authority of Mubarak and reterritorializing justice inasmuch as the people are the ultimate source of authority, they are laying claim to the power that had been usurped and corrupted by Mubarak's regime, especially within the judicial system.

The following object of translation is another depiction of Mubarak, only this time in the form of an elephant mask. The mask represents Mubarak with an oversized head, slouching ears, and bulging red-orange eyes, topped with a hat that seems to have been clumsily stitched together. As

Mubarak Elephant Mask. Photograph by Samia Mehrez

an elephant, the mask emphasizes his thick-skinned attitude toward the Egyptian people's revolution. The notion of Mubarak as thick-skinned was also inscribed in many banners with several synonyms for the word. The translation of this piece happens at the semiotic level in which symbols provide a path to the representations, the intended signifieds.

The oversized head represents an oversized ego. The mask's confounded visage reflects Mubarak's bewilderment at the Egyptian people's revolution. This was recognized in speeches, during which Mubarak was not able to come to terms with the fact that the Egyptian people were rising up to contest his power (chapter 2). Though his red eyes resemble a fury with the revolt sweeping the country, he is incapacitated and helpless in preventing his imminent ousting. The hat, if interpreted as a crown, refers to the title given to him, the modern pharaoh of Egypt. The features of this mask are disproportional as was his power. The elephant was being paraded around Tahrir as protesters surrounded it chanting, "We found Hosni Mubarak!" This work of art gives rise to the notion that street art is not only graffiti and aesthetic formulations of the street, on the street, but also artistic objects displayed on the street, smoothing the visual

Martyrs' Ka'ba at Tahrir. Photograph by Samia Mehrez

discourse in a politics of display. The performance of the object acts as an aesthetic smoothing of head space by deconstructing his image. In deterritorializing Mubarak's image in head space as the dominant authority of the country, the protesters reterritorialize his image as a thick-skinned elephant who does not listen or acknowledge the power and authority of the people. By delegitimizing Mubarak's authority, they are establishing their own through a public performance on the street, an artistic practice that had long vanished during the Mubarak era.

Homage: Memorializing the Martyrs

At this point, we transition to three works of street art that pay homage to the martyrs of the revolution. The first is an installation that was constructed in Tahrir displaying the faces of the martyrs.

More accurately, as the words describe, it is a memorial (chapter 1). The words written atop the cube-like structure say, "Memorial: The Youth Martyrs of the Tahrir Revolution." In the photograph we can see that a multitude of people are gathered around the memorial, drawing parallels to the Ka'ba, the cube-like structure around which Muslims gather and circumambulate

Islam Raafat. Photograph by Lewis Sanders IV

every year in Mecca, Saudi Arabia. An interesting detail of the Muslim ritual is that the process of circumambulation *(tawaf)* is a demonstration of the unity of believers in worship to the one God, moving together in harmony. This brings us to the martyrs' memorial, where thousands of people are gathered, paying respect to the martyrs' lives in a demonstration of the Egyptian people's unity, made evident through their gatherings during the revolution. The act of congregating around the memorial in Tahrir parallels the religious ritual in Mecca by gathering in the spirit of unity of the revolution. The protesters are honoring, appreciating, and paying tribute to the lives of those who died at the hands of the police, the enforcers of Mubarak's brutality. This act of gathering around the memorial reterritorializes head space by reinvigorating the image of the martyrs as well as the protesters, since the regime throughout the revolution depicted them as mischievous youth, who were instigating violence and instability.

Now we begin to shift into the post-Mubarak street art. The following object of translation is a mural memorializing the life of Islam Raafat.

Raafat was an eighteen-year-old protester who was killed by the diplomatic car that plowed into protesters in Tahrir on the night of January 28, 2011, the first Friday of Rage.[38] The initiative to commemorate the lives of the martyrs through murals painted around the city was launched by Ganzeer. He states on his blog, "The goal is to, on one hand, honor the martyrs, and on another hand provide passersby with a reminder of Egypt's struggle for freedom, democracy, and equality."[39] Yet, despite being a memorial to those who fell during the revolution, it was painted over in April, sparking an outrage from activists, artists, and passersby alike, who immediately condemned this act of censorship. They began to ask, "What harm did Islam Raafat's portrait cause our beloved government?"[40] The painting-over of Raafat's portrait in Midan Falaki, less than a five-minute walk from Tahrir, caused a backlash from the community of street artists, and prompting the Mad Graffiti Weekend. The goal was to ensure "that the streets of Egypt belong to the people of Egypt."[41] On the weekend of May 20, 2011, a group of artists and collaborators set off into to the city to reclaim the streets, painting and erecting a portrait of Raafat, as well as other martyrs, along with a massive wheatpasting[42] of a full-size tank confronting a child on a bike carrying the city on a tray that is typically used to transport bread. This piece will be elaborated on in the section of this chapter entitled, "The People and the Military are *Not* One." The function of Raafat's mural, painted on a public restroom, is in its transformation of a public service location into a display case, exhibiting the life of the martyr. By transforming the function of this public utility, the work of art reterritorializes a government service, lending it to the Egyptian people and the passerby. Despite the success of Mad Graffiti Weekend, the mural was removed again in July 2011.

The subsequent piece was created on May 27, 2011, deemed the Second Friday of Rage and the beginning of the second revolution. The work displays the words, 'You are not better than those who died' another reference to the martyrs of the revolution, only this time addressing the people still living, participating in the second day of rage.

The invariant core of this work lies in its confrontational reminder to those still active in the revolution's efforts. It is in not forgetting the lives that the revolution cost to bring about its yet-undetermined success that those protesters still proceeding with the work of the revolution may be edified and humbled in the wake of the martyrs' lives. The picture shows an unidentified white figure surrounded by a white tree, symbolizing that the revolution is not successful because of one identifiable person but by the unity of the Egyptian people. The unity of the people is a significant theme necessary for continuing the people's perception of their power and authority. Their power and authority to smooth and reterritorialize space

"You are not better than the ones who died." Photograph by Laura Gribbon

is only possible in their collective resistance against the state. This piece reterritorializes head space insofar as it deconstructs the image of the revolution as successful and completed, an idea that many had accepted. It became visible that this was not the case from such incidents as the police disrupting a martyrs' memorial service on June 28, 2011, which resulted in a violent clash between protesters and the families of the martyrs against the police. As a result, nearly one thousand protesters were injured in an event that can reasonably be deemed the beginning of the second stage of the revolution. The violent clashes in Abbasiya Square on July 23, 2011, as a result of which activist Muhammad Mohsen died two weeks after being wounded by a large rock thrown from the rooftop of a nearby building, along with the violent military crackdown and eviction of protesters sitting in at Tahrir on the first day of Ramadan, August 1, 2011, show that the revolution is far from over. Mohsen's death is a confirmation of the murals' words by reterritorializing the naive image of the revolution's success. The power and authority of the people are contested by the military state and must remain resistant if the protesters are to succeed in their demands and ambitions. The following section explores street art that showcases and exemplifies the power of the people, united, to manifest their demands, dreams, and ambitions.

Huriya mural. Photograph by Laura Gribbon

The People, United

The following works represent the ability of the Egyptian people to actuate and bring about the changes they desired. The first piece is an intricate mural exhibited on a wall in Zamalek, the largest island in the Nile in Cairo.

The fulcrum of this work is the word '*Huriya*' (freedom) situated in the center. The surrounding symbols activate the word in several contexts. First, there is a figure connected to a machine on its head, wires and tubes extending to other symbols. The figure is holding onto Cairo Tower in one hand and displaying the peace sign with the other hand. The wires and tubes extended from the figure's head are connected to displays of Twitter and Facebook (though Facebook is not visible, it is directly over the figure's head). From these images of two of the social media websites most used in organizing the revolution, another set of wires extends to a light bulb with a brain in its glass bulb. Across the bottom are several structures found in Cairo, such as the Pyramids of Giza, a minaret, and a church spire, to name a few. Rising up from these structures on the right side is a police officer in riot gear with blood smeared across the rim of his helmet. The officer's expression is disdainful. The symbols come together in this piece as a complex and detailed vision of the revolution, owing credit to such tools as Twitter and Facebook for giving the Egyptian people an alternate means for communicating and mobilizing. There is also a television set with the Al Jazeera news channel symbol depicted in the mural. Al Jazeera was influential in mobilizing protesters through their on-the-ground interviews as well as their detailed coverage of events, despite being shut down by the government during the early days of the uprising. These interviews, aired on the channel—on varying satellite frequencies—served as a mapping of safe passageways through which protesters could avoid thugs, pro-Mubarak supporters, and police. By taking the collective elements, it becomes evident that the figure is the agent of change, who uses social media websites as a tool to mobilize and bring about freedom. By using these media outlets as vehicles for social change, the figure is able to channel its intentionality to reclaim and reterritorialize the freedom that the Mubarak regime had monopolized. In head space, the readings of these images showcase the Egyptian people's triumph in smoothing the striated measures imposed by the state on free flows of activity, expression, and aesthetic creation. Within the image, the wall in the background is falling apart, representing the deconstruction of the existing structures that have long encaged the freedom of the Egyptian people.

The next piece is a chessboard painted on one of the walls of the American University in Cairo's former library building. The work epitomizes the power of the Egyptian people's unity.

On the top half, four rows of pawns are confronting the court pieces at the bottom, with the king fallen. Interestingly enough, in *A Thousand Plateaus* Deleuze and Guattari state, "Chess is a game of State," and elaborate, "Chess is indeed a war, but an institutionalized, regulated, coded war, with a front, a rear, battles."[43] This work of art, however, transgresses the rules of the state, the formal coding of movement in the game of chess. The pawns against the court pieces are the same color, black. The pawns' stylized structure is inverted so that they are all gathered on one end, contesting the dominance of the court pieces at the other end. They are still situated in the space of a chessboard, to which we can draw parallels to the striated form of the city, yet their collective assembly, and consequently their movement, is not inhibited by the rules of the game or the rules of the state. Instead, it is in the power and legitimacy of the people that the pieces are able to disregard the institutional logic of the state and contest the regime's legitimacy. The piece depicts the

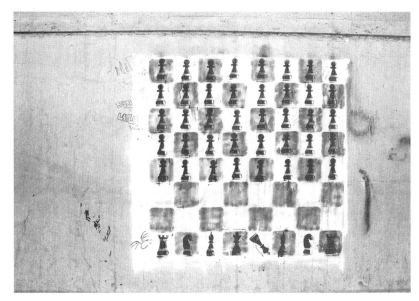

Checkmate. Photograph by Lewis Sanders IV

pawns, the Egyptian people, smoothing the disciplining form of the state, the Mubarak regime. And the final detail, the king-Mubarak, toppled by their resistance to the pressure to conform or be subjugated to the state's discipline. 'Game over Mubarak.'[44] Checkmate.

The following piece is much simpler than the former, though just as powerful. It is a work formed by a stencil, showing the Islamic crescent and Coptic cross together, overlapping each symbol's edges.

The word in the bottom background of the work states 'brothers.' One of the striking spectacles of the revolution was the transcendence of religious differences between Egyptians, which the former regime had constantly manipulated in order to create the appearance of sectarian strife. The Coptic community, which had long been repressed by the former regime and equally misrepresented in cultural discourse, reversed the varying perceptions of differences between them and Egyptian Muslims. This reversal was a reterritorialization of the state's strategies in dealing with these differences. The state's strategy consisted of denial and reconciliation, though the latter consisted of emphasizing stereotypes that created further divisions.[45] For example, the Ramadan special series *Awan al-ward* (Time of Roses), aired on state television, was "intended as a lesson in 'moderate' religious values for both Muslims and Copts,"

Crescent–Cross Unity. Photograph by Laura Gribbon

though it was depicted through the "unacceptable marriage between a Coptic woman and a Muslim man."[46] After four Coptic Christians had filed lawsuits against the Ministry of Information, the script was changed in which the Coptic woman recognized "that her marriage to a Muslim was a mistake."[47] The state's ability to increase social divisions between Coptic Christians and Muslims was reterritorialized during the eighteen days that led to Mubarak's ouster. This stencil represents the smoothing of sectarian images that striated Egyptian head space within their respective religio-public spheres. The word 'brothers' represents an immanent unity of action, where the Egyptian people came together, denying their differences, in order to challenge and bring down the regime: Coptic Christians protecting Muslims during prayers, and vice versa, as well as women protesting alongside men, despite dominant patriarchal values found in Egyptian society, were common experiences shared in Tahrir as well as throughout the country.

The Military and the People are Not One

The subsequent four pieces, though the first is only indirectly linked, express a growing criticism of the military's lack of action and accord with the revolution's demands. The first target of translation in this section is

Ganzeer's 'Mubarak Posse Love.' It is a mural in Zamalek that depicts Mubarak, Ahmed Ezz, Tantawi, and Safwat al-Sherif, the upper echelon of the former regime, in a love quadrangle.

The words atop of the piece are a play on the slogan "*al-Sha'b yurid isqat al-nizam*" with the word '*Habayib*,' or 'loved ones,' interjected at the end. Hence, 'the people want the downfall of the loved ones of the regime.' This goes to show that the revolution was not looking to solely bring the downfall of Mubarak or even the system. It explains that these people, all linked to the former regime, lovers of the regime, and loved by it, should be held accountable for their participation in a corrupt system that repressed the Egyptian people. It incriminates Ezz, an Egyptian business tycoon (owner of Ezz Steel) and a former high-ranking National Democratic Party (NDP) official, Field Marshal Tantawi, and al-Sherif, former Speaker of the Egyptian Shura Council. The piece presents them lightheartedly, all together as lovers. By demanding the downfall of the lovers and loved ones of the regime, the piece extends the demand of the revolution into the representational image of the regime as far more expansive then just the upper echelon of politicians. It identifies the regime's corrupt influence reaching beyond the state and into businesses and organizations, which enjoyed favor and gave favor to the regime.

"The people demand the downfall of Mubarak's loved ones." Photograph by Ganzeer

This deterritorialization of the overarching structure that exists beyond the state, yet within its confines, reterritorializes its image in head space by demanding the downfall of the entire system, lovers included.

The second piece in this section is a street performance, as opposed to the previous selections of graffiti and murals exhibited under the title of street art. A turtle is dragging a cart with bars, a pseudo-transportable prison, carrying cutout faces of members of the former regime.

The turtle, representative of the military's unhurried response to arresting these former members of the regime, is slowly dragging them to an unspecified destination. The same day this turtle was seen, vendors were selling live turtles in Tahrir. The turtle here symbolizes the military's slow response to the demands of the revolution (for example, arresting and trying the members of the regime). The turtle also hides in a shell, which is to say that the military has been hiding from the revolution in its demands and desires, as expressed by the Egyptian people. The tardiness of the trials translates into the failure of the revolution on behalf of the people's ability to claim their power and authority. Inasmuch as the Egyptian people are unable to stake their claims on justice, the process of reterritorialization by the people is deterritorialized and reclaimed by the military state. In this sense, this piece shows that the military is not in

The military, slow as a turtle. Photograph by Samia Mehrez

accordance with the revolution's demands since the trials of the former regime are constantly postponed and deferred while juxtaposing the failure of the people's ability to reterritorialize the revolution, which is being claimed by the military.

The third piece, mentioned briefly earlier, is a product of Mad Graffiti Weekend. The work is a wheatpasting of a full-size tank aiming its tank gun at an Egyptian child, who is riding a bike while carrying the city on a tray that is typically used to transport bread.

This piece can be translated on two levels: first, as a critique of the military's actions against the people, and second as a representation of the city as life—'ish (bread). At the first level of translation, this piece echoes a popular sentiment that the military is, in fact, not in accord with the Egyptian people or the revolution. This is evident in the way the military has treated civilians since Mubarak resigned and turned over his powers to the Tantawi-led SCAF. For example, on March 9, 2011 the military forcefully cleared Tahrir and arrested eighteen women. These women testified that they had been sentenced in a military court and were told that their prison terms would be annulled as long as they did not continue protesting. During their detention, they were stripped of their clothes and subjected to virginity tests. In human rights terms,

Tank, child biking with the city, life. Photograph by Laura Gribbon

'virginity testing' constitutes rape. The military later responded by stating that virginity tests were conducted only in order to curtail any allegations of rape against members of the military.[48] On April 8, 2011 the military forced protesters staging a sit-in at Tahrir to leave. This resulted in a clash in which the military used live ammunition, tear gas, and brute force—in conjunction with the police—against protesters. There are numerous examples of situations in which the military has dealt with civilians inappropriately following Mubarak's resignation. At the second level, the tray that the child is carrying, as mentioned above, is typically used to transport bread. The word bread in colloquial Egyptian Arabic is *'ish*, which also means 'life.' By transposing bread with the city, it comes to show that the city is, in some sense, life. It is the place where millions of Egyptians live; it gives them a space to live, to breathe, to be free. It is in this sense that the military is simultaneously confronting and attacking life—the life of the Egyptian people and the life of the city—and disciplining both, through a war on space and the politics of display. In head space, this piece reterritorializes the dominant narrative of the military state as the steward of Egyptian life and the revolution.

The final piece of this section is as comical as it is serious. Near Talaat Harb Square, this stencil design depicts Tantawi with a long beard, equating him with the Salafi movement, part of the Islamist political current calling for shari'a.

The piece elucidates a phenomenon that occurred after the first eighteen days of the revolution. Before the revolution, the Salafi community of Muslims was scarcely spoken of or acknowledged in the general public because they had been imprisoned by the Nasser, Sadat, and Mubarak regimes. In addition, they had been fighting in Afghanistan alongside the *mujahidin* in order to deter the Soviet invasion. After Mubarak's resignation, the SCAF and the Ministry of Interior decided to release many Salafi prisoners and to provide an allowance to those returning from exile. The arrival of Salafis on the political scene has unearthed a division in the Egyptian public sphere in which they, along with other Islamist political parties like the Muslim Brotherhood, have allegedly given concessions and promises to the SCAF and vice versa. This was evident in the mobilization of the 'Yes' vote during the constitutational referendum on March 19, 2011 spearheaded by Salafi and Islamist organizations along with the former ruling NDP party. In an article published by *AhramOnline*, "What was Religion Doing in the Debate on Egypt's Constitutional Amendments?,"

Tantawi Salafi. Photograph by Sarah Carr

the author states, "Salafis were among the fiercest advocates of the 'Yes' vote, declaring it a religious duty for all Muslims, portraying the 'No' campaigners as Christian and secularist 'enemies of Islam.'"[49] Essentially, the 'Yes' vote was framed as a vote for Islam while the 'No' vote was framed as a vote toward secularism and even the banning of the *Higab*. The hasty decision to hold a constitutional referendum a little over a month after Mubarak's resignation was made by the SCAF. On July 29, 2011 when Islamists and Salafis dominated Tahrir, many were chanting, "*Ya mushir, ya mushir, inta al-amir*," ('Hey, marshal, hey marshal, you are the prince'), naming Field Marshal Tantawi as their leader, since Islamists and Salafis believe in the concept of *wali al-amr*, that is, the legitimate ruler who cannot be contested if he is a Muslim, whether or not he is just or corrupt.[50] Hence, Tantawi depicted as a Salafi represents his desire to create a religious state in which democracy and freedoms for women would not be included. Instead, they would be traded for a strict and literalist interpretation of shari'a.

Connecting Global Struggles

Street art in recent years has become a popular tool for commenting on the urban condition. Street artists such as Banksy and the group Space

Hijackers have contributed to the global spread of street art as a form of aesthetic practice and resistance. This is to say that street art links people, the world over, who are rehearsing their lives in distinction to the commonly accepted practices of their society. Though major corporations have used street art as a medium for advertising reaching out to counter-culture enthusiasts and passersby alike, the street art spoken of here represents a resistance to homogenizing social and state pressures. The following two pieces offer a glance into how the street art of the Egyptian Revolution linked this uprising to other revolutions in history as well as how social commentators outside of Egypt connected the art to other popular struggles.

The first one is a work captured in a photograph on February 4, 2011 that proclaims in French "Vive la révolution" ('Long Live the Revolution'). It is a reference to the French Revolution that brought down the country's monarchy during the ten-year period between 1789 and 1799.

The French Revolution is credited with having brought about the modern era of republics and democracies. The principles of the French Revolution, "Liberté, égalité, fraternité," ('Liberty, Equality, and Fraternity'), compare to those of the Egyptian Revolution: "*'Ish, Huriya, 'adala igtima'iya*," ('Life, Freedom, and Social Justice'). The protester who wrote this must have been aware of the French people's struggle against monarchy and absolute rule, which culminated in the final blow to this system in France. It is commonly perceived in history that the royalty were preoccupied with their wealth and power and far removed from the problems of the French people. The current struggle in Egypt bears an apparent parallel example, wherein the former regime had been perceived by the

"Vive la révolution." Photograph by Sarah Carr

people as absent from their issues, and as robbing them of their social, political, and economic livelihood. It comes as no surprise that Mubarak was charged by the people with allegedly stealing US$70 billion from the Egyptian people. By interlinking these two struggles, protesters are encouraged by an example of the people's ability to overthrow the oppressive authority that has taken hold of what is legitimately theirs: their lives. This piece is a reterritorialization not only of the Egyptian people's lives, but also of the revolution, which counterrevolutionary forces, such as the military state, have attempted to usurp and control.

The second piece in this section is a piano played by five fingers (though only three are evident in the photograph). It was painted over a wall near Tahrir, filled with depictions of police brutality.

In an article titled "Graffiti: Cairo Revolution Painted on the Streets" in *Respect Magazine*'s blog,[51] the author describes and translates its meaning: "On a wall scarred by street fights—punctured with bullet holes and charred by Molotov cocktails—a piano has emerged. This is reminiscent of a slogan that appeared on the walls of Paris during the uprising in May '68—"Sous les pavés, la plage" ('Under the paving stones, the beach')—and speaks to the spirit of collective optimism of the Egyptian Revolution, which toppled a tyrant and is creatively reclaiming the streets."[52] The

Piano. Photograph by Laura Gribbon

author is linking the sentiments of this work to those of the May 1968 uprising in France. Paris circa May 1968 saw one of the largest general strikes, by the people, to take place in an advanced industrial state, bringing the economy to a near standstill. Beginning with students and youth protesting, it later developed and crossed several social and economic classes. Similarly, in the Egyptian Revolution, the people gathered to fight for their social, political, and economic rights, just as the French did in May 1968. Street art was a major component in the contemporary French uprising just as it was in the Egyptian Revolution. A more detailed translation of this work interprets the fingers playing the piano as a representation of the people's ability to create an aesthetic overlay on top of the state's evident violence. This piece paints over the violence. On a wall that still holds the memories of the former regime's brutality against the people, it is the people who are reclaiming their space and who made this revolution possible. It also stands as a reminder to the passerby, who interact with the scars left on the walls, that the people are creating and reclaiming the contested spaces of the revolution.

The Revolution Is Not Over

The last two selections represent a continual presence of participation, a need to continue in the revolution's efforts. They remind the Egyptian people that the revolution is not over. The first is a sketch made with a black marker and a stencil. The image displays a rat at the bottom of three paths.

The path to the left leads to nowhere. The path on the right, the one which leads to a stencil of a journal or book with wings, has "foreign agenda" written over it. This is a play on former vice president Omar Suleiman's accusations that the protesters were supporting foreign agendas and were being directed by foreign forces. This rhetoric has been a strong tool used to delegitimize the opposition and was used by the military state against the April 6 Youth Movement, which has played a critical part in mobilizing protesters throughout the revolution. Yet, in this case, the path is not leading to the representation of the Egyptian people but to a rat. The path down the middle, to which an arrow is pointing, leads to a street sign. It points in three directions. The first sign says 'The people,' the second 'revolution,' and the third 'government.' Above the rat a question is posed: 'Where do I go?' The meaning of this work lies in the rat's predicament. In Egypt, rats are typically viewed as

"Where do I go?" Photograph by Laura Gribbon

dirty animals. They creep and eat at the inner workings of apartments and houses. In this sense, the rat, conceived of as a counterrevolutionary force, is given directions as to what to eat at first. The arrow in front of it is specifying its imminent direction. In this case, the path between the journal with wings and the rat is specifying a relationship between counterrevolutionary forces and foreign agendas in the country. There are no signs pointing to the rat's direction toward the foreign agenda, nor the direction of the foreign agenda to the rat, providing a relational legibility instead of a path. After the resignation of Mubarak, the international community has grown less interested in encouraging the Egyptians' fight for freedom. Instead, it has shifted to a growing concern for stability in the country, seeing as a democracy in Egypt could result in a major shift in power structures within the region. By elucidating the issue of counterrevolutionary forces, the piece reterritorializes Egyptian head space by revealing the existence of these forces and their plans to eat at the 'people,' 'revolution,' and 'government.'

The last selection is a set of two interlinked works, each standing as a translation of the other. The first one states "*'Ish al-thawra*" and next to it, "Enjoy the revolution." *'Ish*, as explained earlier, has connotations of life, to live, and bread, yet it has been translated here as 'enjoy.' Why? This is due, in part, to the word 'enjoy' in English since it can signify at least two different things; first, "to take delight and pleasure (in an activity or occasion)," and second, to "possess and benefit from."[53] By combining these two definitions into one word, one signifier, it expresses several connotations in the Arabic word *'ish*. This is not to say it captures it completely, because no translation does so, but it provides a window into the phrase. The two works operate together in providing signification to each other (see discussion of translation and affinity of language in chapter 6). This work acts as an aesthetic smoothing of head space by reminding those who have grown weary or despondent of the revolution that these events do not occur in all places and at all times. Insofar as it reminds the Egyptian passersby to enjoy and live the revolution, it reclaims the spirit of the revolution as a time of the people's power and authority over their territory and space, which is being contested by the striating practices of the state. It implores resistance to the dominant narrative and asks the passerby to live it out since people have taken their lives into their own hands, and are executing their power and authority by reclaiming and reterritorializing their space. The revolution is now; live it and enjoy it, for "Revolutions are the ecstasy of history: the moment when social reality and social dream fuse (the act of love)."[54]

Conclusion

The street art of the revolution is as much a way of reclaiming and reterritorializing space as it is a glimpse into the several narratives of the people

"'Ish al-thawra—Enjoy the revolution." Photograph by Joseph Hill

contesting the state's desire to discipline, regulate, and striate their lives according to its interests. As Deleuze argues, these attributes of the state, of the former regime and the military state, are inherent in its existence. It would not be a state if it were not for these attributes. Street art of the revolution represents the activity of smoothing striated urban space. As Ganzeer explains, "Creating graffiti [read: street art] involves taking ownership of the streets, just like we did during the uprising. And so of course it's political, and illegal."[55] This is to say it is illegal because it is contesting the state's power over space. Just as the occupation of Tahrir is about physical space, street art is about reclaiming the visual narrative that the state had held for far too long. Like the nomad, the street artist reterritorializes deterritorialized space. But this is not to say that it is all done and over with. Inasmuch as protesters have reclaimed and reterritorialized the striated space of the state, the state has responded in order to reclaim it. The state's response has led to the imprisonment of activists, military trials for civilians (despite the former regime being put on civilian trials), control over media, forceful demolitions of sit-ins, and violent clashes that have taken the lives of Egyptians. Those who rehearse practices of reterritorialization in public are the ones who receive the state's harshest responses. This is to show that the battle over space, whether

Cleaning Up. Photograph by Nermine Hammam

physical or head space, is a dynamic one that will continue between the people and the state. Contested spaces, those striated and smooth, will continue to fold in and out of each other in multiple directions as the battle moves forward. In this sense, let us remember that street art of the Egyptian Revolution signifies the struggles of the protesters both in the same physical locations as their protests and also in the head space offered by visual representation in urban space. These struggles against dominant structures are crucial for the realization of free and smooth spaces and for spaces that are limitless in practice and potential.[56]

Notes to Chapter Four

1   Lyman G. Chaffee, *Political Protest and Street Art: Popular Tools for Democratization in Hispanic Countries* (Westport: Greenwood Press, 1993), p. 4.
2   Umberto Eco, *The Open Work* (Cambridge, MA: Harvard University Press, 1989), p. 4.
3   Jonathan Crary, *Techniques of the Observer: On Vision and Modernity in the Nineteenth Century* (Cambridge, MA: Massachusetts Institute of Technology Press, 1992), p. 31.
4   Gilles Deleuze and Félix Guattari, *A Thousand Plateaus: Capitalism and Schizophrenia* (Minneapolis: University of Minnesota Press, 2005), p. 474.
5   Deleuze and Guattari, *A Thousand Plateaus*, p. 479.
6   Deleuze and Guattari, *A Thousand Plateaus*, p. 478.
7   Deleuze and Guattari, *A Thousand Plateaus*, p. 481.
8   Deleuze and Guattari, *A Thousand Plateaus*, p. 385–86.
9   Deleuze and Guattari, *A Thousand Plateaus*, p. 386.
10 Paul Virilio, *Speed and Politics* (Los Angeles: Semiotext(e), 2006), p. 39.
11 Virilio, *Speed and Politics*, p. 39.
12 Mona Abaza, "Cairo's Downtown Imagined: Dubaisation or Nostalgia?" *Urban Studies Journal* (May 2011): 1076.
13 Abaza, "Cairo's Downtown Imagined," p. 1075.
14 Abaza, "Cairo's Downtown Imagined," p. 1079. Abaza comments on investors' plans to "revamp" downtown Cairo. She explains, "There are already developers who have raised some $80 million to refurbish the centre of town. The al-Isma'ili company, whose shareholders are the Samih Sawiris tycoon family, and a Saudi firm called Amwal el Khalig have already purchased 20 buildings and have plans to buy 12 more.... Opposition journalists like Adel Hammouda have expressed their doubts

about the developers' intentions to preserve the city rather than destroy it with skyscrapers. Downtown Cairo will be then transformed into a residential area with offices, commercial centres and hotels."

15 Abaza, "Cairo's Downtown Imagined," p. 1084.

16 Deleuze and Guattari, *A Thousand Plateaus*, p. 381.

17 Joe Lukawski is a filmmaker and intellectual who works on urban scenes. His film *Paris Underground: Exploring Urban Scenes* (2010) explores the underground as ephemeral spaces of expression and transgression with sociologist Steven Sawyer. His upcoming film titled *Hidden Rivers* explores hydraulic risks and water supply sustainability surrounding the old water system in Fez as mapped by an archaic poem.

18 Joe Lukawski, personal communication, June 27, 2011.

19 "Breaking the 'Ad Complex': The Street as Museum, 'Absolute Advertising' and Performing Territory." Joe Lukawaski's Blog, http://joelukawski.wordpress.com

20 Deleuze and Guattari, *A Thousand Plateaus*, p. 492. Deleuze and Guattari comment on the urban nomad, "[I]t is possible to live smooth even in the cities, to be an urban nomad (for example, a stroll taken by Henry Miller in Clichy or Brooklyn is a nomadic transit in smooth space; he makes the city disgorge a patchwork, differentials of speed, delays and accelerations, changes in orientations, continuous variations). . . . They are nomads by dint of not moving, not migrating, of holding a smooth space that they refuse to leave, that they leave only in order to conquer and die. Voyage in place: that is the name of all intensities, even if they also develop in extension."

21 Edward W. Soja, *Thirdspace: Journeys to Los Angeles and Other Real-and-Imagined Places* (Oxford: Blackwell Publishing, 2004), p. 33.

22 Henri Lefebvre, *La présence et l'absence*, cited in Soja, *Thirdspace*, p. 33.

23 Henri Lefebvre, *The Production of Space*, trans. Donald Nicholson-Smith (Oxford: Blackwell Publishing, 2004), p. 185.

24 Gilles Deleuze, *Pure Immanence: Essays on a Life* (New York: Urzone, 2001). Deleuze explains in the essay "Immanence: A Life" found in the aforementioned collection, "A life contains only virtuals. It is made up of virtualities, events, singularities. What we call virtual is not something that lacks reality but something that is engaged in a process of actualization following the plane that gives it its particular reality. The immanent event is actualized in a state of things and of the lived that make it happen. The plane of immanence is itself actualized in an object and a subject to which it attributes itself. But

however inseparable an object and a subject may be from their actualization, the plane of immanence is itself virtual, so long as the events that populate it are virtualities. Events or singularities give to the plane all their virtuality, just as the plane of immanence gives virtual events their full reality" (p. 31).

25 Angelo Quattrocchi and Tom Nairn, *The Beginning of the End* (London: Verso, 1998), p. 2.

26 Daniel 5:3, New King James Version.

27 Daniel 5:26, New King James Version.

28 Ganzeer, "Does Egypt Need a New Flag?" *Rolling Bulb*, http://rollingbulb. com/post/3784546629/does-egypt-need-a-new-flag

29 Ganzeer, "Does Egypt Need a New Flag?"

30 Ganzeer, "Does Egypt Need a New Flag?"

31 Khairy Shalaby, *The Hashish Waiter*, trans. Adam Talib (Cairo: American University in Cairo Press, 2011).

32 Naguib Mahfouz, *Midaq Alley*, trans. Trevor Le Gassick (Cairo: American University in Cairo Press, 1975).

33 Naguib Mahfouz, *Adrift on the Nile*, trans. Frances Liardet (Cairo: American University in Cairo Press, 1993).

34 Walter Ambrust, *Mass Culture and Modernism in Egypt* (Cambridge: Cambridge University Press, 1996), p. 72.

35 "Crackdown on Hashish Had Country's 7 Million Users Jittery," *Los Angeles Times Blog*, http://latimesblogs.latimes.com/ babylonbeyond/2010/04/egypt-hashish-drought-causes-unrest-among-millions-of-users-1.html

36 Rabab El-Mahdi and Philip Marfleet, *Egypt: A Moment of Change* (Cairo: American University in Cairo Press, 2009) p. 138.

37 Abdallah al-Ghoul is a Palestinian filmmaker from Rafah, Gaza. *Ticket from Azrael* (2009), al-Ghoul's documentary film depicting the lives of Palestinian youth workers in the underground tunnels between Gaza and Egypt, was awarded special mention at the Dubai International Film Festival. He currently lives in Cairo.

38 "The Death of Innocence," *Al-Ahram Weekly*, February 10–16, 2011, http://weekly.ahram.org.eg/2011/1034/sc32.htm

39 Blog Ganzeer, "Martyr Murals Project," http://ganzeer.blogspot. com/2011/03/martyr-murals-project.html

40 Blog Ganzeer, "Martyr Mural for Islam Raafat Gets Censored," http:// ganzeer.blogspot.com/2011/04/martyr-mural-for-islam-raafat-gets.html

41 Blog Ganzeer. "First Mad Graffiti Meeting," http://ganzeer.blogspot. com/2011/04/first-mad-graffiti-meeting.html

42   A wheatpasting, as understood in this chapter, is a product of street art. It is generally put up using an adhesive made of cornstarch and water (wheatpaste). The product put up on walls and other urban surfaces is typically made from paper.

43   Deleuze and Guattari, *A Thousand Plateaus*, p. 353.

44   The phrase "Game Over Mubarak" was a widely distributed message during the first days of the revolution. It was written in graffiti tags across the lions of Qasr al-Nil Bridge. It was also seen on military tanks (chapter 3), and on walls across Cairo.

45   Samia Mehrez, *Egypt's Culture Wars* (New York: Routledge Press, 2008), p. 190.

46   Mehrez, *Egypt's Culture Wars*, p. 192.

47   Mehrez, *Egypt's Culture Wars*, p. 193.

48   "Egypt Must Investigate Forced Virginity Tests: Amnesty," *Al-Ahram English Online*, June 1, 2011, http://english.ahram.org.eg/NewsContent/1/64/13404/Egypt/Politics-/Egypt-must-investigate-forced-virginity-tests-Amne.aspx

49   Salma Shukrallah and Yassin Gaber, "What Was Religion Doing in the Debate on Egypt's Constitutional Amendments?" *AhramOnline*, March 22, 2011, http://english.ahram.org.eg/NewsContent/1/64/8267/Egypt/Politics-/What-was-religion-doing-in-the-debate-on-Egypts-Co.aspx

50   Roel Meijer, *Global Salafism: Islam's New Religious Movement* (London: C. Hurst & Co. Ltd., 2009), p. xvi.

51   *Respect Magazine* is a quarterly publication that seeks to exhibit and comment on hip-hop culture and the urban condition in a sophisticated and intelligent manner. It was launched in 2009.

52   "Graffiti: Cairo Revolution Painted on the Streets," *Respect Magazine* Blog, June 17, 2011, http://respect-mag.com/cairo-revolution-painted-on-the-streets/

53   New Oxford American Dictionary (New York: Oxford University, 2005).

54   Quattrocchi and Nairn, *The Beginning of the End*, p. 2.

55   "Graffiti: Cairo Revolution Painted on the Streets," *Respect Magazine* Blog, http://respect-mag.com/cairo-revolution-painted-on-the-streets/

56   I would like to thank Samia Mehrez, Joe Lukawski, and Alessia Di Basilio for being there when I have needed them most. Your lives provide me with constant inspiration. I would also like to thank all the photographers who have lent me their photographs for this project, especially Laura Gribbon. Last but not least, I would like to thank Ganzeer for hanging out and discussing politics and artistic creation over a beer at Huriya. Without all of you, this chapter would not exist.

5

al-Thawra al-daHika: The Challenges of Translating Revolutionary Humor

Heba Salem and Kantaro Taira

The Egyptian Revolution has been labeled '*al-Thawra al-daHika*' ('the Laughing Revolution') not only because of the avalanche of political jokes that it has generated but, perhaps more importantly, because of the very structure and instant dissemination of the jokes themselves, which were inspired to a great extent by both traditional and social media discourses, forms, and languages. Political humor is always embedded in a political culture and history, which are both key to understanding and appreciating the subtleties, ambiguities, and subversive referential worlds of the political joke.

This chapter will explore the challenges of translating Egyptian political jokes of the revolution and the extent to which notions of fidelity and equivalence may not necessarily 'carry over' in translating humor across cultures.[1] The content of these jokes abundantly involves the Egyptian social, political, and cultural contexts outside the text of the joke itself. This fact suggests that due to different contextual and para-textual constructs, a literal, word-for-word translation (not that one exists) cannot capture the humor or immediacy of these jokes, for the target language's culture does not necessarily always have equivalent jokes. Indeed, as Gayatri Spivak has argued, "the simple possibility that something might not be meaningful is contained by the rhetorical system as the always possible menace of a space outside language."[2] Furthermore, the very function and use of humor and jokes may be different from one culture to another. For example, while an Egyptian joke is exchanged among people as part of a public collective narrative, Japanese culture does not have jokes as narrative texts in the public sphere.[3] Only professional comedians narrate humorous stories as narrative texts. Hence cultural specificities may also become a constraining factor in translating humor.

On the level of lexicon, cultural specificities may also affect the conceptual signification of words themselves from one language or culture to the other. For example, the English word 'cheese' cannot be completely equivalent to the standard Russian 'cheese.' The 'cheese' that English indicates is subtly but crucially different from Russian 'cheese' because of cultural differences in the very status of 'cheese' from one context to another. Roman Jakobson argues that "on the level of interlingual translation, there is ordinarily no full equivalence between code-units, while messages may serve as adequate interpretations of alien code-units or messages."[4] Despite the different connotation of 'cheese' from one cultural context to another, the brief supplemental words, describing 'cheese,' enable translators to 'carry over' the close meaning of 'cheese' to the target language. Similarly, through replacing a source language word with an equivalent word in the target language, the original meaning is not deformed. For example, 'orange cat' in English is equivalent to 'brown cat' in Japanese, and 'brown cat' indicates the same cat as 'orange cat.' In fact, an Internet search engine shows the same picture of an 'orange cat' as a 'brown cat.' The English word 'orange' as a color contains 'burnt orange' closer to the color of chocolate, while the Japanese color 'orange' only indicates 'orange peel' like the color of the ripe orange fruits.[5] In order to correctly 'transmit' the meaning of 'orange cat,' 'orange' is replaced with 'brown.'

The cognitive difference of words, however, may occasionally present us with untranslatable words with specific social connotations. As Jakobson illustrates, Death appears as an old man in German tales because in German 'death' is masculine, while Russians imagine Death as a woman because in Russian 'death' is feminine.[6] To indicate the chess piece that native English speakers call 'queen,' 'male minister' *(wazir)* is used in Arab countries, where male ministers had worked as caliphs' and sultans' right arms while women had not had their place in the political field. Since the gender of the chess piece is different from one cultural context to another, the image that the same chess piece evokes may be different in the two cultures. These examples demonstrate the lack of equivalent words between source language and target language.

In this chapter, we therefore forgo the impossible but also irrelevant notion of equivalence while we attempt to 'translate' '*al-Thawra al-daHika*' itself to the target culture. '*Al-Thawra al-daHika*' is essentially

humorous because it carries and is embedded with Egyptian cultural elements, connotations, and emotions, which may not have an equivalent in
the target language. In order to insist on this constant tension between
source and target language and culture, we have maintained the Arabic
coinage '*al-Thawra al-daHika*' that serves as a reminder of the challenges
of translating humor.

The Politics of Humor

Humor is one of the oldest and most subversive political tools that have
been used systematically and in different cultures to break the monotony
and hardships of life. In his analysis of the relationship between humor and
authority, David L. Paletz emphasizes that "democracies, by their nature,
would seem to invite humor publicly directed at their rulers" because many
democracies have "the tradition and practice of free speech, the most famous
expression of which in the United States is in the Constitution."[7] During
times of oppression and under police state control, however, political jokes
become a very important vehicle for people to express their opinions in
public without fear of reprisal. As Samer S. Shehata rightly noted, citing
Freud's remarks on humor, jokes allow people to indirectly protest against
various authorities and powers that constrain their freedoms, thus becoming a form of liberation.[8] One of the most important aspects of jokes in this
regard is their ability to subvert power relations in ways that are similar to
the subversive powers of the 'carnivalesque.' As the Russian cultural critic
Mikhail Bakhtin succinctly put it "during carnival: what is suspended first of
all is hierarchical structure and all the forms of terror, reverence, piety, and
etiquette with it" and "mock crowning and subsequent decrowning of the
carnival king." Finally, "his crown is removed, the other symbols of authority
are taken away, he is ridiculed and beaten."[9] Hence one liberating aspect of
jokes is that they do away with social and political hierarchies and dethrone
revered figures of power. Indeed, jokes can be considered an alternative form
of sociopolitical sarcasm and critique. According to Shehata, in oppressive
society, political jokes are circulated in the public sphere where freedom of
expression is permitted "because political jokes are oral, censorship proves
to be extremely difficult if not impossible" and the joke tellers are mere
transmitters, not social activists.[10] Similarly, in Matthew Diamond's article
on political cartoons in the Arab world post 9/11, Diamond regards jokes
as the means that undermine the idealized image of authorities. Diamond
argues that as symbolic pluri-textual constructs, jokes can affect the political

context in a broad spectrum of ways, from supporting the prevailing pattern of authority and power relations to undermining or subverting it.[11]

Frustration and Egyptian Political Humor

Jokes have always played an essential role in the everyday lives of Egyptians and have always provided a crucial venue for criticism and a kind of 'safety valve' for the release of pent-up frustrations at the social, economic, and political levels.[12] At the same time, since jokes are transmitted orally, Egyptians have been able to voice their opinion and criticize unjust situations without fear of censorship by telling a joke. A renowned Egyptian actor once said, "The joke is the devastating weapon which the Egyptians used against the invaders and occupiers. It was the valiant guerrilla that penetrated the palaces of the rulers and the bastions of the tyrants, disturbing their repose and filling their heart [sic] with panic."[13] At the same time, Egyptian jokes are inspired by the sociopolitical and discursive order and context of their time and can therefore provide vital information for the authorities. This makes them a kind of political barometer for the state in some instances. The following joke is an example of how humor can become one venue through which the people can expose corruption and injustice and make their voices heard by the authorities. The joke is about having to bribe soldiers in the army because they are underpaid.

Two people were playing chess and many others were watching. One of the players wanted to move the pawn forward, but the pawn refused to budge. The player took a one-pound note out of his pocket and gave it to the pawn, saying: "How about this?" So the pawn moved![14]

(Itnin biyil'abu shatarang wi saHibhum biyitfarrag 'alihum. WaHid biyHarrak il-'askari; il-'askari rasu wi alf sif ma yitHarraksh; fa raH mitalla' luh ginih wi al luh: "Ih ra'yak?" Fa-l-'askari itHarrak!).

Important political events in Egypt have always been the focus of jokes and humoristic criticism, even devastating and tragic events such as Egypt's defeat by Israel in the 1967 War are not spared. Before the defeat, the regime had routinely trumpeted military grandeur, and a whole generation of Egyptians had internalized and believed the 'official' illusions. But along with the tragedy, these illusions were denuded and exposed to the merciless self-deprecating humor. In this process of 'disenchantment,' the jokes served as a constant reminder of the undoing of the myth. The following joke is one example of this black humor.

After the 1967 defeat, a tourist guide led a group of tourists to the Pyramids. During the tour of the monuments, he wanted to propagate the greatness of Egypt so he said: "Indeed, Egypt is the oldest civilization in history." The echo of his voice resounded with the same statement. So he continued, "Egypt is the mother of the world," and again the echo of his voice resounded with the same words. The guide then said, "And we will go to war against Israel!" Here the echo replied sarcastically, "Enough, you idiot!"[15]

(Ba'd il-hazima istaHab murshid siyaHi magmu'a min l-suyyaH il-aganib li ziyarit il-ahram, wi asna' il-sharH arada an yaqum bi-l-da'aya li Masr, fa qal: "Inna misr aqdam Hadara fi-l-tarikh," fa karrar sada-l-sut il-'ibara fa qal-al-murshid: "Wi hiyya umm il-dunya," fa karrar il-sada-l-'ibara. Fa qal-al-murshid: "Wa sawfa nuHarib Isra'il," fa qal sada-l-sut sakhiran: "Bass ya mughaffal!").

Not only did Egyptians laugh at themselves, but they also turned their dismissive humor toward the army whose generals they held directly responsible for the defeat.[16] An immediate target of this black humor was Vice President and Field Marshal Abdel Hakim Amer, whose negligence and irresponsible decisions were believed to be the main reason behind the 1967 disaster.

Abdel Hakim Amer attended the graduation ceremony of a new class of officers and asked one of them, "Where would you like to serve?" He said, "In your office, sir." Amer replied, "Are you crazy?" The graduate answered, "Is this a prerequisite for the position, sir?"[17]

(Kan Abd al-Hakim 'Amir fi Hafl takhrig duf'a gidida min il-zubbat fasa'al waHid minhum: "TiHibb tikhdim fin?" Fa luh: "Fi maktabak ya fandim," fa al luh 'Amir: "Inta magnun?" Fa radd il-zaabit: "huwwa da shart ya fandim?").

This level of audacious black humor was extended to President Nasser himself in the aftermath of the 1967 defeat, especially with news of his failing health and his need for treatment and surgery. The following joke shows the extent to which Egyptians could articulate their disappointment in Nasser's failure to defend what he had propagated from the start, namely, pan-Arabism with Egypt at its very center as defender of the Palestinian cause and future. The core of the joke is a pun on both the verb and proper noun *ghazza* in Arabic, which can at once refer to the Gaza strip that had been under Egyptian administration until the Israeli occupation of the Sinai Peninsula in 1967 and the verb *ghazza/yaghuzzu*, which means to poke or to pinch. The joke basically reduces the loss of Gaza (the territory) to a *ghazza* (a pinch):

> In one of the meetings between Nasser and the 1952 military council after the defeat in 1967, he suddenly screamed in apparent pain: "Aaaah!" The members of the council asked him worriedly: "What's wrong, Mr. President?"
> He replied: "Nothing, just a '*ghazza/Ghazza*,' but it's gone now!"
>
> (*Fi aHad igtima'at maglis qiyadit il-thawra ba'd naksit 67, sarakh Abdel Nasir: "Aaah!" Fa sa'aluh: "Malak ya rayyis?"*
> *Fa al: "Mafish . . . ghazza wi raHit.")*

Humor and Censorship

Before the January 25 Revolution, Egypt witnessed various levels of official and unofficial censorship that effectively constrained freedom of expression.[18] In Marina Stagh's detailed study of censorship in Egypt during the Nasser and Sadat periods, she illustrates how the state constrained the free circulation of the written word. Nasser nationalized most of the private publishing companies and pro-government officials were always appointed as the editors-in-chief.[19] Furthermore, Stagh argues that "many writers during Nasser's period have shared the experience of detention and imprisonment; others have been suspended from employment in media and prevented from publishing. Any calls for restoration of any democratic rights were turned into accusations of plotting to overthrow the regime."[20] The following joke is among the popular ones that used to circulate during Nasser's period and makes fun of the strict repression that prevailed during his rule through play on the idiomatic expression "to open one's mouth":

> One man tells another: "Our friend couldn't get his tooth pulled out at the dentist's."

When asked why, the man replied: "Because no one now can open their mouth!"[21]

*(WaaHid biyul li saHbu: Fulaan ma'dirsh yikhla' dirsu.
SaHbu: Lih?
Al-luh: huwwa fih Hadd yi'dar yiftaH bu'u dilwa'ti!)*

After Nasser, both Sadat and Mubarak sought to cultivate a façade of a more liberal attitude toward basic freedoms but essentially followed the same repressive policies to varying degrees and through different strategic tactics.[22] Specifically during the Mubarak period (1981–2011) official control over the written word seemed to be loosened and there was more freedom of expression in the press.[23] However, the limits and boundaries of freedom of expression allowed by the state remained undefined and unpredictable, and therefore always volatile, causing many crises in which well-known authors and other cultural actors were implicated.[24] The fluid and unpredictable repressive measures and reprisals that the more 'liberal' Mubarak regime could enforce are captured in the following joke in which God himself could become a target of state reprisal:

God summons Azrael (the angel of death) and tells him, "It's time to get Hosni Mubarak."
"Are you sure?" Azrael asks timidly.
God insists: "Yes, his time has come; go and bring me his soul."
So Azrael descends from heaven and heads straight for the presidential palace.
Once there, he tries to walk in, but he is captured by State Security. They throw him in a cell, beat him up, and torture him. After several months, he is finally set free.
Back in heaven, God sees him all bruised and broken and asks, "What happened?"
"State Security beat me and tortured me," Azrael tells God. "They only just sent me back."
God goes pale and in a frightened voice says, "Did you tell them I sent you?"[25]

But violation of political rights and basic human freedoms were not the only aspects of the Mubarak rule that provided food for humor. Indeed, during the past thirty years of the Mubarak regime, the economic pressures with high unemployment rates as well as increasing state corruption represented major frustrations for Egyptians, who found their partial release in humor, both oral and in print. For example, most cartoons drawn by a famous Egyptian cartoonist, Nagui Kamel, in newspapers between 1994 and 2003 were about low salaries, money and marriage, and corruption.[26] These economic frustrations and political corruption generated a series of self-deprecating jokes of which the catch phrse *"tib'a inta akid fi Masr"* ('then you are definitely in Egypt') is made to confirm the most absurd situations that could only happen in Egypt where corruption was rampant. The following joke is a notable example:

> When you have to pay a traffic ticket unjustly, because you don't own a car to begin with, then you are definitely in Egypt!

> *(RuHt tittalla' mukhalfat 'arabiyitak wi la'itha ghir SaHiHa la'inn bi-l-fi'l ma'andaksh 'arabiya! Tib'a inta akid fi Masr!).*

Mubarak himself also had his fair share of jokes. He has been labeled *"al-ba'ara al-daHika"* ('the laughing cow') and made fun of since the beginning of his rule in order to express the utter disrespect that Egyptians had for his abilities as a president.[27] With his prolonged period of rule, the jokes harped increasingly on how fed up Egyptians were with his persistence in holding on to power. For example, during the 'Eid (feast), one of the widely circulated jokes was a pun on the traditional greeting *"'Eid mubarak"* ('a blessed feast') playing on the Arabic word *'mubarak'* ('blessed') and the proper name Mubarak, the name of the president himself. The joke goes like this:

> O God, please make this an 'Eid Mahmoud,' an 'Eid Ahmad,' anybody's 'eid, but not 'Eid Mubarak!

> *(Allahumma ig'alhu 'id MaHmud, 'id AHmad, 'id ayy Hadd bass mish 'id Mubarak!).*

Another joke targets what seemed like Mubarak's never-ending presidency:

> When you ask someone, "Who is going to be the president during the third millennium?" and he answers without giving it any thought: "Mubarak" . . . then you are definitely in Egypt.

(Law sa'alt Hadd: "min Haykun il-rayyis fi kull il-alfiya il-talta," wi radd wi al bidun tafkir: "Mubarak," tib'a inta akid fi Masr!).

Humor and the Revolution

During the January 25 Revolution, people used jokes as a venue to freely express their opinion and to sustain the ongoing uprising by absorbing unfolding events and making fun of them. Throughout the eighteen days leading to the resignation of Mubarak, an incredible number of jokes were instantaneously and consistently produced while being embedded in, and interwoven with the Egyptian cultural narrative at large. Thus, positive and negative reactions to the events that took place during the revolution could be brought together under a cohesive umbrella of comic relief. As columnist Fahmy Howeidy correctly remarked, referring to thugs who threw stones at demonstrators, "Mubarak's people threw rocks" and in response "the people charged at Mubarak with jokes and comedy."[28] Indeed, one of the jokes that circulated in Midan al-Tahrir articulated the same explosive effect of jokes that were circulating on cell phones in Tahrir:

A thug to Al Arabiya satellite channel: The kids are hurling "blue-tooth" bombs at us.
(Baltagi li qanat al-'arabiya: il-'iyal biyirmu 'alina qanabil blututh).

The steady stream of comedy flowing through Midan al-Tahrir allowed people to defy the regime in nonviolent ways. The tougher things got, the more the jokes seemed to grow in number and break the fear barrier. The longer Mubarak remained in office, the longer and more frequent the jokes became. This irony was ruthlessly revealed in many jokes that called attention to the disconnect between the regime and reality. Activist and university professor Laila Soueif gave a significant example of people's retaliation against Mubarak's oppressive tactics when military jets swooped overhead, terrifying the crowd in Tahrir during the early days of the January 2011 sit-in. She reported that the young people "started jumping up and down, chanting, 'Hosni has gone mad, Hosni has gone mad,' so they made it a joke, and everyone stopped being scared."[29] These comments show that Egyptians overcame fear with jokes that called on the subversive powers of the carnivalesque.

In his article "The Poetry of Revolt," Elliott Colla has noted that "the act of singing and shouting with large groups of fellow citizens has created a certain and palpable sense of community that had not existed before" and "protesters began to lose their fear."[30] Similarly, one important outcome of the carnivalesque power of jokes is that they provide a venue for establishing and cementing solidarity between the people in the face of oppression. In her dissertation on urban jokes in Egypt, Nadia Izzeldin Atif analyzes the function of jokes in enabling the assimilation of individuals or whole cliques from out-groups through sharing humor.[31] Thus, the jokes born in Tahrir allowed people to create a sense of camaraderie. *al-Sha'b yurid* (The People Demand), a small book that was published to commemorate the revolution, records plenty of jokes, chants, and slogans used in demonstrations.[32] Jokes are represented as part of a communal memory, producing solidarity through a common collective narrative during this revolutionary movement. One demonstrator articulates the political communal impact of jokes in the following terms: "I went to the square every day looking for a new joke."[33]

But then, Egyptians didn't necessarily need to go to Midan al-Tahrir every day for a new joke to boost the sense of community or renew the sense of solidarity since the very mode of circulation and dissemination of humor was being transformed through this technologically savvy revolution. In the past, jokes used to be exchanged orally among people in coffee shops or on social occasions among friends. With developing social media, which enabled Egyptians to mobilize tens of thousands of people, this mode became outdated for many. Facebook, mobile phones, and Twitter became the primary means of circulating the jokes; jokes thus became one of the revolution's most crucial weapons. Hundreds, even thousands, of Egyptians exchanged jokes in less than one minute. Indeed, new media proved to be the perfect forum for political satire, particularly Twitter, in which users capture the moment in 140 characters or less. Mubarak, who has supposedly never sent an email in his life, appeared on a fake Twitter site, @HosniMubarak, as did his son @GMubarak, and wife @SuzanneMobarak. A fake 'Installing Freedom' screen grab on the website http://www. streetartutopia.com/?p=1228 showed files copied from the folder /Tunisia, overlaid with the pop-up message, "Cannot install 'Freedom.' Please remove 'Mubarak' and try again." There were also several versions of "Mubarak is Offline" or "Delete Mubarak" references. As the situation has continued to unfold on the ground over the past several months, new jokes are being circulated and updated on joke pages on Facebook. The more recent jokes involve new actors such as members of the ruling Supreme

Council of the Armed Forces (SCAF) and the many ministers who have come and gone through the interim government's revolving door.[34]

Translating Humor

There is little doubt that, although "translating the revolution" through jokes is an original approach, the question remains: Is this revolution really '*al-Thawra al-daHika* ('the Laughing Revolution') for foreigners or others who do not share the same collective narrative that is embedded within these jokes? True, many demonstrators transferred the humor to tweets in English, which allowed the wider world to get in on the jokes and further circulate them. But if we were to consider the larger repertoire of jokes that continues to be produced, one will stumble against several blocks that may not necessarily enable the task of the translator in carrying across the humor to a target culture. The experiences of the two authors of this chapter, one Japanese and the other Egyptian, are instructive in this regard.

As a Japanese student of Arabic, my first encounter with Egyptian jokes was when I read a collection of Arabic jokes collected in Egypt and published in Japan in 1978. The title of the introduction was "Cultural Fruits: The Jokes" and the first chapter dealt with political jokes that the editor had collected in Cairo about presidents Nasser and Sadat. I remember that I started reading the collection with curiosity but I quickly felt that it was not interesting at all and I quit reading it after the first chapter. Since I started studying Arabic, I have heard that jokes are a very important aspect of the very being of the Egyptian people, so much so that they have been called '*sha'b ibn nukta*' ('the people of the joke'). But as a Japanese person, I really cannot understand these jokes. Not that we do not have a sense for jokes or humorous stories in Japan or that I cannot read Arabic, but rather because I simply do not understand Egyptian jokes. Even the Japanese editor of the collection of Arabic jokes admits that he could not understand a joke that he got from an Egyptian writer until he was provided with its explanation.[35]

Likewise, as an instructor of Arabic as a foreign language, I share my Japanese co-author's frustrations when it comes to translating humor. I have to admit that I find that teaching an Arabic joke is one of the most difficult tasks. It is also equally difficult for those learning Arabic as a foreign language. Teaching a joke actually means that I have to unpack its elliptical and intertextual form and language, and to provide the unwritten narratives that lie behind it in the hope of 'translating' why it is funny, why it elicits laughter. Laughing at a joke needs more than just understanding each and every word. An Egyptian joke might sound funny to one of my language students only after introducing its context and explaining what it all means. This basically means that I always find myself having to undo the joke and turn it into a long-winded story, an explication that drowns its very essence: immediacy. This process is of course doubly complicated by our attempt to translate Egyptian jokes of the revolution into another language since the problems of translating humor lie beyond the word for word and confront us with the challenges that translators must undertake as they carry across a whole cultural context.

What is a Joke?

The Oxford English Dictionary defines a joke as "something that you say or do to make people laugh." Its reason for existence is to set the audience laughing. The joke that does not produce laughter is no longer a joke but a mere sentence. But what is it that produces laughter in jokes? According to Immanuel Kant, "Laughter is an affection arising from the sudden transformation of a strained expectation into nothing."[36] This means that a joke provides a sudden and different answer from one that might be expected by the listener. This is an explanation of the mechanism of jokes, how they work and how they produce their immediate impact: laughter. But what makes a listener have expectations? An answer to this question is provided by 'reader response theory,' which focuses on the relationship between texts and readers and assumes an "interpretive community"[37] in the interpretation of texts, thus explaining what H.R. Jauss has labeled the "horizon of expectation" in readers.[38] This horizon of expectation is formed through collective knowledge in a society and is indispensable for the interpretation of texts. In the same manner, the horizon of expectation in jokes is formed by culture and education.

So how can we translate humor to a target culture with a different interpretative community that is not necessarily familiar with the inter-textual narrative embedded in a joke? In his important discussion of the merits of foreignizing, rather than domesticating, a translated text, Lawrence Venuti addresses the problem of intertextuality in the source language and ways in which such embedded texts may be *translated* into the target language. He says, "a translator may find that the very concept of the domestic merits interrogation for its concealment of heterogeneity and hybridity which can complicate existing stereotypes, canons, and standards applied in translation."[39] It is for these reasons that Venuti insists on the importance of commentary or what he refers to as "the reminder" of the foreign in translation. He says, "In the reminder lies the hope that translation will establish a domestic readership," and then again "it is only through the reminder, when inscribed with part of the foreign context, that the translation can establish a common understanding between domestic and foreign context."[40] To transmit intertextuality to another culture, the reader needs the commentary explaining the intertextuality that permeates the text itself in the source language and culture. The remark of Kaoru Yamamoto, a Japanese scholar who translated Palestinian writer Emile Habiby's classic, *The Secret Life of Saeed: The Pessoptimist*, provides an interesting case of such intertextual transmission. Concerning the huge number of annotations, which totaled 265, in the translation, Yamamoto points to the community of her Japanese readers who need annotations for a comprehensive understanding of the text. She remarks, "these readers believe that, since human life itself is difficult, it is natural that the literature that expresses this life will be equally difficult."[41] Yamamoto's remarks illustrate that the background of the text, Palestine itself, can be 'transmitted' to a Japanese 'interpretive community' only through annotation, that is a reminder, to use Venuti's formulation once more.

In the case of jokes also, a translator needs commentary to explain the background because a joke packs cultural intertextuality into one short sentence. Here is an example of an Egyptian joke that elucidates what we have been arguing, rendered in two attempts at translation, both of which fall short of producing laughter.

Version one:
They asked the president what he thought about change.
He replied that change is *sunna* in life.
They asked: Well, will you not change then?
He said: I'm *Fard*, not *Sunna*.
(*Sa'alu-l-rayyis 'an ra'yu fi-l-taghyir; al: il-taghyir da sunnit il-Haya; alu luh: Tab wi siyattak mish Hatitghayyar? al: ana fard mish sunna!*).

Version two:
They asked the president what he thought about change.
He replied that change was the essence of life itself (*sunnat al-Haya*)

but also a reference to *Sunnat al-Rasul* or the guiding sayings and actions of the Prophet Muhammad that are not obligatory in Islam). So they asked him: "And how about you, sir? Aren't you going to change?"

He replied: "I am a must (*fard*—a reference to the Islamic concept of religious duty), not an option *(sunna)*.

Using a Japanese lexicon, I will attempt to translate this joke into Japanese. First, we do not have the same words or a similar concept to '*sunna*' and '*fard*' in our lexicon. These are Islamic words and concepts. Moreover, historically, Japan did not have strong relationships with Islamic countries,[42] and consequently, we have not considered developing words equivalent to '*sunna*' and '*fard*.' Even if a translator were to find the proper words for them, we still would not understand and capture the dense ingenuity of this joke. Of course the word '*rayyis*' in the joke is a metonymy for Mubarak, and Mubarak is a symbol of oppression. But, beyond that, in order to understand part of this joke, we need knowledge of the Egyptian context, which Mubarak had ruled Egypt for thirty years like a despotic monarch. Also, the signifier '*fard*' is different from the signified; or to put it differently, there is a pun on the word itself. '*Fard*' not only means the literal '*fard*' (that is, obligation or duty), but it also references the Islamic religious obligation and duty. Indeed this punning on the literal signifier is an essential part of the joke. In addition, readers should know something about Mubarak's demeanor, for he hardly ever smiled. Even when he tried to be humorous, people generally found his jokes either forced, misplaced, or inappropriate, making him a target for satire and stigmatizing him as thick-skinned and humorless. This adds to the impact of the word '*fard*.' This is just one example of a joke that shows us that paratextual cultural elements complicate the translation of humor. It is not a linguistic problem. In order to translate jokes, we have to 'transmit' the paratextual and the intertextual that provide the context of the joke. Only then might we begin to partake of the humor.

To understand the meaning of a joke, the readers need commentary, but what is a joke with commentary and explication? If laughter arises from treachery against a collective strained expectation, then the explication of a joke makes us lose any expectation. The main purpose of jokes is to set the audience laughing. Explaining a joke makes it lose its very purpose already. The following joke is an example of this loss. The joke is woven around a well-known Egyptian movie[43] by the famous comedian Muhammad Heneidi. In the film Heneidi disguises himself as a prostitute, who pretends that she is well educated and fluent in English. It is well-known that many Egyptians mix and confuse the sounds 'b' and 'p'; for example: '*banda*' (for 'panda'), '*combuter*' (for 'computer'). To show that she is educated and fluent in English and can pronounce the sound 'p' that does not exist in Arabic, this prostitute pronounces the word 'mobile' as '*mopile*.' The word 'mobile' has entered the Egyptian colloquial lexicon and is treated and behaves like an Arabic word. It therefore has a plural form: *mobilat*. The punch line in the joke is borrowed from the movie where the prostitute says: "*Byeee, mopailat ba'a*." It means that we will not see each other again, but let's stay in touch via mobile phone. When Mubarak finally stepped down on February 11, 2011 and left for Sharm al-Sheikh, the joke that circulated was that Egyptian people said to Mubarak: "*Mubarak, mopailat ba'a*" ('Mubarak, let's keep in touch by cell phone').

Al-Thawra al-DaHika

As seen from the example above, with cumulative cultural common knowledge from the present and past, jokes absorb current political and social events and incorporate them into the joke itself. One of the jokes that was widely circulated in the early days of the revolution tried to capture the power of new media and its devastating impact on the regime. It called upon a classic formula that Egyptians have repeatedly used in many jokes made prior to the revolution to ridicule the powers that be: a meeting of and conversation between deceased Egyptian presidents in the afterlife. Its elliptical form carries within it the whole history of modern Egypt and it is expected that the listener would know the paratextual and intertexual narratives surrounding the joke, that is, the fate of the two former presidents Nasser and Sadat: the first was rumored to have been poisoned and the second was assassinated during a military parade. In the joke, the third president (Mubarak) has just arrived to join the other two in the afterlife. They compare notes on the reasons for their respective fates:

Nasser and Sadat ask Mubarak: "Poison or assassination?" He replies: "FACEBOOK!"

(*Mubarak ba'd ma mat abil il-Sadat wi Nasir. Sa'alu: Simm walla manassa? Alluhum: Facebook!*).

Just as new communicative technology and social media informed the jokes of the revolution, so did traditional media and news broadcasts with their own formulaic language and discourse. One rather long joke parodied the authorities' empty discursive pronouncements in the daily press in which the dominant strategy is to blame the victims—the Egyptian people themselves—for the government's failings. The joke amasses imaginary cliché statements from prominent Egyptian cabinet members and former ministers belonging to the National Democratic Party (NDP), as well as regional and international statements in reaction to the self-immolation of a number of Egyptians on the eve of the revolution.[44] All the statements reproduced in the joke are parodies of familiar official discourse that are meant to violate the expectations of the listener, given the tragic context, namely, people setting themselves on fire to protest subhuman living conditions.

> Ahmed Ezz [former chairman of Egypt's National Assembly's Budget Committee]: The solution to self-immolation is to increase the price of gas.
> [Yusuf] Botros Ghali [former minister of finance]: A new tax will be enforced on families if one of their members sets himself on fire.
> Minister of the Environment: Self-immolation is the reason behind the black cloud.
> Minister of Employment: Self-immolation of citizens will secure new jobs for Egyptian youth as firefighters.
> Ahmad Nazif [former prime minister]: The people do not understand their own self-interest. The proof is their abuse of petrochemical products.
> Rashid Muhammad Rashid [former minister of commerce]: There is an increase in petroleum imports as a result of the rise in consumption due to the self-immolation of citizens.
> Habib al-Adli [former minister of interior]: It is prohibited for more than three people to set themselves on fire in the same place.
> The Sheikh of al-Azhar [highest religious authority]: Self-immolators are sinful and, as a punishment, should not be saved.
> Hilary Clinton [US secretary of state]: The United States urges the protection of Egyptian citizens from self-immolation and calls upon the Egyptian regime to take all measures to decrease popular discontent.

Ahmad Abul Gheit [former minister of foreign affairs]: Self-immolation of Egyptian citizens is an internal affair. All Egyptian citizens are free to set themselves on fire.
Mubarak threatens to set himself on fire and demands the change of the people.

The joke actually goes on to include sarcastic reactions from many other regional and international actors but this selection should suffice to make the point clear: the extent to which Egyptians have mobilized an entire collective narrative in order to ridicule their own regime and its transparent and empty discursive practices, which were totally insensitive, unsympathetic, and abusive of the people and their genuine daily hardships.

Another new form of joke that surfaced with the revolution was the parody and imitation of the style of satellite media broadcasts that deploy the now familiar TV screen banner 'breaking news' *('agil)* to update viewers on important and urgent political developments. The format adopted the dense, formulaic language of the news announcement that follows the banner. The joke below was circulated after February 11, 2011 when Mubarak finally stepped down, a moment that coincided with the very beginning of the Libyan uprising. Fridays were, and continue to be, significant mobilizing days during all the revolutionary movements taking place in the Arab world, since Friday is at once the day for rest and the day for heavily attended Muslim noon prayer. Hence Fridays have regularly witnessed the largest number of demonstrators and have been crucial turning points in the Tunisian and Egyptian revolutions, which dethroned dictators and toppled regimes in both countries and took the lead in reshaping modern Arab history. The successive Friday demonstrations have, throughout the duration of a revolution, been given different names, which have been copied by other demonstrators in Libya, Yemen, and later in Syria. These have ranged from Friday of Rage, to Friday of Victory, to Friday of Resilience, and so on. After Mubarak stepped down, this 'breaking news' joke spread throughout Egypt right away.

Breaking News: After Friday of Victory in Tunis, and Friday of Liberation in Egypt, Qadhafi orders his men to cancel all Fridays in Libya.

(Khabar 'agil: ba'd gum'it il-nasr fi Tunis wi gum'it il-taHrir fi Masr, al-Qadhafi ya'mur bi ilgha' yum il-gum'a fi Libya.)

The joke obviously ridicules Arab rulers and the absolute power that enabled them to oppress and control people as they liked. A variation on this theme lay at the core of another joke about Mubarak, who was still holding on to power even after the sweeping triumph of the revolution. The following jokes mock the 'power' that they believed they still wielded. Before the revolution, policies were always decided from the top down, starting with Mubarak himself of course. After the January uprising and its success in deposing him, the joke reported an important decision from Mubarak to the people, via his prime minister who remained in his post less that one month after Mubarak's fall.

Based on presidential directives, Prime Minister Ahmed Shafik announced that the revolution has succeeded.

(SarraHa Ahmed Shafiq, ra'is al-wuzara' annahu bina'an 'ala tawgihat al-ra'is, nagaHat al-thawra).

The following joke illustrates the Egyptian people's image of Mubarak, who seemed to believe that he and his family owned Egypt and its people. It also demonstrates how thick-skinned and totally isolated he was from the severe problems that led to the uprising.

The head of parliament asked President Mubarak to prepare a farewell speech for the people of Egypt.
The president replied: "Why? Where are the people going?"

*(Talab ra'is maglis al-sha'b min al-ra'is Mubarak tahdir kalimat wada' li-l-sha'b al-masri.
Radd al-ra'is wi al: Lih? Huwwa il-sha'b rayiH fin?)*

Not only do jokes make fun of the authorities, but they also deprive rulers of sovereignty. To subvert the regime, the following jokes transform the former ruler from an absolute authority to a normal Egyptian, and then mock Mubarak, who was holding on to power. The next joke came in response to the revolution's main slogan "The people demand the change of the regime," one of the largest banners that fluttered in Tahrir during the January–February sit-in. The joke inverts this demand as a way to mock Mubarak's shock and refusal to accept the people's uprising against him.

Breaking News: President Mubarak was seen holding a big banner that read: "The president demands the change of the people."

(*'Agil: Zuhur Mubarak bi lafita kabira maktub 'alayha: al-ra'is yurid taghyir al-sha'b*).

The next joke offers another variation on Mubarak's denial and refusal to abdicate his position as president. This joke is actually quite layered: it makes reference to a hit song by one of the Arab world's most popular young female singers, Nancy Ajram. Interestingly, the joke portrays Mubarak, who is eighty-two years old, as a fan of this stunning thirty-year-old star. The song in question is characterized by its elusiveness, inconclusiveness, and deferral of a real decision in rupturing a relationship that in this instance is displaced on the relationship between Mubarak and the Egyptian people.

Breaking News: Broadcasting a special request from President Mubarak to the Egyptian people: Nancy Ajram's song, "Shun you, yes; leave you, no."

(*'Agil: al-ra'is yuhdi-l-sha'b al-masri ughniyat Nancy Ajram 'Akhasmak ah, asibak la"*).

Cell phone messaging and tweets also influenced the mode of circulation and length of jokes that made their rounds in Tahrir. Tweets and SMS messaging effectively led to chain-jokes focused on specific subjects and events of the day. A particularly rich and quite hilarious chain of jokes followed after former vice president Omar Suleiman's statement to the people in which he announced that Mubarak had decided to step down. These provide a particularly good example of the extent to which jokes were responding interactively to political developments at an amazing speed, made possible by tweets and the very form that tweets imposed.

In the still image below, taken from Suleiman's address to the Egyptian people, an unknown, gloomy-looking man, who was later identified as a member of the military special forces, stands behind him throughout the speech. This man's unexplained presence was the cause of hundreds of jokes that began with the simple question circulated among thousands of people: "Does anyone know who the man standing behind Omar Suleiman is?"

The chain of jokes about the man behind Omar Suleiman came in all forms and modes. For example, one of these jokes parodied the discourse of military communiqués of the SCAF. The first part of the joke copied verbatim the SMS message sent by the SCAF to the Egyptian people after Mubarak stepped down on February 11, 2011. The irony arises from the tension between the first half of the joke, which imitates the tone and formal language of the military communiqués, and the frivolous second part, which violates the listener's expectations from the first half. The first half is in elevated, *fusHa* (formal, classical Arabic); the second half is in *'ammiya* (colloquial Arabic). Although this discrepancy between the formal/classical and the colloquial may not be apparent in translation, it is still important to note that such linguistic-register divergence produces a comic effect.

A call to all the honest and responsible people of Egypt: Can somebody tell us who's this guy standing behind Omar Suleiman?

(Nida' ila gami' al-shurafa' wa l-mas'ulin fi Misr: ayy Hadd yitla' yu'ul lina min il-ragil illi wara 'Umar Suliman?)

The following joke combines the 'breaking news' joke formula and the 'Who's this guy standing behind Omar Suleiman' chain of jokes, showing the endless possible substitutions and combinations that Egyptians have

Omar Suleiman and the unidentified man

deployed to produce new jokes. It is also a joke that exposes conflicting and misleading media reporting by imitating it. In this case the 'breaking news' item reports on the various contested locations of Mubarak after he had stepped down.

> Breaking News: Al Jazeera: Mubarak departed for Dubai.
> Breaking News: Al Arabiya: Mubarak departed for London.
> Breaking News: Egyptian TV: Mubarak departed for Sharm al-Sheik.
> The truth is: Mubarak is at the house of the man standing behind Omar Suleiman.

> (ʿAgil Al-jazira: Mubarak safara ila Dubai.
> ʿAgil Al-arabiya: Mubarak safara ila London.
> ʿAgil il-tilivisyun il masri: Mubarak safara ila Sharm al-shikh
> Al-Haqiqa: Mubarak fi bit il-ragil illi wara ʿUmar Suliman).

The following "man behind Omar Suleiman" joke makes fun of singer Tamer Hosny, who had been contracted by Pepsi Cola for its advertisement campaign because he was so popular among the youth. During the revolution, Hosny, who was among the pro-Mubarak celebrities, went to Tahrir and asked the protesters to go back home and talked to them about how the regime would help them find jobs and so on. But the protesters in Tahrir beat him up and he lost his credibility and popularity. Here is the joke:

> Breaking News: Pepsi terminates its contract with Tamer Hosny . . . and signs a new contract with the man standing behind Omar Suleiman.

> (ʿAgil: Pepsi talghi taʿaqudaha maʿa Tamir Husni wa tataʿaqad maʿa-l-ragil illi wara ʿUmar Suliman.)

The chain of jokes about the man behind Omar Suleiman ultimately culminated in a hilarious song that makes of him a role model to be emulated by any one contemplating what they might want to become when they grow up.[45]

The next joke emerged after news of the acquittal of former first lady, Suzanne Mubarak. She had been under house arrest and was accused of corruption and the misuse of state funds, like former president Mubarak himself and many of his ministers and high-profile businessmen. The joke is constructed around the *"mahragan al-qira'a li-l-gami'"* ('Reading for All Festival') that was one of the many national projects carried out under the auspices of Mrs. Mubarak to encourage Egyptians, of all ages, to read. The project, which was also marred by the misuse of funds, offered many classics as well as translated books, at very affordable prices. Once more, the joke uses formulaic media language, "Breaking News," and makes it sound like a new military communiqué. The joke actually says that Suzanne Mubarak is still there and that her projects are still going on; only their names have changed. The joke reflects the disappointment of most Egyptians with her acquittal. It also implicates the ruling SCAF in this decision since in the joke the 'communiqué' is issued by them. Furthermore, the joke suggests that other corrupt figures who are in jail will also be acquitted. The first 'all' in the joke that appears in 'Reading for All' refers to all Egyptians, while the second 'all' in the joke can refer to 'all' of Suzanne Mubarak's family and entourage who are in prison.

Breaking News: The Military Council announces that the name: "Reading for All Festival" will be changed to "Acquittal for All Festival"!

('Agil: qarrara l-maglis al-'askari taghyir ism mahragan al-qira'a li-l-gami' ila mahragan al-bara'a li-l-gami'.)

One of the very interesting and innovative aspects of the use of humor and jokes during the revolution was the didactic one. Very quickly activists came to realize that there were a large number of people who had not participated in the uprising. These people had been following distorted reporting by state media and had not taken an active part in the events and their implications, let alone the role that they could play in shaping them. Activists took the initiative to simplify and explicate the important demands and aspirations of the revolution and the protesters through humor, rather than hackneyed political discourse, which would have immediately turned off the uninitiated or the unsympathetic. Besides the use of political puppet shows and stand-up comedy in Tahrir itself, a humorous Socratic dialogic text circulated on the Internet with the title "Risala ila Hizb al-Kanaba" ('A Message to the Party of the Couch') written by activist Ezzat Amin.[46] '*Hizb al-kanaba*' refers to all those who watched the revolution unfold as they sat on their couch at home drinking tea. The expression itself, '*Hizb al-kanaba*' ('The Party of the Couch'), eventually became a household one that everyone uses. The dialogue that is constructed out of twenty questions and answers tries to address many of the anxieties and misconceptions of "the party of the couch." These ranged from identifying the youth involved in the January 25, 2011 demonstrations and the demands of protesters after Mubarak's departure to Sharm al-Sheikh, to why the demonstrations had to continue, whom to vote for in the upcoming elections, what was meant by "counterrevolution," and fear of intervention by the United States, Israel, and Iran, and so on. For example:

> Question number one: Who might be described as the 'January 25 Youth'?
> Answer: There is no specific description . . . if you guys mean the representatives of the revolution . . . there is no particular representative because this is a new kind of revolution for us. . . .

> *(Al-su'al al-awwal: Min "shabab 25 yanayir"?*
> *Mafish wasf muHaddad li-shabab 25 yanayir, law asduku 'ala mumassilin il-thawra, famafish bardu mumassil mu'ayan, wi da la'inn il-thawra di gidida 'alina).*

> Question number eleven: O.K. Then, whom should I vote for?
> Answer: This revolution happened so that no one can ever again tell you whom to vote for. Make the effort to read the different electoral campaign programs while you are sitting on the couch!

> *(Al-su'al al-Hadi 'ashar: tab antakhib min?*
> *Il-thawra amit 'ashan maHaddish yib'a wasi 'ala Hadd wi y'ullak intikhib min, it'ab shuwaya wi i'ra-l-baramig il-intikhabiya wi inta a'id 'ala al-kanab!).*

The text typically used actual questions that were on the minds of many people and tried to provide logical, informative, but also humorous responses. Here is one example that addresses people's economic concerns:

> Question number sixteen: So, will the price of pasta be lower after the revolution?

Answer: Let's think beyond pasta and chicken. . . . The demands of January 25 were bread, freedom, and social justice. If you feel that these demands will not fulfill your needs, I'll try and explain it your way: when your employer doesn't have to bribe the corrupt public officer because he ran away or has been arrested, the money your employer saves should come your way or go toward expanding his business.

(Al-su'al al-sadis 'ashar: ya'ni ba'd il-thawra kis il-makaruna Hayib'a bikam?
Yarit nibuss li ab'ad min kis il-makaruna wi-l-farkha. . . . 25 yanayir il-matalib kanit 'ish, Huriya, 'adala igtima'iya. Law Hasis in il-kalam da may akkilsh 'ish Ha'ullak bi l-tari'a illi inta tifhamha: lamma mudirak mayidfa'sh rashwa 'ashan il-mas'ul il-fasid hirib ba'd il-sawra aw it'abad 'alih, il-fulus il-ziyada illi ma'a mudirak da mafrud yshabra'ak biha aw yikabbar il-biznis.)

Other questions revolve around Mubarak's departure and the sense of guilt that some were feeling toward having deposed the nation's 'father' figure, the reputed hero of the 1973 war who launched the first air strike against Israeli troops in the occupied Sinai.

Question number seventeen: They should be ashamed of what they've done to Mubarak. . . . He's our big man.
Answer: I would call him "our big man" if we were a gang. . . . I really don't need to show you the amount of corruption. Suffice it to say that Muhammad Hassanein Heikal declared on Egyptian television, which is now controlled by the army, that the story of the "first air strike" is ridiculous and that what Mubarak effectively did was to overshadow the real heroes of the October war as a jealous wife would her rivals.

(Al-su'al al-sabi' 'ashar: bass 'ib illi 'amaluh fi mubarak . . . da kibirna.
Mumkin a'tibru kibirna law kunna 'isaba. Ya'ni mish miHtag awwarrilak kamm il-fasad wi l-nahb wi yikfi inn MuHammad Hasanin Hikal al 'ala l-qana il-masriyya illi hiyya taba' il-gish inn mawduu' il-darba il-gaw-wiya da kalam mudHik wi innu azaH abtal Uktubar kama tuziH il-mar'a il-ghayura durritha.)

Another interesting aspect of revolutionary humor was how it drew upon formulaic one-liner jokes from the self-deprecating prerevolutionary series *"tib'a inta akid fi Masr"* to signal important changes in attitudes and the change of political consciousness specifically where notions of national belonging, identity, and pride were concerned. The following joke took on the Egyptian passion for soccer, which was actually manipulated by the Mubarak regime to channel the people's emotive communal solidarities away from political activism—a situation that changed radically after the revolution (chapter 1). The joke addresses the radical change in the status of soccer in Egypt since the revolution; here, it is represented by Egyptians' disengagement with and indifference to the successive victories of al-Ahly (the national team), which has won the African soccer championship three times.

When al-Ahly scores five goals and plays in the African championship and still no one talks about soccer, then you are definitely in Egypt.

(Lamma yib'a il-ahli faz khamsa wi Hayil'b fi butulit afriqiya wi maHaddish biyitkallim 'an il-kura, tib'a inta akid fi Masr.)

Another joke addresses how the revolution transformed social mores and choices even in personal relationships where, in the joke, revolutionary values are upheld instead of economic interests:

When the main criterion for choosing the future bridegroom is that he's been to Tahrir and was part of the popular committee that patrolled the neighborhood, then you are definitely in Egypt.

(Lamma yikun min muwasafat il-'aris li ay 'arusa innu yikun raH il-taHrir wi wi'if fi-l-lagna il-sh'biya, tib'a inta akid fi Masr.)

And finally, this joke presents another example of the euphoric revolutionary moment that salvaged the very essence of being Egyptian from a global map peppered with instances in which so many millions of Egyptian immigrants and migrant workers around the world had been treated with contempt:

When you have an Egyptian passport and foreigners applaud you at the airport, then you are definitely in Egypt.

(Lamma yikun ma'ak gawaz safar masri wi-l-aganib yisa'afulak fi-l-matar, tib'a inta akid fi Masr).

One of the most interesting aspects of these chain jokes is that they are being constantly updated and combined with the latest events via mobile phones, Facebook, and Twitter. In such a public space, all Egyptians can be editors and can participate in updating jokes with their own concerns. The feelings of hope and dramatic mood changes throughout the eighteen days of the revolution and beyond can be traced through these jokes. Indeed, jokes have become a venue through which to translate the revolution itself: its developments, dreams, frustrations, and victories. They are also a real measure of the agency that Egyptians have acquired since January 25, 2011 despite repeated setbacks, tragedies, and confrontations between the protesters with both the Central Security Forces and the Military Police. Despite the fact that jokes represent one of the more difficult aspects of translating revolution, they remain—even as we find ourselves having to explicate them—one of the most important weapons used to sustain Egypt's revolution.

Notes

1   The jokes this chapter deals with were mainly collected by our colleagues in Samia Mehrez's seminar "Translating Revolution," American University in Cairo, spring 2011; we also gathered some of them from the Internet. Part of what the seminar group has accomplished in this respect is available to the public via the class blog, which was created by the seminar's participants: http://translatingrev. wordpress.com/. The jokes collected from other sources are mentioned in the notes.

2   Gayatri Chakravorty Spivak, "The Politics of Translation," in Lawrence Venuti, ed., *The Translation Studies Reader* (London: Routledge, 2000), p. 398.

3   This does not imply that the Japanese do not have a sense of humor. The Japanese have several forms of laughing entertainment and enjoy listening to humorous stories. For example, in order to gain a high audience rating, television production companies use comedians in most of their programs, occasionally even for the news and political talk shows. In most cases, 'jokes' in Japanese are puns, unlike Egyptian jokes. The nuance of the meaning is different from '*nukta*' in Arabic and 'jokes' in English.

4   Roman Jakobson, "On Linguistic Aspects of Translation," in Lawrence Venuti, ed., *The Translation Studies Reader* (London: Routledge, 2000), p. 113.

5   Takao Suzuki, *Nihongo to Gaikokugo* (Japanese and Foreign Language) (Tokyo: Iwanamishinsyo, 1990), pp. 12–13.

6   Jakobson, "On Linguistic Aspects of Translation," p. 117.

7   David L. Paletz, "Political Humor and Authority: From Support to Subversion," *International Political Science Review* 11, no. 4 (1990): 483–84. Paletz's analysis seems to be based on the relationship between the state and censorship. He admits subversive power in political humor against authority holders, and thus politicians care for the humor in public space. However, his opinion that democracy invites political humor does not always describe the humor found in all democratic countries. He mainly analyzes the humor that American comedians relate in public spaces. But Japanese comedians tend not to select political issues for their humorous stories and jokes. He does not at all refer to the reason American comedians choose political humor rather than direct criticism.

8   Samer. S. Shehata, "The Politics of Laughter: Nasser, Sadat, and Mubarak in Egyptian Political Jokes," *Folklore* 103, no. 1 (1992): 76.

9   Mikhail Bakhtin, *Problems of Dostoevsky's Poetics* (Minneapolis: University of Minnesota Press, 1984), pp. 122–25.

10 Shehata, "The Politics of Laughter," pp. 75–76, 88. Shehata lists the articles dealing with political jokes in oppressive societies. He notes the articles about Russian, Czechoslovakian, East German, Romanian, Polish, Cuban, Chinese, Spanish, and Mexican political jokes and humor.

11 Matthew Diamond, "No Laughing Matter: Post-September 11 Political Cartoons in Arab/Muslim Newspapers," *Political Communication* 19, no. 2 (2002): 251.

12 Nadia Izzeldin Atif, "Awlad al-nokta: Urban Egyptian Humor" (Ph.D. diss., University of California, 1974), p. 282. According to Atif's interview with a random sample of Egyptians, 97 percent of the interviewees (total fifty-five) answered that jokes serve as a 'safety valve' in releasing pent-up frustrations and anxieties.

13 Issandr El Amrani, "Three Decades of a Joke that Just Won't Die," *Foreign Policy* 184 (2011): 2. http://www.foreignpolicy.com/articles/2011/01/02/three_decades_of_a_joke_that_just_wont_die

14 *'Askari* in the Arabic language means both 'soldier' and the pawn in chess.

15 Muhammad al-Baz, *Nuktat al-Sayyid al-Ra'is*, December 4, 2008, p. 15. Available online at http://www.kotobarabia.com/Library/documentinfo.aspx?ref=5327

16 al-Baz, *Nuktat al-Sayyid al-Ra'is*, p. 14.

17 al-Baz, *Nuktat al-Sayyid al-Ra'is*, p. 15.

18 For a comprehensive discussion of various levels of censorship in Egypt, see Richard Jacquemond, *Conscience of a Nation: Writers, State, and Society in Modern Egypt* (Cairo: American University in Cairo Press, 2008).

19 Marina Stagh, *The Limits of Freedom of Speech: Prose Literature and Prose Writers in Egypt under Nasser and Sadat* (Stockholm: Almqvist & Wiksell International, 1993), pp. 20–21.

20 Stagh, *The Limits of Freedom of Speech*, p. 65.

21 In the jokes Shehata collected, a man had his teeth pulled out through his nose and another had to expose his belly to have his tooth pulled out at the dentist's. Both jokes mean that these people cannot 'open their mouth' because of oppression during Nasser's period. See Shehata, "The Politics of Laughter," p. 81.

22 For a discussion of censorship strategies in various cultural fields, see Samia Mehrez, *Egypt's Culture Wars: Politics and Practice* (Cairo: American University in Cairo Press, 2010 and 2011).

23 Jacquemond, *Conscience of a Nation*, p. 39.

24 See Mehrez, *Egypt's Culture Wars*, in which several examples of censorship cases are provided.

25 El Amrani, "Three Decades of a Joke."

26 Lilia Labidi, "Truth Claims in the Cartoon World of Nagui Kamel," in Maha Abdelrahman, Iman A. Hamdy, Malak Rouchdy, and Reem Saad, eds., *Cultural Dynamics in Contemporary Egypt* (Cairo: American University in Cairo Press, 2006), p. 30. In Kamel's work, 130 cartoons out of 179 drew on these topics as their themes.

27 Similarly, he has often been compared to a donkey, a symbol of idiocy and stupidity. See Shehata, "The Politics of Laughter," pp. 85–86.

28 Michael Slackman, "When a Punch Line Is No Longer a Lifeline for Egyptians," *The New York Times*, April 6, 2011, http://www.nytimes.com/2011/04/06/world/middleeast/06cairo.html?_r=1&pagewanted=all

29 Slackman, "When a Punch Line Is No Longer a Lifeline."

30 Elliott Colla, "The Poetry of Revolt," *Jadaliyya*, January 31, 2011, http://www.jadaliyya.com/pages/index/506/the-poetry-of-revolt.

31 Atif, *Awlad al-Nokta*, p. 89.

32 al-Sha'b al-Masri, *al-Sha'b yurid* (Cairo: al-'Arabi, 2011).

33 Slackman, "When a Punch Line Is No Longer a Lifeline."

34 The Facebook page "Sha'b ibn nukta" records images of the jokes that were circulated in Tahrir on banners during the revolution:

http://www.facebook.com/pages/%D8%B4%D8%B9%D8%A8-
%D8%A7%D8%A8%D9%86-%D9%86%D9%83%D8%AA%D
8%A9/191060150911764

35 Yoshiro Mutaguchi and Haruo Hanawa, *Arabu jouku syuu* (A Collection
of Arabic Jokes) (Tokyo: Jitsugyounonihonsha, 1978), p. 33.

36 Immanuel Kant, *Critique of Judgment* (New York: Cosimo, 2007), p. 133.

37 As for the discussion about the relationship between texts and interpretive community, see Stanley Fish, *Is There a Text in This Class?*
(Cambridge, MA: Harvard University Press, 1980), pp. 14–15.

38 Hans Robert Jauss, *Chouhatsu toshiteno Bungakushi* (Literaturgeschichte
als Provokation), trans. Osamu Kutsuwada (Tokyo: Iwanamisyoten,
1976), pp. 37–40.

39 Lawrence Venuti, "Translation Community, Utopia," in Lawrence
Venuti, ed., *The Translation Studies Reader* (London: Routledge, 2000),
p. 484.

40 Venuti, "Translation Community, Utopia," p. 485.

41 Kaoru Yamamoto made this comment in an international conference
about translation held in Cairo in March 2010.

42 For example, *Kaikyouken* (Islamic World), a Japanese magazine, insists
on the necessity of Islamic studies in the first issue in 1938 because
of the lack of understanding. See Kouji Ookubo, "Kaikyouken Ken-
kyujo Setsuritsu Shushi (The Purport of Establishing Islamic World
Researching Center) in *Kaikyouken* 1, no. 1 (1938): 10.

43 The title of the film is *Ga'ana al-bayan al-tali* (Egypt: Aflam al-Nasr
li-l-Intag wa-l-Tawzi', 2001), starring Muhammad Heneidi and Hanan
Turk.

44 The first example of self-immolation occurred in Tunisia when
Muhammad Bu 'Azizi set himself on fire to protest his living conditions. At least four Egyptian citizens later followed his example of
protest.

45 The song is available online at http://www.youtube.com/watch?v=-
Ci1D3hz0jM&feature=player_embedded#at=19

46 See Izzat Amin, "Risala ila hizb al-kanaba al-'azim," *Masrawy*, February
23, 2011, http://www.masrawy.com/News/Writers/General/2011/
February/23/hezb_kanaba.aspx.

6

The Soul of Tahrir:
Poetics of a Revolution

Lewis Sanders IV and Mark Visonà

Poetry as the Soul of a Revolution[1]

The soul is usually spoken of as an immaterial substance, the transcendental essence of a human. Yet, its shelter is the body, which occupies a physical space. In some ways, the poetics inspired during the January 25 Revolution served as the 'soul' of the revolutionary moment. Even though Midan al-Tahrir provided the physical epicenter of uprising, poets and musicians did not have to be physically present to participate. Poets were moved to write about this historic moment and their work quickly became part of Tahrir itself, despite the physical absence of the authors. One example is Tamim Al-Barghouti, an Egyptian-Palestinian poet who resides and teaches in the United States. He wrote his poem "O Egypt, We Are So Close" in Washington D.C. in the early days of the revolution, but thanks to new media, the poem immediately circulated in Tahrir in the days leading up to Mubarak's resignation. Likewise, the revolution shaped the verses of Egyptian poet Hisham al-Gokh, who was competing in an international poetry competition in Abu Dhabi. The opening lines of his poem also quickly became part of the lyrical landscape of the *midan*. The work of Tunisian poet Abul Qasim al-Shabbi was also resurrected in Tahrir when an equally distinguished Egyptian poet, Ahmed Abdel Muti Hijazi, used the opening lines of his classic ode to freedom, *Idha-l-sha'bu yawman arad al-Haya/falabud an yastajib al-qadar* (If someday the people will to live, then fate must an answer give), to write a new ode to the Egyptian Revolution.[2] Similarly, old and largely forgotten patriotic songs that had lost their original meanings were also brought back in the *midan*. These antiquated songs were broadcast to millions of demonstrators who sang along, thereby investing them with new signification and a

213

reinvigorated meaning. New songs spontaneously sprang from the hearts of protesters in the *midan*, as they sang their demands to the rhythm of the *tabla*, the strings of the *'ud*, and the chords of the guitar. This soul of Tahrir knew no bounds, in neither space nor time. While the body of the revolution was the people, the *midan* was its heart, and the poetics its soul.

The relationship between the poet and the revolution is critical in understanding how protesters' demands, emotions, and experiences were relayed to the general public. During the eighteen days leading to Mubarak's resignation, the poet rose to the foreground of the social landscape. This became evident in the multitude of chants, songs, and poems erupting in Tahrir as well as throughout Egypt. These works were documented and distributed via YouTube videos, newspapers, blogs, and tweets. When the Internet was cut off on January 28, 2011 these poetics spread through word of mouth, echoing the oral tradition found in Arab culture. The role of the poet was to appropriate the experience, make sense of it, and communicate it to others. This communicative aspect of the poet's role manifested itself in two ways. First, the poet became a speaker for the protest community, creating revitalizing expressions of solidarity for the protesters. Second, the poet shaped the transmission of the experience to others outside the situation. These two aspects were communicated through various mediums. The first was circulated through the voices of the protesters, whether in chants, songs, banners, or even on scrap pieces of paper with the words written on them. The second aspect was circulated through modern channels of mass communication, especially via the Internet—in tweets, blog posts, and Facebook updates. Even if these poets were dead, they arose like the phoenix from the ashes during the first eighteen days of the revolution, this time with fire on their tongues. Their immortal words shaped, rejuvenated, and sustained the discourse of the revolution, which in turn sustained the determination of the revolutionaries. Poetry appears naturally in times of emotional discord as ordinary people try to express themselves in extraordinary circumstances. As Lord Byron said:

The dead have been awakened—shall I sleep?
The world's at war with tyrants—shall I crouch?
The harvest's ripe—and shall I pause to reap?
I slumber not; the thorn is in my couch;
Each day a trumpet soundeth in mine ear, its echo in my heart.[3]

k

In such times of calamity and inspiration, the return of the poet is inevitable. Poets dream of such moments.

In the blog post "The Era of Arabic Poetry is Over, Long Live Arabic Poetry," published after the revolution, writer and blogger M. Lynx Qualey challenged literary critics for declaring the end of poetry's relevance in the Arab world:

> It was poets who shook the stage in Tahrir. It's poetry that rocks television screens showing *Million's Poet* and *Arabs Got Talent*. And while the IPAF winner may have captured more Western attention, the Egyptian poet who won *Arabs Got Talent*, Amr Katamish, won 500,000 Saudi riyals, a new car, and a contract with MBC.[4]

Interestingly enough, though, there may be a half-truth to the literary critics' predicament found in the title of the article. It is, for the most part, widely perceived that poetry in recent years has become subordinate to prose. Is this due to the end of the poet as spokesperson for the community, or to the end of a literary tradition? Or has the poet assumed other forms, utilizing other mediums in which poetry is masked under various genres? Poetry may not be dead, but it may be changing—taking form in the words of a singer-songwriter or in the lyrical swagger of a hip-hop artist.

It is important to note the strong legacy of poetry in the Arabic language and poets' social influence, in particular. Since the *jahili* (pre-Islamic) era, Arab poets have been important figures in society with clearly defined social roles. In *jahili* times poets served as the spokesmen for Arab tribes; some conflicts were even settled with poetry contests rather than violence.[5] As a long-standing form of Arabic literature, poetry has played a significant role throughout the history of the Arab people. Under the Islamic caliphates, various genres and types of poetry were developed and expanded upon, with many poets under direct sponsorship of the caliph. Forms of poetry were often classified by structure and content, such as praise *(madH)* and invective *(hija')*. However, Arab poets have always criticized the elites in their society. A modern example of this criticism in action is found in the work of renowned Palestinian poet Mahmoud Darwish, who was the voice of Palestinian resistance against Israel's occupation. In his comprehensive study of the role of literary producers in Egypt, cultural critic Richard Jacquemond labeled poets the "conscience of a nation" despite the various levels of possible censorship on their activities.[6] However, as recent events have shown in Egypt and other Arab nations undergoing revolutions, poets and singers may be reclaiming this title.

Poetry appeared in many forms during the first eighteen days of the revolution, from long odes published in newspapers to lengthy chants shouted on the streets. Ordinary Egyptians became talented and creative poets as they led rhymed chants often emerging spontaneously among groups of people in public.[7] While some call-and-repeat chants were prepared beforehand, many protesters simply shouted rhymed couplets that succinctly captured their feelings and demands, such as this example from early March 2011:

> *'Alli w 'alli w 'alli-l-sut*
> *Illi Hayihtif mish Haymut*

> Raise, raise your voices high
> Whoever chants will not die!

Such chants both inspired protesters and spread the revolution, for Egyptians on the street and in their homes first heard the chants of the protests before actually seeing them. The rhymed chants in particular allowed protesters to voice their grievances in a musical and catchy way, and even mere spectators soon found themselves repeating the chants, both privately and to others. These 'minor' poetic works contributed to the rapid spread of the Egyptian protests and their demands. More critically, this poetry raised the popular awareness of the motivations behind the protests.

Alongside poetry, songs also played a large role in the lyrical tapestry of the revolution. Prior to the January 25 Revolution, Egyptian artists could only speak out against the government by singing songs written to criticize previous governments, such as the works of popular musician Sayyed Darwish during the early twentieth century and the revolutionary blind bard of the sixties, Sheikh Imam.[8] In the second week of the protests, stages were set up in Midan al-Tahrir and artists played freely for the first time in fifty years. Songs served to maintain people's spirits in the *midan* while also articulating the demands of protesters. Often, these songs would set chants to music, creating a catchy way to remember important slogans. An example of the power of these songs to spread awareness of the protests was the popularity of "*IrHal*" ('Leave'), one of Ramy Essam's songs, which is translated in this chapter.[9] First captured in early February, the song went viral on the Internet and was then broadcast on satellite channels including Al Arabiya and Al Jazeera so that the entire world could hear it and sing along. The songs from the time of President Nasser were not discarded, but revised to fit the themes of the revolution. Even children's songs like "Dhahaba-l-laylu, tala'a-l-fagru" ('Night is Gone and the Day Has Come') were appropriated to deliver revolutionary lyrics critical of the regime. Through singing in Midan al-Tahrir, protesters were able to increase the sense of solidarity and patriotism, which allowed them to outlast the regime. Ultimately, songs helped win the battle for popular opinion, which no doubt played a major part in the victory of the Egyptian people.

It should be noted, before shifting to our theoretical approach, that the selections included in this chapter are not all-inclusive, as there are many other songs, poems, and chants that emerged from the revolution. These poetics cover many of the themes and ideas that made up the rich lyrical tapestry of Tahrir, yet in order to comprehensively cover these works, an entire book would have to be written. Instead, the selections in this chapter offer a glimpse into the revolution's discourse concerning identity, particularly through the concepts of '*al-sha'b*' (the people) and '*al-watan*' (the homeland/country). This chapter will occasionally refer to such key concepts in both Arabic and English to emphasize certain thematic elements in the overall narrative of the revolution as well as the repetition of these words across texts. The selections in this chapter map the transformations of these signifiers, as they were given new meanings and significance during the course of the first eighteen days of the revolution. The authors of this chapter, two non-native speakers of Arabic, have translated these pieces to better inform English speakers about these terms and about the Egyptian Revolution in general. It is also hoped that by highlighting some of the thematic complexity present in these poetics, both native and non-native speakers of Arabic will better appreciate the creativity and talent that flourished in Midan al-Tahrir.

Translation Theory and Poetry

Even though this lyricism represented the very soul of the revolution, translating the poetry and songs of the uprising is not a simple task. According to theorists, translations are based on 'interpretations' of the original text as well as the translator's 'shaping' of those interpretations.[10] In order to first interpret a poetic text, the translator must abandon the concept of "invisibility" of the translator and the desire for "transparency" and "domestication" in a translation, as explained by Lawrence Venuti.[11] The aim of his book *The Translator's Invisibility* is "to force translators and their readers to reflect on the ethnocentric violence of translation and hence to write and read translated texts in ways that seek to recognize the linguistic and cultural difference of foreign texts."[12] The ethnocentric violence of an "invisible" translation happens when the translator creates a product in the target language that naturally subjugates the meaning of the source language text in an attempt to create a text that can be described as "fluent" and "smooth" in the target language.[13] The weight of the original text is succumbed to the lingual-cultural framework of the source-language text. This approach to translation inescapably results in an ethnocentric distortion of the original text since the translator alters the original text in order to make it conform to the target language, despite the language's social, cultural, and linguistic nuances. For example, changing the syntax of an Arabic text so that it sounds more like natural English speech could add a large dimension of cultural bias to a translation as the translator domesticates the source text. The strategy followed in this chapter preserves as many elements of the original Arabic as possible in English, yet also modifies the source text to create a poetic product in English. In translation theory, efforts to preserve these original elements of a source text are described as the 'transparency' of a translation.

The impossibility of creating a 'transparent' translation of poetry is best outlined by André Lefevre, who identifies seven approaches that inevitably lead to a forced manipulation of the text:

- Phonemic translation that attempts to capture the source language sound in the target language
- Literal translation that has word-for-word translation
- Metrical translation that reproduces the source-language meter
- Translating the poetry as prose, distorting the source-language syntax
- Rhymed translation that captures meter and rhyme
- Blank verse translation with restrictions caused by structure
- Interpretation of the source text by changing form and creating original poetry.[14]

However, "the overemphasis of one or more elements of the poem at the expense of the whole" can lead to a "demonstrably unbalanced" translation.[15] Such attempts to preserve one element of a poetic text usually lead to distortion of meaning. These efforts also aim to create either a transparent or domesticated translation; however, the poetics of Tahrir are made up of a tapestry of voices—different language registers, styles, tones, and themes. This polyphony of voices forces the translator to approach each text as both the product of an individual and as part of a larger whole—the common epic of Tahrir.

The translations in this chapter are primarily influenced by a "structuralist" approach, which "conceives of a text as a set of related systems, operating within a set of other systems."[16] This approach requires the translator to view the poem or song in the source language at an intertextual level, noting in particular the way that the text may draw on other texts at a structural or thematic level. In translating these poetic works, it was particularly important to utilize this structural or intertextual approach in order to capture how certain elements became part of a common narrative across poetic mediums during the revolution. Yet, this is not to say that the methodology has been confined to the structuralist approach since we acknowledge, as Hans-Georg Gadamer does, "[T]he poem itself will decide nothing."[17] In other words, the interpretations in this chapter were developed acknowledging that a poem may have different meanings depending on the reader.

In discussing Ezra Pound's conception of translating a Greek poem, Donald Davie rightly states: "There may be some rules about how to translate: but there are no rules about how to make poems."[18] Some of the translations echo the patterns and rhythms of Arabic, while others create a new rhythm and rhyme scheme in English. Yet, the overall attempt has been at creating continuity in our translation method: preserving as many of the elements found in the original text as possible while creating a poetic product in English. As Anton Popovič identifies in an essay in Holmes' *The Nature of Translation*, while poetic translations may differ, it is necessary to preserve an "invariant core": an inner meaning communicated via the transposition of theme, tone, and style present in the original.[19] In a way, this is what is described as a process of "semiotic transformation"; "The replacements of the signs encoding a message by signs of another code, preserving invariant information with respect to a given system of reference."[20] This process is also described as "creative transposition."[21] However, the new context of the poem must retain the original poem's intended meaning even though form and language may be greatly different. As the new code's signifiers are particularly associated with other signifiers within the language system, creativity and caution must go hand in hand to retain this core.

The invariant core that we speak of may be best described as the collective signified of all the signifiers of the text, the signification of the whole text. In other words, this core is the collection of meanings provided by the many poetic elements and symbols within a text without which the overall meaning would be compromised. While not all elements of a poem may be captured in translation, the invariant core consists of those elements most central to the identity of a text. In this chapter, references to the "invariant core" of a piece will reflect the authors' interpretation of the necessary poetic characteristics that must be present in a particular translation. This is why it is important for the translator to consider the work in its entirety before embarking on its transformation. Yet, a pertinent question to address here is: what is the purpose, or more so, what is the task of the translator when approaching the transposition of the invariant core? In Walter Benjamin's essay "The Task of the Translator," the author addresses the task of the translator as ensuring the survival of the original text.[22] Thus, translation becomes a way of freeing the invariant core insofar as it allows the growth of the original text as the ontology of its structure, its survival. Its growth is only made possible through translation, transmitting its invariant core embedded in one system of signifiers, the language it was written in, to another. Hence, in *The Ear of the Other*, Jacques Derrida explains in a rereading of Benjamin's essay:

> Given the *surviving* structure of an original text—always a sacred text in its own way insofar as it is a pure original—the task of the translator is precisely to respond to this demand for survival, which is the very structure of the original text. To do this, says Benjamin, the translator must neither reproduce, represent, nor copy the original, nor even, essentially, care about *communicating* the meaning of the original.[23]

Derrida's remarks guide us to understand the act of translation as not necessarily communicating, reproducing, or representing the original, but as the process of ensuring the texts' survival. This also leads us to the overarching narrative of the act of translation, namely the kinship of languages. The transposition of the invariant core as the act of translation touches the affinity of languages since languages share a kinship in their mode of intention, not in the intended object of their signifiers, which are culturally embedded.[24] Benjamin provides a case in point:

> The words *Brot* and *pain* 'intend' the same object, but the modes of this intention are not the same. It is owing to these modes that the word *Brot* means something different to a German than the word *pain* to a Frenchman, that these words are not interchangeable for them, that, in fact, they strive to exclude each other. As to the intended object, however, the two words mean the very same thing. While the modes of intention in these two words are in conflict, intention and object of intention complement each of the two languages from which they are derived; there the object is complementary to the intention.[25]

The kinship of languages lies in their mode of intention and not the intended object to which language provides signifiers that are culturally embedded. Translation is much more than the conversion of a text in the original language to a foreign one. It is the promise and the presentiment, a glimpse of the horizon of a pure language.[26] In dicussing 'pure language,' it should be understood in the act of translation (translating). By translating, the kinship between languages is located in the mode of intention. Thus, in emphasizing the mode of intention (and not the intended object) in translating texts, the affinity between languages is discovered. Inasmuch as an affinity between languages exists, translation appeals to a notion of a pure language, in which texts may be transformed given their culturally laden contexts as well as in the mode of intention of the word, phrase, paragraph, or collective narrative. A pure language is thus an overarching language of significance which only manifests in glimpses, those found in the affinities and kinships between languages. Hence, when emphasizing the mode of intention in a translated text, the text is allowed to navigate through the affinities and kinships of languages as it is being translated and surviving as a new original. This is where the mode of intention of language skims upon the ocean of a pure language. Derrida expands on this idea by suggesting transformations of texts instead of translations:

In the limits to which it is possible or at least appears possible, translation practices the difference between signified and signifier. But if this difference is never pure, no more so is translation, and for the notion of translation we would have to substitute a notion of *transformation:* a regulated transformation of one language by another, of one text by another.[27]

In this sense, translation—or transformation—operates between the spaces of language, in the kinship of languages, as mutually regulating, transforming, and augmenting. This is why this chapter considers translations to be interpretations of the structure of the original text, always interpretations and transformations of the invariant core vis-à-vis its liberation, growth, and survival. The beingness of the text's existence is "to-be-translated," living on.[28]

Egypt as Muse: Poetics and the Nation

An interesting process that took place during the revolution was the appropriation of old songs. These songs had lost their appeal to the Egyptian public, having grown worn and stale. The muse, or object they were inspired by and were sung to, was the idea of 'Masr' or Egypt. Egypt signified a static, geographically situated country bound by borders—a territory. The songs echoed this corporeal embodiment of the country. Abdel Halim Hafez, a singer and actor who was famous in the 1960s, expressed this representation in the verses of "Watani habibi-l-watan al-akbar" ('My Beloved Homeland, the Greatest Homeland'), a song written in 1958 by Ahmad Shafiq Kamil.[29] The verses follow:

> My homeland, whose love possesses my heart
> My homeland, the homeland of the Arab people
> You who called for the great unity
> After you saw the beauty of revolution
> You are grand
> Far greater than existence
> Far greater than eternity
> My homeland
> My homeland, my beloved homeland

The core of this song lies in the focus on the word *watan*, which signifies 'homeland' or 'country.'[30] Yet, this reappropriation process contextualizes it by evoking the word '*muwatin*' (citizen), thereby accenting the human aspect of country—that is, the people. In this poem, Hafez sings, "My homeland, the homeland of the Arab people," and positions his homeland as a space that people inhabit.

A famous Egyptian singer of the 1960s, Shadia, also sang to her country in her song "Ya Habibti ya Masr" or 'O Darling Egypt.'[31] She personifies the tangible elements of Egypt by describing various aspects of her country as people. This is evident in her lyrics "In the embrace of the trees" and "The incantation/In moon-filled nights," giving the country a voice to sing and arms to embrace. In her first verse, she addresses her country while also expressing her fidelity to it:

Verse 1:
O my country
The prettiest country
O my country
I give myself
My children to you
O my country.
Chorus:
O darling, lovely
Egypt, my country.

Verse 2:
He has not seen the hope
In the eyes of the children
And the little girls of the country
And he has never seen the work
All night in the countryside
As will was born
Nor has he seen the Nile
In the embrace of the trees
Or heard
The incantation
In moon-filled nights
For he has never come to Egypt.

The song's invariant core revolves around the portrayal of Egypt as her beloved. In the third verse, she describes to her beloved country a man who has never experienced Egypt. In this verse she also contrasts the experiences of her people, such as "And he has never seen the work/All night in the countryside/As will was born" with this man's inexperience: "For he has never come to Egypt." Thus, she is speaking to her country as an ideal but does not speak directly to its people. In other words, this praise of an ideal results in a land-oriented patriotism to an Egypt that is praiseworthy because of its romanticized characteristics rather than for the accomplishments of its people.

Another song that was revived during the revolution was "Ya Masr umi" (Egypt, Rise), sung by Sheikh Imam and written by the poet Naguib Shihab al-Din.[32] This song speaks to the country uniformly as "Masr," as does "Ya Habibti ya Masr," yet describes and focuses on the actual people who make up the country. Sheikh Imam became immensely popular among leftist circles in the Arab world at large in the 1960s and 1970s, when he performed political songs, predominantly written by 'ammiya poet Ahmad Fuad Nigm. These songs were highly critical of the government and the ruling classes, and much of his work was banned under presidents Nasser and Sadat. As mentioned previously, while it was permissible to perform these traditional protest songs during Mubarak's rule, they became newly popular in society during the revolution. The first stanza of "Ya Masr umi" sheds light on how these songs were given renewed significance:

> Egypt, rise and pull yourself together
> I have all you could wish for, ever
> Neither grief nor the night swallows me
> *Aman, aman*, Biram Effendi
> Now they raise their noble foreheads, free
> Extending their hands to fulfill holy duty
> Without a caliph or a muezzin
> And light between heaven and earth.

This stanza opens with a direct appeal from the poet to his fellow citizens with an idiomatic colloquialism, '*shidd il-Hil*,' ('gird yourself,' 'be strong,' or 'pull yourself together'). The line "*Aman, aman*," is a common refrain in traditional songs and is here used to preface a salute to the poetry of Bairam al-Tunsi (referred to as Bairam Effendi in the poem), one of Egypt's most prominent 'ammiya poets in the twentieth century; it was kept unaltered in the target language to preserve this formulaic reference.

This old song was quickly appropriated to fit revolutionary themes, as the poet describes the strength of the nation as coming from the strength of its citizens (who rise with "noble foreheads" to take part in shaping Egypt's destiny). For protesters, this song also highlighted the urgency of being an active participant in the revolution, for the opening stanza labels this participation as *al-fard*, the Arabic word for a Muslim's mandatory religious duty. This concept of self-reliance is expanded in the line "*na'sin mu'azzin wi khalifa*," missing (or without) a *muezzin* or a caliph. The first traditional religious authority, a muezzin, issues the Muslim call to prayer, while the second, a caliph, is the traditional ruler of the Muslim *umma* or community. In this song, Egyptian citizens act without these leaders to preserve their nation, demonstrating the power of the people. The song also later describes the sacrifices of these citizens in this process.

> Blood runs into the water of the Nile
> And the Nile opens onto my prison.

Two words in this verse, 'blood' *(damm)* and 'prison' *(sign)*, gained new significance in the context of the revolution. This concept of *damm*, or the blood of the people, was an emotional catalyst for protesters during the January 25, 2011 uprising, who were inspired by the often mortal sacrifices made by many while supporting the revolution. While Sheikh Imam sings to Masr (Egypt) primarily in this song, the mention of *damm* further identifies the country as being made up of a *sha'b*, that is, people, made up of flesh and blood. Protesters could also relate to these lines in their message of hope to those imprisoned in '*sign*,' as many were during the initial weeks and months of the revolution. As the Nile "opens onto" the prison in the song, the people retain a link to the *damm* and sacrifice of their compatriots, even while in jail.

In addition to songs that addressed the country with the concept of Masr, some personified the nation and created specific relationships between the singer and country. For example, in Muhammad Mounir's song "Ezzay?" (How Come?)," he purposefully sings to Egypt as an unfaithful counterpart.[33] The song begins:

> How do you accept this for me, my love?
> To be in adoration of your name
> When you continue to confuse me

And you don't even feel my goodness, how?
I have no motive in my love for you
But my faithful love has brought me no salvation
How can I be the one to hold your head up high
When you continue to hold my head down low
How?

In this song, Mounir personifies Egypt as the beloved and challenges her love for him and her people. The core of this song is found in its disappointment in Egypt's ability to love and comfort her people. Interestingly enough, this song was released during the revolution despite the fact that it was written in November of the previous year. It may be for this reason that the song does not cast Egypt in the new light it gained during the revolution. By describing citizen and country as the lover and his beloved, this song helped protesters to explain their motivations to participate in the revolution. As long as their country was governed by a dictator, protesters would be like scorned lovers unable to succeed in their pursuit of the beloved.

In translating these songs, it was important to understand the new meaning attributed to them during the revolution. A song is appropriated when it is lifted from the past, infused with meaning related to current events, and rereleased. For example, in Mounir's "Ezzay?," what seems to be a love song is made into a song about the nation. When walking by Talaat Harb Square in early February, one would be engulfed by the voices of the protesters, or hear Shadia's "Ya Habibiti ya Masr" being blasted on loudspeakers. Her song's lyrics, along with Abdel Halim Hafez's "Watani Habibi" and Sheikh Imam's "Ya Masr umi," represented a revised blossoming of nationalist sentiments centered around the people (al-sha'b) rather than a spatial entity (that is, al-balad [the country] or al-watan [the nation]). This appropriation of old songs represented an early transformation in the relationship between the Egyptian people and their country during the revolution. Thus it is important to translate these songs because they are representative of the shift from an old-fashioned land-focused nationalism to one that is people-focused.

Addressing 'Masr' as 'al-Sha'b': A Nation Made Up of People

"Ya Masr hanit wi banit" ('O Egypt, We Are So Close') is a poem by Tamim Al-Barghouti that ardently heralded this shift.[34] The poet speaks to the people about the situation they are facing, thereby reflecting the experience to those experiencing it. Specifically, the poem calls for patience, as it was written when the protesters waited, day after day, for former President Mubarak to resign or announce real change in the government. In the following stanza, Al-Barghouti praises the people's accomplishments and perseverance:

O Egypt, we are so close
Today will be the day
Nothing remains of the regime save some sticks and batons
If you don't believe me, go to the *midan* so you can see
The oppressor only exists in the imagination of the oppressed
So those who stay home after this are deserters

The invariant core of this poem lies in the declaration of an optimistic future for Masr or Egypt. Even in his last line of the stanza, Al-Barghouti declares "So those who stay home after this are deserters." The word 'deserters' was chosen rather than 'traitor' or 'tyrants' since it implicates those protesters who have succumbed to apathy, not only the counterrevolutionaries. Similar to Shadia and Abdel Halim Hafez, Al-Barghouti addresses the country as a person, in this case one who has been waiting *(hanit)* for a long time. The declarative tone of Barghouti's work invigorated protesters in those crucial days in February, which is captured in this interpretation through the structure of the phrases and personal tone in the target language.

In addition to personifying the concept of Masr as the addressee of a poem or song, several artists began to use the word to signify *'ahlaha*,' or the Egyptian people. While Hisham al-Gokh's poem "Mashhad ra'si min Midan al-Tahrir" (A View of Midan al-Tahrir) was circulated through a different medium than most of the poetic works of the revolution, it quickly grew in popularity.[35] Composed in *fusHa*—unlike Barghouti's poems, which were composed in *'ammiya*—it was distributed through satellite television and YouTube videos. In contrast, Barghouti's "Ya Masr hanit wi banit" was distributed throughout the *midan* on sheets of paper, but his work was no less important. Within the first lines, a modern renaissance in poetry is heralded, transitioning to the familiar reminiscence of Egypt's beauty. The first half of the poem follows.

Hide all your old poems
Tear apart all your old journals

And write poetry for Egypt of her worth
As of today, no more silence that imposes fear
Write of Egypt,
Her people and the peace of her Nile
Your eyes, two beautiful young girls
Decide this fear is of the past
Done, finished with
The streets used to cuddle us
With frost and bitter breeze
And we knew no reason back then
Yet, we warmed each other up
In seeing you smile, we forgot the cold

At its core, the poem expresses a tone of intimate reverence for the country, a mélange of instruction and nostalgia. A noticeable oddity among the elevated language used in this translation is the word 'cuddle' for 'tuda'ibbuna.' This word was chosen over 'joke,' 'play,' or 'toy' because it conveys an intimacy understood in the target language and juxtaposes the harshness of the following line "With frost and bitter breeze." This interpretation remains committed to the tone of the original text by using the imperative tense in English, which conveys the urgency and strength of voice in the original. After the success of this poem, al-Gokh was accused of plagiarizing Upper Egyptian poet Abdel Sattar Selim, and was even threatened with a lawsuit. Yet this borrowing and expanding from one poet to another is a sign of intertexuality and is evident in other poets' work related to the revolution. The soul of Tahrir—the poetics of the revolution—was being expanded as a collective effort.

Interestingly enough, this poem, along with "Ya Masr hanit wi banit," was not created in Egypt. Al-Gokh's was recited at a Prince of Poets competition in Abu Dhabi and Barghouti's was written in Washington D.C. This demonstrates that the soul of Tahrir was not a local phenomenon but an existential expression that transcended physical space. It also exemplifies the reinvigorated shift in perception to where the term Masr was infused with new meaning—that is, the term no longer referred only to Egypt's land but, more importantly, to its people.

Many poets, such as al-Gokh, wrote about revolutionary themes in the classical poetic style. Again, several poems began to address 'Egypt' not as a monolithic ideal, but as a term equivalent to the Egyptian people. The

Arabic word *sha'b* ('people') became invested with new meanings during the course of the revolution as it became a term used to identify protesters. In the poetics that used the word *al-sha'b*, the listener or reader would immediately make a connection with the ability of the people to challenge the regime—true 'people power.' The work of the Tunisian poet Abul Qasim al-Shabbi was perhaps the first poetry to be appropriated by protesters that infused the term *al-sha'b* with revolutionary connotations among the narratives of the revolutions sweeping across the Arab world.[36] The youthful poet's eloquent attacks against French colonialism, such as "To the Tyrants of the World," were contained in verse and reapplied to express modern grievances. The Tunisian Revolution greatly inspired the Egyptians, and the resurrection of al-Shabbi's words gave agency to the people *(al-sha'b)*, and articulated their power as 'the will of the people' *(iradat al-sha'b)*. The poem describes this power and presents the choice between action and apathy as a life-or-death struggle. The first stanza of al-Shabbi's "Iradat al-Haya" (The Will to Live), follows:

If one day the people will to live
Then Fate must an answer give
Night will have to recede, and the chains will have to be broken
If you do not embrace love for life, you will evaporate into air, forgotten.
So woe to whoever is not split by life from the blow of victorious nothing
So the living things said to me, their hidden soul speaking

In addition to the meaning, the invariant core of this poem is the elevated style and music found in the source language. The poem is in *fusHa* and is organized with each line ending with the rhyme of the Arabic letter 'raa' with a *sukun*, which represents a silent stop in Arabic. This interpretation of the poem captures in English a poetic sound and structure in the order of certain phrases and in an AABBCC rhyme scheme. This poem's central theme—giving the people the power to choose—is highlighted by the use of opposing images throughout this stanza: "night/recede (dawn)," "chains/broken," "embrace/evaporate." The overall effect emphasizes the role of the people as agents of their own fate, with 'will' as the instrument of the people. Echoes of the poem's opening line can also be found in perhaps the most prevalent slogan of the new revolutions in the Arab world: "*al-Sha'b yurid isqat al-nizam*" ('The people demand the end of the regime').

The well-known Egyptian poet Ahmed Abdel Muti Hijazi was inspired by this poem's first lines and created a tribute to al-Shabbi, in which he also addressed the people in an elevated style.[37] Hijazi's work is often published by major Egyptian newspapers and distributed on satellite television and the Internet. Hijazi used these lines to expand on the poem by directly telling the people how to achieve their object of life—freedom. This intertextuality of poems from two nations further confirms the renewed solidarities that were being constructed between people in different Arab countries, as will be discussed below. In this poem, as al-Shabbi does, Hijazi addresses the people directly. However, Hijazi provides specific advice on the means to execute their will to obtain life. Here are the first two stanzas of "Iradat al-Haya" ('The Will to Live: A Tribute to Abul Qasim al-Shabbi'):

If the people will to live today
Then they must be free from fear
And carry in the palm of their hands
Their soul
And follow it deeply into danger
In order to earn their fate!
If the people will to live today
Then the slaves must rise
In fury
Endure the bite of hunger
But not endure the bite of the shackle
They die in the first hours of the night, if they must
Because they will rise again in the breaking dawn
In order to be born again tomorrow!
Return, O risen dead
O shackled slaves, rise in fury
O residents of the graves!
For the life that has long awaited you remains delayed
And you miss seeing suns without number!
And ages pass while you slumber!

Like al-Gokh and al-Shabbi, Hijazi writes this poem in *fusHa*. The poem emphasizes particular words to stress their meaning—*'ruh'* ('soul') and *qiyamatuhum* ('fury')—to affect the reader's emotions. The invariant core of this poem lies in these separated meanings, as well as the serious tone and language used in the poem. Hijazi develops the themes of al-Shabbi's first stanza—freedom and chains—by stating that the people must no longer tolerate the "bite of the shackle." This version also preserves the directness and no-nonsense tone of the source language by using formal English phrasing, such as "They die in the first hours of the night, if they must" instead of a more colloquial "If they have to die in the night's first hours, they will." The poem is an official call to arms, motivating *al-sha'b* to action.

Another song that gained new popularity during the revolution further defined the agency and inherent power of *al-sha'b*. One of Umm Kulthum's songs, "Ana-l-sha'b" ('I am the People'), written by Kamil al-Shinnawi, seems to have been composed in the first days of the revolution.[38] The song's chorus best captures the revolutionary spirit that swept the Egyptian populace:

> The people let out a voice set free
> Strong, ancient, deep, and lofty
> Saying: I am the people and the miracle
> I am the people
> I do not know the impossible
> I am the people
> I will accept no less than eternity

The invariant core of this poem concerns the characteristics of the people's *sawt* (voice). The song does not address the people but rather speaks for them in a *sawt* of a unified populace that is empowered and confident. While the song was originally written to celebrate Egypt's 1952 anti-monarchy revolution, it became a way for protesters in 2011 to celebrate their successes and better define themselves, for the rest of the country and the authorities, as a unified and unbeatable power stretching throughout history. When singing this song, protesters categorized themselves as the same *sha'b* that arose to defeat the corruption of the monarchy, a unified force made up of all segments of Egyptian society. Consequently, this mythology of the Egyptian people across time placed the protesters in a positive historical context for those Egyptians who were still undecided about the revolution. These lyrics also define the characteristics of the people by describing their voice as *taliq*, *qawiy*, *abiy*, *'ariq*, and *'amiq* (liberated, strong, unyielding, ancient, and lofty). The song thus gives comfort and reassurance and portrays the actions of *al-sha'b* as part of a historical tradition of the Egyptian people, whose authority trumps all others.

Speaking to the Regime: Asking Why

In addition to poems that addressed the people, one strong voice in Tahrir's polyphony addressed the regime and its enforcers. This boldness came from the belief in the power of *al-sha'b* and increasingly, in the power of *al-shabab* (the youth). The well-known *'ammiya* poet Abdel Rahman al-Abnoudi celebrates the youth in his poem "al-Midan" (The Midan) and daringly challenges the regime.[39] Al-Abnoudi uses a stylized form of *'ammiya* to contrast the old ruling elite with this young dynamic force. Here are the first twelve lines of that poem:

> Egyptian hands, tawny and wise
> Smashing the frames, in thunder they rise
> Flared in one voice, see Egypt in the sun
> O state of old men, your time is now done
> You ravaged our lands, rabid and old
> One like the other, in greed, filth, and mold
> Wondrous buds bloomed, turned fall into spring
> Raising the dead, the miracle youth bring
> Shoot me! My murder won't bring back your state
> For my people I write in my blood a new fate
> My blood or the spring, both they are green
> I smile—in joy or sorrow, remains to be seen

The invariant core of this poem must contain the oral nature of the piece, as this poem is meant to be recited in the source language. The translation used both a rhythm and rhyming pattern to capture the easy flow of the original, with lines composed of two metrical phrases such as "Egyptian hands, tawny and wise" and "Raising the dead, the miracle youth bring." Also, the themes of youth versus old are found in the allusions to the corruption of the old regime ("state of old men") and the violence perpetrated by the regime against the young protesters ("My murder won't bring back your state"). The brave tone of the original is also conveyed in the directness by which al-Abnoudi addresses the regime's crimes: "You ravaged our lands" and "Shoot me!" The sacrifices of *al-shabab* and their triumph allow the poet to speak out freely against those in power, and there is no longer fear of the old *dawla* (state).

Another example of *'ammiya* poetry that celebrated the youth is rendered by Ahmed Tharwat, better known by his stage name ZAP Tharwat, a young Egyptian DJ, who rose to prominence during the revolution.[40] ZAP Tharwat recasts the established *'ammiya* poetic tradition, in the work of poets like al-Abnoudi, into an alternative musical medium: hip-hop. Interestingly, his poem "Naharna nadi" ('Our Morning is Dew') is an expansion of Barghouti's "Ya Masr hanit wi banit" thereby establishing further dialogic relations between the poetic voices of Tahrir. ZAP Tharwat's poem speaks to Egypt as it has been redefined—as the people, rather than the land itself—describing their predicament while encouraging them. However, ZAP Tharwat also challenges the regime's motivations and actions. The first half of ZAP Tharwat's "Our Morning is Dew" follows:

> To the words of Al-Barghouti, I come to add
> O Egypt, we're so close and it's so clear
> We are but days away
> Our morning is dew
> But the villain's is gloom
> You of cap and rank, is my blood worthless to you?
> We could have been friends or brothers
> Maybe you don't even know me
> But I know that if you knew me, you wouldn't beat me with your weapon
> Your weapon to me is safety, not for beating or abuse
> O Egypt, are we not your children? Or are you selling us off?
> Suddenly we became heroes, people cheering us on
> From one demonstration to another, people calling us
> Then suddenly they turned against us and damned our names
> Some of them tried to beat us with shoes
> Are you saying we've been deceived? Have you understood?
> You were right here on the streets, sleeping next to us
> Muslims and Christians, hand in hand
> Then we became traitors, infiltrators, Muslim Brothers, and Iranians?
> Red and green agenda, a book and two notebooks
> Come down and see with your own eyes
> Ask them who they are

...
You'll hear a collective voice
We are all Egyptian

This poem sheds light on the shift that occurred during the eighteen
days preceding the resignation of Mubarak, especially on the events of
February 2, 2011. On this day the regime's supporters attacked protesters on camel-back and with Molotov cocktails in the evening. Egypt's
state television channel deemed the protesters Muslim Brothers, Israeli
spies, and foreign infiltrators with agendas. This poem challenges these
identities projected by state television onto the pro-democracy protesters. Hence, ZAP Tharwat's proposition at the end of the first half of his
poem: "Come down and see with your eyes/Ask them who they are." The
poem calls out the people who make up the regime, asking them why
they are not "friends" or "brothers." The music video that introduced the
world to this work showed images and video clips of the people who were
in Tahrir Square to contrast the claims of the regime, which had lost the
ability to connect with the people.[41]

Like ZAP Tharwat, Ahmed Mekky, an actor, director, author, and
rapper, also chose hip-hop as the medium for sharing his poetic reflections
of the revolution.[42] His work "January 25" showcases the Egyptian Revolution by describing the achievements of the youth to the uninformed
spectator. The chorus and first two stanzas of Mekky's "January 25" follow:

The dignity of the Egyptian is worth much to him
He wants it back, and for corruption to fly away [again]
January twenty-five
Anniversary of the greatest Egyptian revolution of all time
Not wearing a collar, the youth held Egypt's head high
He needs his legal rights
And demands them respectably
Take a tour of Tahrir and you will see
You'll find a smile on your face
And your heart flying
The youth understood the meaning of unifying
United and made the change
My son, the Egyptian
Is much greater after the revolution

Despite the strong masculine imagery found in the song, the lyrics focus on the active contribution of young people to the success of the revolution. The core of this poetic work is thus discovered in its admiration of their participation, their demands, and their ability to bring about their desired change to the oppressive political climate in Egypt. Yet the song is not meant to credit the success of the revolution to the youth, as the following works will show.

The transformation of *al-shabab* during the revolution became another theme present in several works, including that of Amr Katamish, winner of the television program *Arabs Got Talent*. In one performance on the show, Katamish presented a humorous poem in colloquial Arabic about the revolution, composed of a series of different voices of ordinary Egyptians. The first verses highlight the changes in young people's behavior as a result of the revolution and addresses the concerns about the potential for sexual harassment to occur as men and women mingled in the free space of Tahrir. While sexual harassment on the streets was relatively common before the revolution, this poem jokingly points to its absence among the youth as a result of the revolution.

> My nickname is Nora but my real name is Azza
> And they say I'm a babe
> All my pants are tight
> So I look like a chick
> If I walk and some guy sees me
> With leering eyes he stares at me
> But after the revolution when I walk I look proud
> I don't hear any catcalls or meows
> I don't see guys blinking and winking
> For this I am proud of my country and know honor's meaning
> Now I'm convinced that someday soon we'll purify Gaza.

The core of this poem lies in the sassy tone that Katamish adopts as the voice of a teenage girl and in the shift from the frivolity of the opening lines to the seriousness of the description of her life after the revolution. This section highlights how the meaning of *al-shabab* changed during the revolution from one that indicated inexperienced and rude youth to one that signifies proud patriots who can liberate or cleanse Gaza *(sanutahhir Ghazza)*. In the source language this terminology evokes the imagery of health, and depicts young people acting to 'cure' the sickness of a war-torn land. The revolution succeeded because of the efforts of these youths, and this poem expresses how the identity of *al-shabab* shifted to reflect this victory. The poem compares these glorious youths with the regime's supporters, as it later mocks the regime by speaking in the voice of a government minister, who visits a doctor after he had lost all will to live.

> I love my life
> I always steal what I like
> But after the revolution's success
> I'm feeling inclined to perish
> What do I do, Doctor?
> Give me an answer.

The core of this poem lies in the clipped nature of the phrases in the source language and in the humor created by these short rhyming statements: "*UHibbu Hayati*" ('I love my life') and "*Asriq ma yaHlu li*" ('I steal what I like'). This interpretation in English uses near rhymes in an attempt to capture the musicality of the original. The contrast in the poem between Nora and this minister highlights the negative aspects of the old guard and the new feelings of pride experienced by the youth as a result of their success in the revolution. The boldness of this poem's humor also reveals the new sense of freedom felt by those opposed to the regime. Notably, while Katamish had been using this poetic style for seven years without gaining much notoriety, the revolution may have increased the popularity of this non-traditional form of creative expression.

Addressing the President: Challenging Mubarak in Verse

As the voice challenging the regime gained strength in the polyphony of Tahrir, the poetics began to reflect a growing boldness and anger condensed against former President Mubarak. The protester's demands came to be expressed by one word: *irHal* ('leave'). This demand was included in the literary and oral tapestry of Tahrir in chants, poems, and songs. In particular, songs and poems in *'ammiya* spread like wildfire, since Egyptian artists could easily connect with the general populace via entertainment. These songs 'went viral,' spreading quickly via the Internet, cell phones, and satellite television. With their new styles, these songs particularly appealed to the youth, as many of these artists came from their same generation. As discussed above, the virtual platform provided by YouTube allowed these artists to perform live in Tahrir and affect even those who stayed at home, in addition to those who were present in the square. While relatively few well-known groups played during the first eighteen days in Midan al-Tahrir, individual artists and some bands did perform on stage. One of the earliest and best-known songs performed was Ramy Essam's "IrHal," which was widely disseminated via the Internet and major television news channels. Essam played several times in Midan al-Tahrir, incorporating popular chants and jokes into his songs. Here is the full text of "IrHal":

> All of us, one hand, our demand, one stand: Get out! Get out! Get out! Get out!
> All of us, one hand, our demand, one stand: Get out! Get out! Get out! Get out!
> All of us, one hand, our demand, one stand: Get out! Get out! Get out! Get out!
> All of us, one hand, our demand, one stand: Get out! Get out! Get out! Get out!
> Down with, down with Hosni Mubarak!
> Down with, down with Hosni Mubarak!
> Down with, down with Hosni Mubarak!
> Down with, down with Hosni Mubarak!
> The people demand the downfall of the regime
> The people demand the downfall of the regime
> The people demand the downfall of the regime
> We won't leave, he's gonna leave!
> We won't leave, he's gonna leave!

The invariant core of this piece is in the meaning and musicality of the chants that make up the song. The power of this piece lies in these chants, as their viral spread allowed any protester to instantly realize the words of this song and sing along, and to condense their motivations into a few lyrics. The song alludes to several thematic elements in these chants, including "all of us" (referencing the "We are All Khaled Said" Facebook group that originally called for protests on January 25), "one hand," which makes reference to the people's connection to the military, and "get out," which was the protesters' main demand. This version captures the rhythm of the original by creating phrases that are easily chanted in English. These phrases directly addressed Mubarak rather than just the regime. The poetics were now personal, fearlessly targeting the individual held responsible for the injustices—former President Mubarak—in the common voice of every Egyptian: *"Talabna, Haga waHda, irHal"* ('Our demand, one stand: Get out.')

As the voices turned against Mubarak, poets used *'ammiya* to mock the president's speeches and his supporters. These works, using the common tongue, openly disdained the president and ridiculed his actions. With their new power, *al-sha'b* could now deal with Mubarak on their own terms. One famous colloquial Arabic poet, Sayyed Higab, vilified the president with the language of the street in his "Waslit radH" (Catfight).[43] In this poem, Higab presents Mubarak's arguments in the voices of low-class women having a verbal spat. The verbal finger-pointing illustrates the real absurdity of Mubarak's actions. Here is the beginning of the poem:

> They said to What's-His-Name
> Hey What's-Your-Name
> Leave
> Don't just sit there
> The thing is . . . they said
> What's-His-Name, his dignity's hurt!
> This guy's got dignity?
> His sleazy lies are in his eyes.
> And our lives and our children's blood were spilled by his hands.
> If he has dignity why'd he rob us, why?
> Why'd he destroy us, why?
> And why'd he betray our soil?
> And why'd he kill our youth?
> If our father's a traitor and a thief we'll flip him around
> And bury him with his shame with no one to pray for his name

The core of this poem is in the strong tone and dismissive language found in the source text. Higab read this poem on the talk show *Akhir kalam* ('The Last Word') in a series of starts and stops, mimicking a real argument. The theme of the youth being killed—*"Wi atal shababha lih?"*

('And why'd he kill our youth?')—reflects the intertextuality of the poem and the sacrifice of young martyrs at the hands of the regime is another common thread in the lyrical tapestry of Tahrir. This interpretation attempts to capture the strong tone of the original in Higab's repetition of the word *lih* (why), creating a punctuated rhythm throughout. This question of 'why' addresses the *Hizb al-kanaba* ('Party of the Couch'), Egyptians who had not joined the rest of *al-sha'b* in protests but merely watched them on television. By highlighting the absurdity of this support for someone with no *karama* (honor/dignity), the poem makes a strong statement against Mubarak and calls for *al-sha'b* to unite against him.

al-Sha'b al-'arabi: Shifts in Identity of the People

The works selected for this chapter trace the theme of identity found in the poetics of the revolution. With the evolution of the concept of Masr from a term that describes the land to one that identifies *al-sha'b*, these works demonstrate how the discourse concerning these meanings developed in Tahrir. In some ways, the shifts in meaning of *al-sha'b* have occurred in a circular pattern. The term was first appropriated in Tunisia through al-Shabbi's poetry to indicate that the people made up a state, not its rulers. When *iradat al-sha'b* ('will of the people') was incorporated into the lyrical tapestry of Tahrir, the term came to mean *al-sha'b al-masri* ('the Egyptian people'). However, as the revolution has progressed in Egypt, the term has expanded to *al-sha'b al-'arabi* ('the Arab people'), crossing borders as it did from Tunisia to Egypt to include the entire Arab world. Egyptians were highly aware of the conditions in other Arab countries during and after the Egyptian revolution. It has also been only half a century since the era of Nasser and the philosophies of pan-Arabism, and many Egyptians recall this period favorably. Egyptian poet Muhammad Bahgat wrote a poem several years ago that criticized the armies in the Arab World through humor. This poem was also appropriated as a song during the revolution and sung in Midan al-Tahrir by Ramy Essam. While a strong pro-military sentiment existed during the first eighteen days of the revolution, not all Egyptians were happy with the actions of the army. Essam in particular had cause to criticize the military, because he endured torture at the hands of the Military Police (see note 9). This poem jokingly evaluates of the role of the army, which in some countries is typically viewed as the protectors of the Arab people. It also serves as an example of the unity that Egyptians felt for Arabs in other countries,

especially for their respective plights. Here are the first three stanzas of
"Al-gish al-'arabi fin?" ('Where's the Arab Army?'):

> One, two, where's the Arab army?
> The Arab Army in Egypt
> Lives up in Nasr City,
> Wakes up in the afternoon
> To poor bread and tea.
> The Arab Army in Syria,
> Hair cut to the latest fashion,
> And like the times of Victoria
> Have double-decker trams.
> The Arab Army in Libya
> Is just like art that's Cubist
> All eggplant and weird faces yeah
> I think they caught evil-eye-itis!
> The Arab Army—the Gulfies
> Can't fight, they got no energy
> It's a strategic tranquillity
> What's up with that, you crow?
> The Arab Army in Tunis
> Green just like fresh-picked parsley
> 'Cause when Aziza loves Yunis
> They let all other wars be.
> The Arab Army's Sudani,
> With my ear I hear their voice
> "I've got to attack alone?"
> "No, I'm retreating, boys!"
> Arab Army got no dignity
> Lost it when they hit Afghanis.
> What's more, they didn't speak in Bosnia.
> Now they're eating the debt.

The central theme of this song is the Arab army not doing its job,
but rather doing odd things in odd places. The poem makes reference
to the Egyptian army living in Madinat Nasr (Nasr City), an upper-class
suburb of Cairo, and criticizes them for being lazy rather than defending
the people. The line "hair cut in the latest fashion" depicts the Syrian

army as being obsessed with image, in this case portraying an image of "being cool." In Libya, the army has caught the "evil eye" and everything is *bitingan* ('eggplant'), which alludes to how messed up the situation is. The armies of the Arab states in the Gulf maintain a "strategic tranquillity," even while the people suffer. The army in Tunis is "green" and is fresh and beautiful, and when "Aziza" (a girl's name) loves "Yunis" (a boy's name), then the country is at peace. The verse about the army in Sudan uses a cultural stereotype of laziness to explain the army's behavior. The final verse ends on a serious note: while there have been grave injustices against Muslims and Arabs, such as in Afghanistan and Bosnia, the Arab Army "didn't speak," and must either eat or swallow their "debt." Even though the poem was written prior to the revolution, these references were appropriated by Essam to describe the current situation facing many regimes in the Arab World. Prior to the wave of revolutions, *il-gish il-'arabi* was supposed to protect *il-sha'b il-arabi*, but this song rightly points out a widespread dereliction of duty. The repetition of the term *il-gish il-'arabi* demonstrates the renewed feelings of pan-Arab solidarity felt by the Egyptian people *(al-sha'b al-Masri)* with other revolutionaries throughout the region. On a linguistic level, the repetition shows that *al-sha'b* now signifies *al-sha'b al-'arabi*. In order to retain the tempo of the song, the interpretation features a rhyme scheme common to those found in English songs, with short lyrics making up each stanza. As a result, an audience reading the song in English is able to 'sing along,' evoking the participatory nature of this work.[44] The shifting discourse of Tahrir is evident today as protests begin to focus on more regional concerns, such as breaking the Gaza blockade and supporting revolutions in Syria and Libya.

Conclusion

While this chapter has concentrated on the development of songs and poetic works of the Egyptian Revolution, the lyrical tapestry of the revolution spans numerous themes, subjects, and genres. The evolution of the discourse concerning identity has been explored via the concepts of *al-sha'b* and *al-watan*. The aim of this chapter has been to highlight how quickly themes develop and continue to change in the larger narrative of the revolution. These aesthetic arrangements also display the interlinking views of the revolution, which is evident in the intertextuality of the texts. ZAP Tharwat's work was an expansion of Al-Barghouti's, Hijazi's a revival of al-Shabbi's, and even al-Gokh's with its borrowed lines from the Upper

Egyptian poet Abdel Sattar Selim. In the search for equivalence in these translations, while certain poetic elements in the source text unavoidably become lost in translation, at the same time new elements emerge in the target language. The intertextuality and structural complexity of the texts in their source language results in a resistance to the process of translation. The invariant core is transformed in the ecstatic moment of transposition, traveling from one code to the next, in hopes that its new attire embraces this inner meaning. This is to say that the work done in this chapter reflects the view of translation as an act of creative design rather than the orthodox practice of an invisible translator. In the traditional concept of translation, the translator is subjugated by the text and loses his or her human touch in exchange for a mechanical one. Yet, the translator—not just the text—is also transformed by this interaction as he or she fords the channels of translation and engages the various issues that arise in creative ways. As non-native Arabic speakers, the authors faced several limitations, such as not recognizing certain references or shifts in language as quickly as a native speaker might. However, through creativity, flexibility, and consistent methodology, we have endeavored to create an acceptable synthesis of these texts.

This chapter has traced one thread in the larger tapestry of the revolution's poetics. Numerous other songs, chants, and poems were produced on a variety of subjects and themes, which make up the polyphony that is the soul of Tahrir. Also, while large segments of these poems were translated or at least read in the original language, they remain to be translated fully, either in the framework presented in this chapter or in other innovative ways. It is hoped that these translations allow English speakers a glimpse into the rich and creative world of Arabic poetry while better revealing the underlying narratives of the Egyptian Revolution.[45]

Notes

1 The original Arabic texts of poems and songs appear in Appendix 2 and Appendix 3, respectively.

2 Abul Qasim al-Shabbi (1909–34) was a Tunisian poet best known for writing on patriotic themes, including part of the Tunisian national anthem. His best-known works are "To the Tyrants of the World" and "The Will to Live." These poems attacked French colonialism and the occupation of Tunisia. Excerpts of these two works became popular chants during both the Tunisian and Egyptian revolutions.

Ahmed Abdel Muti Hijazi, born in 1935, is a contemporary Egyptian poet who is one of the pioneers of the movement of renewal in contemporary Arabic poetry. He was managing editor of *Sabah al-Kheir* magazine. He spent several years in exile in France during the Sadat period where he worked as a professor of Arabic poetry at the new Sorbonne University. When he returned to Cairo during the early eighties he worked as a columnist for *al-Ahram* newspaper and was editor-in-chief of the literary magazine *Ibda'*. Among his best-known poetry collections are *Elegy to a Beautiful Life* (1972) and *Creatures of the Kingdom of Darkness* (1978).

3   From "Revolution Quotes," http://www.quoteland.com/topic/Revolution-Quotes/128/.

4   From "The End of Arabic Poetry is Over, Long Live Arabic Poetry," M. Lynx Qualey Blog, April 17, 2011, http://arablit.wordpress.com/2011/04/17/the-era-of-arabic-poetry-is-over-long-live-arabic-poetry/. Amr Katamish (b. 1987) is a stand-up comedian and performer, who graduated with a degree in geology from Helwan University in Cairo. On the 2010–11 season of the show *Arabs Got Talent* on MBC4, Katamish won first prize for his poems that express the perspective of Arab youth during and following the revolution. His poetic style is known as *sh'ir Halamantishi*, a blend of colloquial and formal Arabic that covers ordinary subjects in a humorous fashion.

5   While there are no specific examples of poetry ending a war in the pre-Islamic Arabian Peninsula, poets were widely considered to be ambassadors and spokesmen of their tribes in this period. "Arabic Poetry," Wikipedia, http://en.wikipedia.org/wiki/Arabic_poetry#Pre-Islamic_poetry

6   Richard Jacquemond, *Conscience of the Nation: Writers, State, and Society in Modern Egypt* (Cairo: American University in Cairo Press, 2008), p. 133.

7   An amazing example of this practice of spontaneous chanting is available online at "The Bravest Girl in Egypt," YouTube, January 29, 2011, http://www.youtube.com/watch?v=wTTGPym-9rU

8   Imam Muhammad Ahmad Issa (1918–95), known as Sheikh Imam, was a poet and singer who gained a large following in the 1960s and 1970s through his folk songs and political works. His collaboration with noted Egyptian *'ammiya* poet Ahmad Fuad Nigm on political songs about the poor and the 1967 War led to their imprisonment by the Egyptian government. Prior to the revolution, musicians performed his songs to indirectly criticize the Mubarak government.

Sayyed Darwish (1892–1923) was a composer from Alexandria. He gained a large following as a singer and composer of popular songs rendered in a new style, one that was less similar to that found in Egypt under the pashas. Importantly, Darwish composed in Egyptian *'ammiya*, alluded to political events in his songs, and specifically addressed issues from the 1919 Egyptian Revolution. Darwish also set the Egyptian national anthem to music. His works have been sung by popular and famous Arabic singers such as the Lebanese superstar Fairuz. From "Sheikh Sayyed Darwish," http://almashriq.hiof.no/egypt/700/780/sayed-darweesh/index.html

9   Ramy Essam, born in 1987 in the village of Mansoura, is a songwriter and musician who formed a protest band, Mashakil ('Problems'), in 2009. During the Egyptian Revolution, Essam's performances in Midan al-Tahrir quickly went viral on YouTube. According to National Public Radio, Essam was among a group of protesters arrested in early March outside the Egyptian Museum and tortured by the Military Police in the same building. See Steve Inskeep, "Ramy Essam: The Singer of the Egyptian Revolution," *NPR Music*, March 15, 2011, http://www.npr.org/2011/03/15/134538629/ramy-esam-the-singer-of-the-egyptian-revolution

10   Susan Bassnett, *Translation Studies* (New York: Routledge, 2002), pp. 84–85. In this work, Bassnett discusses seven strategies for approaching the translation of poetry created by André Lefevere, and interpretation is one of these strategies. For more on this approach, consult the original: André Lefevere, *Translating Poetry: Seven Strategies and a Blueprint* (Amsterdam: Van Gorcum, 1975).

11   Lawrence Venuti, *The Translator's Invisibility: A History of Translation* (New York: Routledge, 1995), p. 6.

12   Venuti, *The Translator's Invisibility*, p. 41.

13   Venuti, *The Translator's Invisibility*, p. 21.

14   Bassnett, *Translation Studies*, pp. 83–84. See note 10 of this chapter on the original work by Lefevere.

15   Bassnett, *Translation Studies*, p. 84. This remark by Bassnett alludes to Lefevere's vindication of Anne Cluysenaar's establishment of unbalanced approaches to translation.

16   Bassnett, *Translation Studies*, p. 80. Bassnett is reasserting Cluysenaar's statements on the structuralist approach to literary translations. For further information on this approach, see Anne Cluysenaar, *Introduction to Literary Stylistics* (London: Batsford, 1976) and Robert Scholes, *Structuralism in Literature* (New Haven, CT: Yale University Press, 1974).

17 Jacques Derrida, *Uninterrupted Dialogue: Between Two Infinities* (Leiden: Research in Phenomenology, 2004), p. 12. Derrida is situating Gadamer's thoughts of the poem within the infinity of dialogue between the reader and the text. This is reminiscent of Gadamer's discourse on the infinite process. For further discussion of this concept, see Gadamer's work *Research and Method* (London: Continuum, 2004) and a volume on his works titled *Language and Linguisticality in Gadamer's Hermeneutics* (Lanham: Lexington Books, 2000).

18 Donald Davie, *Ezra Pound: Poet as Sculptor* (London: Routledge & Kegan Paul, 1965), p. 86.

19 Anton Popovič, "The Concept of 'Shift of Expression' in Translation Analysis," in James Holmes, ed., *The Nature of Translation* (The Hague and Paris: Mouton, 1970); quoted in Bassnett, *Translation Studies*, p. 89.

20 A. Ludskanov, "A Semiotic Approach to the Theory of Translation," *Language Sciences* 35, April 1975; quoted in Bassnett, *Translation Studies*, p. 25. See Ludskanov's essay for further discussion on semiotic transformation.

21 Bassnett, *Translation Studies*, p. 91. The term "creative transposition" was originally used by Roman Jakobson. Consult Roman Jakobson, "On Linguistic Aspects of Translation," in R.A. Brower, ed., *On Translation* (Cambridge, MA: Harvard University Press, 1959) for more on transference of messages and meaning from source language to target language.

22 Lawrence Venuti, *Translation Studies Reader* (London: Routledge, 2000), p. 17. See Walter Benjamin's essay "The Task of the Translator" (1923) for more on his conception of translation.

23 Jacques Derrida, *The Ear of the Other: Otobiography, Transference, Translation* (New York: Schocken Books, 1985), p. 122.

24 Venuti, *Translation Studies Reader*, p. 17.

25 Walter Benjamin, "The Task of the Translator" (1923), as quoted in Venuti, *Translation Studies Reader*, p. 18.

26 Derrida, *The Ear of the Other*, p. 123. This debate over the task of the translator and its rereading by Derrida opened a new era in the field of translation studies during the latter half of the twentieth century. By situating the original's structure as survival, it gave hope to a new promise in translation as a shared affinity of languages as well as the positive assurance of "the after-life of a text, a new 'original' in another language." (Bassnett, *Translation Studies*, p. 9) For more details on translation as survival of the original text and its promise of pure language, a kinship between languages, read "The Task of the Translator" by

Walter Benjamin (1923); "Des Tours de Babel," translated by Joseph F. Graham in *Difference in Translation* (New York: Cornell University Press, 1985); and "The Ear of the Other" by Jacques Derrida.

27 Jacques Derrida, *Positions* (Chicago: University of Chicago Press, 1981), p. 20.

28 Beingness requires action, where existence does not necessitate action (though we could probably argue round and round this statement). This suggests that in order for the text to survive, it must be translated. The text should be understood "independently of its living conditions—the conditions, obviously, of its author's life—and to understand it instead in its surviving structure," as stated by Derrida in *Ear of the Other* (p. 122). The text's surviving structure, its beingness, is "to-be-translated." The text's existence, on the other hand, does not require translation, for it exists already. See Derrida, "Des Tours de Babel," for more on the concept of "to-be-translated."

29 Abdel Halim Ali Shabana, better known as Abdel Halim Hafez, is one of the most celebrated singers of Egypt and the Arab world. He was also an actor, conductor, and film producer. He passed away in London on March 30, 1977.

30 For an interesting reading of this song and the relationship between nationalism and song in general, see Joseph Massad, "Liberating Songs: Palestine Put to Music," *Palestine, Israel, and the Politics of Popular Culture*, ed. Rebecca Stein and Ted Swedenburg (Durham, NC: Duke University Press, 2005), pp. 175–201.

31 Fatima Ahmad Kamal, better known as Shadia, is a famous Egyptian actress and singer. Her most popular works in film and song arose during the 1950s and 1960s. She has performed in over one hundred films and featured in over six hundred songs.

32 Naguib Shihab al-Din, a prominent *'ammiya* poet who wrote several lyrics for Sheikh Imam but whose literary production and name remained practically unknown to many Egyptians until the January 25 Revolution, during which his poem "Ya Masr umi" was propelled to the very center of the poetic polyphony in Tahrir.

33 Muhammad Mounir is a popular Egyptian singer and actor with Nubian roots. His musical career began in the late 1970s and continues today. He is known for incorporating political and social commentary into his lyrics.

34 Tamim Al-Barghouti is an Egyptian-Palestinian poet and political scientist. His father is the famous Palestinian poet Mourid Barghouti and his mother is the Egyptian academic, activist, and novelist Radwa Ashour.

He has taught at the American University in Cairo and Georgetown University in Washington D.C. He writes poetry in *fusHa* as well as in Egyptian and Palestinian dialects.

35 Hisham al-Gokh is an Egyptian poet who rose to prominence during the revolution. He won second place in the Prince of Poets competition in Abu Dhabi with his poem "A View of Midan al-Tahrir."

36 For more on Abul Qasim al-Shabbi, see note 2 of this chapter.

37 For more on Ahmed Abdel Muti Hijazi, see note 2 of this chapter.

38 Umm Kulthum Fatima Ibrahim al-Sayyid al-Beltagi (1898–1975), better known as Umm Kulthum, may be the best-known and most popular female singer in the Arab World. Umm Kulthum's songs often lasted for hours and were known for mesmerizing audiences. While King Farouk was an early sponsor of her career, her songs often introduced the public events held by Gamal Abdel Nasser after the 1952 Revolution.

39 Abdel Rahman al-Abnoudi (b. 1938) is an Egyptian 'ammiya poet, who first became known for collecting and publishing an epic folk poem, *Sirat Bani Hilal* (concerning an Egyptian tribe in the time of the Fatimid Dynasty). Al-Abnoudi first began to use political commentary in his poetry with his attacks on Sadat's peace deal with Israel in several poems. Before the revolution, he took up various causes such as attacking the ruling party's corrupt ruling style. Parts of the song translated here, "al-Midan," were also used in "Sut al-Huriya," one of the most popular songs on YouTube during the revolution.

40 Ahmed Tharwat Zaki, better know by his stage name ZAP Tharwat, is a young Egyptian hip-hop artist and poet whose lyrics reflect strong political commentary. Like many young artists, he gained notoriety from the revolution and continues to perform and record politically engaged work.

41 See ZAP Tharwat, "Tribute to the Heroes of 25 January," YouTube, February 8, 2011, http://www.youtube.com/watch?v=NAgxK-e0zzY

42 Ahmed Mekky is a prominent Egyptian actor, film director, film producer, and rap artist. His acting career began in the early 2000s. He is an alumnus of the American University in Cairo.

43 Sayyed Higab was born in 1940 in a small Egyptian village and was raised in the port city of Alexandria. He joins poet Abdel Rahman al-Abnoudi in promoting poetry composed and recited in Egyptian 'ammiya. Higab has been a member of several political movements, including the Muslim Brotherhood and Marxist movements in Egypt, and agitated against the Mubarak government.

44 For a performance of this song in English by the authors, visit "Translating Revolution," YouTube, March 22, 2011, http://www.youtube.com/watch?v=yC3uscSqiRk

45 We would like to thank Samia Mehrez for inspiring us in this critical moment and our classmates for their enthusiasm and critiques. We would like to thank Adham Zidan, Amor Eletrebi, Riham El Sayed Mohamad, Abdallah al-Ghoul, and Obada Ashraf for their contributions to our understanding of the original Arabic texts.

7

The People and the Army Are One Hand: Myths and Their Translations

Menna Khalil

January 25 has been designated as "National Police Day" in Egypt
since 1952. In 2011, the date marked an uprising against a heap of
sociopolitical conditions in Egypt: the thirty-year despotism of
Hosni Mubarak (the longest presidential mandate in Egypt's history);
the grooming of Gamal Mubarak (the former president's younger son)
for succession, or rather inheritance, of power; press and speech censorship; uncontested police brutality (through the continued reactivation of
the 1958 Emergency Law);[1] corruption among government officials; a
deteriorating economy, and an ever-widening gap between the upper and
lower classes of the country. As people who took to the streets in January
of 2011 chanted "*thawra*" ('revolution'), the term, which was recognized
from prior resistance movements in the country such as 1919 and 1952,
became a lived reality.[2] In turn, the events created a new arena of possible encounters in Egypt between citizens and regime, protesters and the
police and army, and people and public space.[3]

After three days of intensifying demonstrations, the Egyptian army
was deployed into the streets of Cairo on January 28, 2011 to control
and restore order over protests, fires, looting, and violence taking place
across the country. Some police and state security forces were pulled off
the streets while others continued to engage demonstrators as the army
was deployed. As the withdrawing riot police continued to fire tear gas,
protesters began to swarm around what appeared to be a military truck,
with its faint beige color distinguishing it from that of the blue and green
police vehicles used to capture and detain demonstrators. Very quickly,
Midan al-Tahrir and other public spaces within the heart of Downtown
Cairo were flooded with army tanks, vehicles, and personnel.

However, this was not the first time the army had been deployed onto the country's streets—more specifically, the streets of Cairo. In 1977, former President Anwar Sadat sent the army to disband the Bread Riots, led by many across the country against the World Bank and International Monetary Fund's termination of food subsidies. And again, in 1986, thousands of underpaid conscripts of the Central Security Forces (CSF) violently protested the potential one-year extension of their three-year mandatory service by the Ministry of Interior. Former President Hosni Mubarak ordered the army to use whatever means necessary to quash the riots and restore order to the streets of Cairo. Although these are two of the main incidents in which the army was ordered to repress demonstrations, other protests in the last decades on any number of sociopolitical issues were met with severe violence from the Central Security Forces. It is important to note that in the last ten years, Mubarak has increasingly militarized the CSF (or riot police) through sheer numbers (now amounting to more than 350,000), equipment, power, and budget. This expanded the regime's control over domestic life, by slowly decreasing the involvement and public visibility of the army as an institution.[4]

On January 28, 2011, what army soldiers encountered with civilian protesters were not localized demands for reform (as in the above examples), but a people's demand for political change expressed through the widely chanted slogan "*al-Sha'b yurid isqat al-nizam*" ('The people demand the fall of the regime'). This direct demand called into question the position of the army—itself a political instrument of the regime with Mubarak presiding over the military institution as its chief commander—in relation to the people and their historic allegiance to the army. It is important to note here that demonstrators' initial encounter with the army on that day was characterized by the appearance of conscripted army soldiers, not high-ranking officials or representatives of the institution, but the body of troops that is *of* the people. Moreover, throughout the January 28, 2011 encounter, a discursive strategy was applied by many demonstrators: the army was confronted with its past image and discourse as protector and liberator from illegitimate monarchical rule, outside invasion, and war.

Whether an intentional strategy or an internalized perception, the collective memorialization of the army as protector against foreign imperialism and liberator of the nation, as a force having *always* stood by and guided the will of the people, gave it almost godlike qualities. Yet on the ground, protesters finally faced the soldiers—imagined as superheroes or saviors coming from afar—who left their common roles of serving the nation, protecting its borders, and building its structures to occupy and preside over public territory as they sit atop tanks with a dual function: protection and threat.

Set against this backdrop, crowds of protesters began to chant in intense and unified cadence as the army took its position in the streets of the capital: "*Silmiya . . . silmiya*" ('Nonviolent . . . nonviolent'). Protesters vigorously and anxiously chanted "*silmiya*" as a plea of sorts to establish an urgent, nonviolent rapport with the army, as the latter's position was still unclear. People further welcomed the army troops with open arms while clapping, hugging, and cheering as they chanted: "*al-Gish wa-l-sha'b id waHda*" ('The army and the people are one hand').

This chapter is not offered as an exhaustive, empirical account of the Egyptian Revolution; rather, it is interested in *translating*[5] the new possibilities of encounter created by exchanges between the people and the army—as more generalizing, almost reifying categories of 'demonstrators' and 'soldiers/officers,' respectively—since the revolution began. Reference to demonstrators and soldiers as 'the people' and 'the army' is relied upon for the purposes of analyzing popular rhetoric and characterization of the two bodies albeit not making them fixed. Since the language of the present events is constantly in motion between the quintessence of the past and a potential future, it makes the undoing and doing of prior associations and the maneuvering of exchanges between the two bodies all the more fluid. The chapter is anchored in understanding this new realm of possibility through the varying terms of language (slogans, gestures, songs, images) as they are negotiated in moments of ephemerality. In many ways, such terms of language can be used to interpret the complex relationship between the people and the army—vis-à-vis conscripts of the latter's encounter with 'the people' as protesters—as it continues to unfold on the ground.

In translating these modes of signification, the chapter will try to make sense of how such terms of language can transfer the historical notion of unity that founds the relationship between the people and the army onto new terrains as the two bodies transform, come together, and separate over the course of the events. The chapter will examine the shifting role of the army from a cited guardian of the people, an institution composed of sons and fathers of the nation, a political instrument of prior regimes, to a hovering menace. The Supreme Council of the Armed Forces (SCAF) represents the latter as it replaced the Mubarak

The Supreme Council of the Armed Forces attending a military show. Photograph by Amgad Naguib[6]

regime—itself an heir to thirty years of military rule in Egypt since 1952—and took on the responsibility of transitioning the country into stability. More specifically, and despite rising suspicion and ambivalence surrounding the evolving relationship between the ruling SCAF and the revolutionary forces, it will draw upon the concept of unity as it continues to be chanted through the slogan: *"al-Gish wa-l-sha'b id waHda"* ('The army and the people are one hand').

The Making of Unity

"Limadha ista'badtum al-nas wa qad waladathum ummuhatuhum aHraran?" ('Why have you enslaved people when their mothers birthed them free?')

The notion of unity at the level of new discourse created between the people and the army since the beginning of the January 25, 2011 events can be broached through what Roland Barthes calls "mythical speech":[7]

We are no longer dealing here with a theoretical mode of representation: we are dealing with this particular image, which is given for this particular signification. Mythical speech is made of a material, which has already been worked on so as to make it suitable for communication: it is because all the materials of myth (whether pictorial or written) presuppose a signifying consciousness that one can reason about them while discounting their substance.

With no fixity, myth becomes a malleable form, a mode of signification that can come, go, integrate, or decontextualize. It is a speech genre conveyed by a discourse to mediate particular messages. And in it resides a kind of tokenism—an effortlessness in establishing new possibilities for signification and exchange through banal actions—stratified in utterly familiar social orientation and dialogue, for they have been ostensibly taught/learned, and in turn, bank on being recognized.[8]

Where does myth fall into the establishment, reference to, or constant citation of unity between the people and the army? How do we choose to invoke popular characterizations of the army in certain moments and not others? And is such use of slogans, gestures, objects in line with the intentions of the protesters' aims or reflective of the convoluted discourse between the people and the army? How do such mythical signifiers lend themselves to the making or unmaking of unity in the context of the revolution?

The unity between the people and the army is directly tied with the conceptualization and instrumentality of this political entity as a national body. I cannot give a full historical account of the place of the army in popular imaginations, but one might still look to this discourse to understand the complex and ambivalent relationship between the people and the army. This unity, rather the intersection between civilian and military life, begins with Muhammad Ali's conscription of masses of Egyptian peasants to form his new army in the early nineteenth century.[9] The conscription of the army in Muhammad Ali's day was top down, which is quite contrary to the popular perception of the army as being comprised of forces from within. Since its inception, the army has been represented (and campaigned) as an interior institution of power extracted from and resonating with ordinary civilian life. Inherited from Muhammad Ali's conscription is today's draft system, which obliges every household with multiple male children to enlist their sons for service. In turn, a lineage with the army is created, making it difficult to not identify with its soldiers on a familial and social level.

Yet how is the image of the army soldier so close to home, so familiar, despite their visual absence from everyday life? Historical accounts of the army's evolution from a conforming body that exists to protect and sustain the imperial power to a resisting, anti-imperial force are vital to its characterization today. In prior revolutions and moments of popular resistance (1882, 1919, 1952), the army (an institution as well as a body of conscripts) is historically defined as liberator or savior of Egypt from corrupt rule, hegemonic dominance, and foreign invasion. Of course, that is not to say the army was involved as a leading actor in all these events, nor did all these events really have the removal of foreign dominance as their central theme. However, it is the army's process of conscription (in the early 1800s) and its centrality as a *national* defense force that give it such resonance of unity and belonging with 'the people.'

In 1882, Ahmad 'Urabi led a national rebellion against Khedive Tawfiq and European imperialism. Coming to prominence in 1879, 'Urabi was the first officer of Egyptian background to reach higher ranks of the modern Egyptian army created by Muhammad Ali in the 1820s.[10] He uniquely straddles a position of unity between people and army: a peasant from a wealthy rural background, who became an officer and later a revolutionary. 'Urabi can be seen as a prime example of the intersection between militarism and civility: He not only led the resistance against corrupt foreign powers, but was *of* the people. In collective memory, and especially under Gamal Abdel Nasser's (an army man also of rural background) rule, 'Urabi is regarded as a patriot and national hero, who through his revolt between 1881 and 1882 planted the seeds for the country's independence from imperialist forces (achieved through the 1919 Revolution in the early 1920s). The famous saying that opens this section is attributed to him in his confrontation with the khedive and the British occupiers and has become (especially through the *writing* and teaching of history in Egyptian schools) a household idiom against oppressive authorities.

Much like the 2011 uprising, the 1919 Revolution meant different things to different social and political groups in Egypt. For instance, 1919 marked a people's uprising, mainly led by national activists—elite students, peasants, workers, and merchants. After a two-year period of prolonged negotiations with the British, independence came to effect in 1922. Centered more around territorial nationalism and self-determination and less on transforming the social and class structure, the uprising is cited as the official *thawra* ('revolution') against British colonial rule. Although the army was not a leading actor in 1919, as it was still a force under British command, much of its foundation for the 1952 military coup d'état against King Farouk's corrupt monarchy—deemed a descendant of the Muhammad Ali dynasty (itself a foreign rule), an ally of the British and other imperial powers, and an aristocratic ruler not representative of the people—came from such nationalist discourse of resistance. With worldwide economic depression in the 1930s and a polarization of wealth and economic exploitation, student-, worker-, and peasant-led demonstrations began to spread. In 1952, Muhammad Naguib, Gamal Abdel Nasser, and a group of high-ranking military men known as the Free Officers capitalized on such popular resistance to carry out the revolution and overthrow the monarchy.

It is precisely through this period that one begins to understand the treatment of the army soldier as a type of celebrity. In photographs, songs, and films the army soldier is personified to strike the unusual balance between myriad, at times contradictory, qualities: revolutionary, fearless, fierce, gallant, yet handsome, refined, compassionate, poetic.[11] His image becomes engraved in collective memory as the star of Egyptian glory, the force that intersects (people and army, governed and governing), defends, and protects the nation.

Photograph of Gamal Abdel Nasser in a public parade, early 1950s. Photograph by Amgad Naguib

The Reappearance of the Army

"al-Gish wa-l-sha'b id waHda"
('The Army and the People Are One Hand')

In the context of the January uprising, mythical speech (for example, *"al-Gish wa-l-sha'b id waHda"*) is considered as one that cites, transports, or postulates past signifiers onto an unstable present, enabling their reappropriation by society. Throughout the revolution, time and history were inevitably conflated: the constant insertion of *past* feelings of apathy leading to a kind of present timelessness was shot through with uncertainty. In turn, the language of authority—that of the regime as a political structure that characterizes itself as patriarchal or almost parental,[12] commanding the protesters, in the words of former Director of General Intelligence Omar Suleiman: "Youth of Egypt, heroes of Egypt, go home and go to work so that we can build and create"[13]—was met with chants, gestures, and nationalist songs that translate past discourses of national identity and resistance in Egyptian history onto present moments.

This mythical speech concerning the army is one that was immediately revived in Midan al-Tahrir starting January 28, 2011.[14] The blasting of nationalist songs throughout the 2011 revolution can be read as a form of citation and revitalization of a historic alliance between the army and the people.[15] For instance, Abdel Halim Hafez's song "Hikayat sha'b" (The Story of a People)—originally written and performed in 1960 in celebration of the completion of the Aswan High Dam (itself a project that thrives on national unity)—was played and repeated throughout the 2011 demonstrations. The song essentially constructs a mythical narrative that intertwines the 'story of a people' and the story of its army with the late president Gamal Abdel Nasser as the ultimate bearer of victory and liberation. Joseph Massad analyzes the use of nationalist music in the context of the 1952 Revolution: "the role of the state in revolutionary Egypt was instrumental in the funding and support of song, especially through the new medium of state-owned television."[16] The lyrics and the video clip of "Hikayat sha'b" were and continue to be stunning in their ostensible praise of Nasser and *his* nationalist project to unite the Egyptian people as a self-determined, unified body that takes pride in its alliance with the Arab world against imperial forces of the west.

Imprinted in a collective national memory since the 1960s,[17] the significance of such songs' renewed appearance during the January 2011 uprising can be interpreted as a means of consolidating the mythical bonds between the army and the people. What might the nationalist songs of the 1960s and 1970s, now transposed to a very different political scene—that of popular uprising against an unjust regime—evoke? Not only do the lyrics of "Hikayat sha'b" represent the army as liberator, they depict it as the force that cleansed and purged the country of corruption: "we have overcome, we have overcome, we have overcome, the day the army rose up, the day we declared a revolution of light and fire, the day we ousted corruption, the day we achieved liberation from the occupier." Moreover, the army is characterized as a force seeking to restore ownership of the country to the people, symbolized here by the nationalization of the Suez Canal, '*ammimna al-qanah*,' articulated in the plural form of the verb, emphasizes the collective act of the army (represented by Gamal Abdel Nasser) and the people as one hand.

Another song by Hafez from the 1970s, "Sikit al-kalam" ('There is no more to be said'), romanticizes the soldier and the rifle along with the path of resistance the people and the army wrote unanimously as their destiny.[18] Once again, in the song the trope of unity or one hand (*id waHda*) is prominent for the lyrics give the rifle precedence over words; indeed, the rifle becomes the final word: "*Sikit il-kalam wi-l-bundu'iya itkallimit*" ('There is no more to be said; the rifle has spoken'). A recent exhibit titled "Dystopia" by Egyptian artist Nermine Hammam exceptionally portrayed the idea of the army as a silent force during the first eighteen days—besieged and besieging, innocent and godlike. Once again, the counterpoint to the innocence of the soldiers in Hammam's images (below) and the compassion she expresses toward them in her artist statement is the army tank, whose rotating turret and heavy gun were directed at protesters at all times. Duality, anxiety, and ambivalence were present from day one when protesters chanted in apprehension, "*Silmiya . . . silmiya*."

The sight of thousands of people chanting on January 28, 2011 "The army and the people are one hand" might have come as a surprise to a global spectatorship that had been anxiously watching the Egyptian uprising as it unfolded for three violent days. It may have been a surprise that countless demonstrators who had taken to the streets in the uprising were cheering the arrival of a military machine in full gear when they had just succeeded in taking over the contested and symbolic space of their freedom: Midan al-Tahrir (chapter 1). However, for the demonstrators, the slogan "*al-Gish wa-l-sha'b id waHda*" seemed to encapsulate and

Images from the exhibit
"Dystopia." Photograph by
Nermine Hammam

translate a long-standing relationship between the people and the army whose tanks and soldiers had just been stationed in various vital spaces in Cairo such as Midan al-Tahrir, the State Radio and Television Building in Maspero, and other public areas in the capital and around the country. The almost frantic reiteration of the slogan during the night of January 28, 2011 and well beyond the following months must therefore be read within a historical and symbolic context of the relationship between the two bodies in which the latter is considered family. Not to say that the Central Security Forces do not come from Egyptian families, but the army has historically been characterized as having protected the people against foreign enemies (see above section).

The insistence of establishing unity between the army and the people also reverberates with the notion of *"asham,"* which translates within Egyptian cultural contexts as a history of expectations—in this case, from the people of the army and vice versa. Such expectations have been made possible and generated through distant as well as recent collective memorialization and characterization of the status and place of the military institution within the Egyptian imagination. In the context of this relationship, the concept of *"asham"* becomes all the more complex and layered, for it is entrenched with uncertainty, desire, anxiety. Similarly, whether in the form of speech, gesture, or object, tokens of nonviolence and *maHabba* ('amiability') were time and again offered to negotiate a new relationship between the two bodies. As mentioned earlier, upon arrival in Tahrir on January 28, 2011, the trucks were flooded with more and more protesters clapping, singing, and greeting the soldiers coming from afar to investigate their circumstances. In this moment of ambiguity and while the position of the army was still unclear, protesters showered the officers with roses, Kitkat chocolates, hugs, and kisses—all of which

Egyptian army officers tearing an Israeli flag, date unknown. Photograph by Amgad Naguib

illustrated welcoming and celebratory customs.[19] Therefore, to say "the army and the people are one hand" is not simply a statement but an aspiration and an expectation grounded in prior significations and meanings.

Since demonstrators identified Mubarak, the old regime, and their security forces as no longer with 'us,' no longer of 'us,' they became outsiders. The deployed army force was interpellated by protesters as they hailed its personnel: a body recognized by many and differentiated by some as not having brutalized or forsaken them, but one that intervenes to halt violence and restore order, and in turn, remains of them, of their lineage.[20] As protesters chanted and pointed to one another *"Irfa' rasak fu' inta masri"* ('Raise your head up high, you're Egyptian') to claim the ability to redefine (almost authenticate) their identity as Egyptian and revive their sense of pride in it, they invited the army to become a pure vessel: one that fulfills their familial and political role in representing the people, in sharing their demands for justice and salvation. Soldiers were invited to stand along with 'the people,' to become redeemed and purified souls—no longer broken, succumbing to the callousness of the Mubarak regime had turned them into. And once again, so as to establish unity with a force identified as a 'redeemer' of sorts, the chant *"al-Gish wa-l-sha'b id waHda"* was repeated, intensified, even reduced to a commanding call: *"Id waHda, id waHda"* ('One hand, one hand').

Yet how did the army become a pure force or redeemer, especially in a space contaminated with corruption, abuse of power, and violence from internal security forces, to thugs,[21] to pro-Mubarak protesters—all of which, at times can be overlapping actors? As previously mentioned, in Tahrir, encounters between the people and the army became a temporary discursive space with its own lexis and copula of language that can join things together to sustain moments of exchange between the two bodies. But what happens when demonstrators, caught between past and future discourse, equally draw upon speech and gestures to combat unprecedented dominance by the SCAF? How are protesters to address the presence of 'the protector' well knowing that state security of all shape and form (central, intelligence, special operations, thugs) is mixed and brought to violently disband their demonstrations?

Although deployed by the Mubarak regime, somehow, and based on its past discourse of unity with the people, the army was identified as a force that should and must embody its role as an ally and protector of the people. In a striking contrast, the protesters mocked the CSF's retreat as they greeted the army: "*Yala al-'ar yala al-'ar . . . fat al-'askar khat al-nar . . . gum darabu 'alina Hisar*" ('Shame, shame, you brought us shame . . . the army soldier left the fire of the front lines to besiege the people'). Initially, the army soldiers stood in silence, reluctant to engage in verbal or physical exchanges with those interpellating them, serving their passive role as shields or symbolic referees between protesters and state security forces, between citizens and the regime.

This passivity can be understood in the army's visual absence from the streets (with the previously cited exceptions), which was consequential to Mubarak's ongoing restructuring of security forces in the last two decades, leaving matters of everyday order to the police and Central Security Forces—the former being more notorious for its brutality and uncontested corruption than the latter. Yet, such absence and infrequent encounters between the people and the army worked to preserve its conscripts' image in collective memory as the sons and fathers of families sacrificing everyday comfort and security for the sake of protecting and building the nation. And so, with the help of the eerie scene of large clunky tanks on the urban streets of Cairo throughout the events, soldiers became a somewhat supernatural force that may very well act as one with civilians and their resistance; if not protecting, then at the least shielding them from the violent hands of State Security Forces and Mubarak's corrupt allies. The populace's honoring of the imagined and often venerated heroism of the army was challenged by the appearance of soldiers as overwhelmed and disoriented young men—rife with inexperience, especially in dealing with the very public their institution is supposed to have protected and liberated.

After the initial encounter between the army and the people on January 28, 2011, these 'celebrities' seemed quite uncelebrated. Sitting atop their tanks for days on end, the young soldiers began to look like awkward and abandoned children overwhelmed by a sea of cheering demonstrators. The awkwardness may have been due to the context itself: military men in the heart of the city with strict orders of neutrality. The army had been mobilized to protect public institutions, not to protect the demonstrators or engage in any kind of action with or against them. With the long and difficult hours of January 28, 2011 that witnessed the looting of the Egyptian Museum and the burning of the National Democratic Party (NDP) headquarters, these soldier 'celebrities' looked worn out, hungry, exhausted, and embarrassed about their neutrality and their inability either to act or to respond to those around them. Timidly at first, then with more confidence and familiarity over the continuing days of the eighteen-day sit-in, some began to accept water, food, and flowers, and posed for photographs with demonstrators, who were indeed treating them like family.

In some ways, Hammam tests this familial connection in "Dystopia:" through her images, she transported soldiers to more friendly, uncertain, even absurd spaces almost reflective of their varying expressions throughout the events, and as she stated, "the mechanisms with which panicked teenagers deal with the multiple confusions of an uncanny world of consequential role playing and serious masquerading."[22] One can almost interpret such binaries as a dialectic between the making and unmaking of this relationship, its progression, and the ongoing negotiation between the two bodies as they encounter one another on the ground.

To be sure, there was the memory of the past moments of army deployment on the streets of Cairo discussed above, but there was also an understanding that these soldiers, who were sitting neutrally atop their tanks, obeyed orders from the new ruling entity SCAF, whose loyalty to Mubarak and his regime continues to be an enigma. By deploying the tanks and soldiers in the heart of Cairo and around the country, was the SCAF protecting the legitimate demands of the revolutionaries or was

Images from the exhibit "Dystopia." Photo credit left, Nermine Hammam. Photo credit right, Amgad Naguib

it protecting the interests of a counterrevolution? What did it mean for F-16 fighter jets to whip over Midan al-Tahrir in broad daylight with the square packed solid with demonstrators? What did it mean for protesters to be attacked on February 2, 2011 in what has come to be known as 'The Battle of the Camel' as the army stood in silence and neutrality? Inversely, what did it mean for these young soldiers to be in the midst of millions of potentially and justifiably angry protesters? To be caught in the crossfire between protesters and state thugs and still under orders to be neutral?

For instance on January 28, 2011, protesters descriptively chanted—without question, and in the form of contingency: "*Ya 'askari yabu bundu'iya, inta ma'aya walla 'alaya?*" ('You! Soldier with a rifle, are you with me or against me?'). Postulated in that moment was the general characterization of 'soldier' as armed with a rifle, applicable to all security forces that had indeed attacked and killed the demonstrators. And for the January 28, 2011 episode, a different kind of inquiry was made of the army soldier: will you be 'my protector' or 'my enemy'? The historical reference was subtle and fluid; to be manipulated by the tense present moment and the recognition of the rifle made violence apparent, confronting the soldier with it. Once again, "You!" here hailed the soldier, not as part of an army institution *(al-gish)* hierarchically distinct from the people *(al-sha'b)*, but as one interpellated subject juxtaposed with another—the citizen.

As events progressed and encounters continued, the chants of protesters seemed to reflect an increasing tone of apprehension, fear, and distrust (unlike the initial ones of urgency and willingness on January 28, 2011) over the continued attempts at establishing unity with the army. Soon after (and even during) the eighteen days, people began to reverse the initial greeting of the army as its leader and protector, "*al-Gish wa-l-sha'b id waHda,*" to "*al-Sha'b wa-l-gish id waHda.*" In the latter version of the chant, *al-sha'b* (the people) became the active subjects, preceding the army and conditioning or rather actualizing the notion of unity in relation to them. In some ways, this reversal can be seen as an unmaking or calling into question of this relationship between the people and the army. Albeit complex and rooted in particular moments of popular allegiance or a prior history binding the two bodies, the relationship is constantly shifting: while the army is viewed as "protector and liberator" or "of us, our family" by some, it is contested by others, who might characterize it as an institution of power—once supportive of the old regime, capable of perpetrating as much as protecting.

The Unmaking of Unity: Attacks and Apologies

"DiHku 'alina wi alu taghyir . . . Shalu Mubarak Hattu mushir"
('They tricked us and said change. . . . They removed Mubarak and put in a field marshal')

The popular discourse of unity that continued to bind the two bodies showed the relationship between the people and the army as contradictory, in flux, but necessary and more or less inescapable. It is interesting to note here that even the construction of both bodies is unfixed, relative, and needs ongoing translation: who was the body citing or invoking this unity—*"al-Gish wa-l-sha'b id waHda"*—on January 28, February 25, and April 9, 2011? Who attacked the protesters on March 9, April 9, and August 1, 2011? Who protected which groups on June 28, 2011?

After eighteen days of ongoing resistance leading to the ouster of Mubarak, a rupture occurred vis-à-vis the relationship and semiotic mediation (through speech and gesture as genuine sentiment or tactic) between the people and the army as *one hand*. On February 25, 2011, many witnessed army soldiers using force to disperse a protest outside of parliament against the new cabinet and in solidarity with Libya. Tanks were moving, soldiers were rapidly marching, and protesters were being attacked—punched, kicked, and clubbed with electric prods. And army soldiers were arresting and detaining protesters in high numbers. Here, a shift in chants, slogans, and gestures as well as the corporeal occurred in light of increasing violence, and the army, its soldiers, rifles, and tanks were no longer standing in silence as symbols of benevolence, as passive protectors or shields, but as threatening and combative ones. This was the first episode whereby the army used force and violence to disperse crowds of protesters. To some protesters, especially those critically using slogans of exaltation and shaming, gestures, and gifts as a tactic to establish unity, the army was showing its true colors, its malevolence.

The army was in an impossible position: it was supposed to be the protector and guarantor of the revolution, but at the same time the SCAF conditioned the official and permanent removal of revolutionaries so as to gain full control over the country's affairs. If soldiers were to keep their image as protectors, they needed to be protecting the people from something. What was that something? Two things come to mind: protection from thugs and protection from chaos. To many others at home and on the street yearning for stability, the protesters needed to stop demonstrating and let the transitional government—*Hukumit tasyir al-a'mal*—and the SCAF do their jobs. Stability is needed and the army is thought of as guardian of the revolution and its demands, as armor against 'counter-revolutionaries.'

And yet again on March 9, 2011, the rupture, the unmaking of this unity began to unfold all the more as the army attacked forcefully to disband protesters and later came to apologize. In Tahrir, many witnessed the destruction of tents, the removal of the martyrs' memorial, the disbanding of crowds, and the beating and expulsion of protesters by unidentified forces. A bit later, the uniformed army soldiers intervened, taking those remaining in the square to the Egyptian Museum to be interrogated, tortured, and detained by a variety of security forces. Prior to the army's intervention, who could have carried out such destruction and in what interest? Was it thugs or state security? Rumor and state television had it that those occupying the square at the time *were* thugs, not January 25 protesters. One cannot help but recall: somehow, plainclothed individuals removing and destroying tents combined forces with army officers to expel protesters and/or thugs from the square.

Once again, the myth was unmade and the spell of '*id waHda*' was broken, calling into question the very notion of unity, especially as army soldiers began to take on characteristics usually belonging to other state security forces of the Ministry of Interior: arresting, detaining, torturing, trying civilians, and issuing sentences (in this case under martial law) without investigation. The people and the army were no longer blindly cited as a single hand, and many began to separate the army from the SCAF. However, an ambiance of chaos and fear overtook many public spaces of demonstration across the country, and to many others unity was still not in question: the army (as a trusted, coherent institution still functioning to serve the people) must have been protecting people against 'thugs' and 'outlaws.' Besides, why were protesters still in the streets? Now that Mubarak is gone, let the army do its job and restore order, many said. It had been agreed that Issam Sharaf, the new prime minister, and his cabinet would have two weeks to meet some demands and prove their good intentions to the people. The SCAF had also ordered protesters not to sit in Tahrir, as their presence fostered instability, disrupted the order of everyday life, and inevitably harmed the economy.

The next day, the council issued a statement: "thugs" and "outlaws" have infiltrated the square; "we apologize for the violence used against civilian protesters; again, our reservoir of good deeds for the sake of the nation should compel you to trust and cooperate with us." Many staunchly refused to accept apologies for such violent attacks; they felt that ongoing pressure needed to be placed on the government and the SCAF until *real* changes were made and demands of the revolution were fully realized and achieved. In turn, demonstrations have been ongoing against corruption, passivity of the new government, lack of security presence in the streets, violence by Central Security Forces and the army; and in solidarity with Libya, Syria, Palestine, and Yemen. Such ongoing attempts by protesters have been met with threats from the council, indefinitely vowing to empty the square using "firmness and force."

We began to see a shift in this silent discourse when the SCAF, initially addressing the public (on television talk shows, the radio, the Internet, cellphones) with loving, comforting messages, became the same body that issued threats and warnings, inheriting the role of Ministry-of-Interior-like security forces. For instance, the council circulated the first of these messages (in the form of a text message) immediately after January 28, 2011 (the 'Friday of Rage'), addressing "honest and loyal men" to protect Egypt against "traitors." SCAF also launched a Facebook page dedicated to "the people, the honorable youth and martyrs" of the January 25 Revolution. In its first statement,[23] the council reasserted its proper role as protector of the people, disclaiming any political ambitions for power. It cited and banked on the reservoir of credit *(rasid)* and trust given to the army by the people for all their past victories and aims to liberate and protect the nation. In turn, the SCAF addressed the January 25 youth, asking them to trust and cooperate with its army as *dir' al-amn wa-l-aman* ('the shield of security and peace') by leaving Tahrir, in an effort to stabilize the country and preserve the interests of the people and the revolution.

Such forms of communication used by the SCAF began to show the banality of the institution. For one thing, this was the first time the army had communicated with the people, let alone in such an unusual method. For another, the ambiguity of the content—not making it at all clear who is "honest and loyal" and who is a "traitor" in this context—drove many to interpret the message as a sign of the army's alignment with the regime, especially coming at a time when the army had not made any clear statements as to whose side it was on.[24] For instance, upon announcing the council's sixty-ninth statement on July 23, 2011, General Mohsen al-Fangary warns the public of the rumors spread by protesters around the army's use of violence against demonstrators in "Ismailiya, Suez, or any other city."[25] What does it mean for the army to become a body that issues statements via Facebook, text messages, and talk shows? If it is a new discursive space, then they are creating new modes of signification. As previously mentioned, such signifiers are no longer banking on the reservoir of protection, the relationship of unity between the people and the army; instead, they are triggering a perception of governance. The army is no longer identifying itself as one with the people, but a body that reigns over them. In turn, unity is once again transformed or unmade, diffusing the mystique of the army as protector of the people . . . as one with them.

With growing distrust in the intentions and new place the SCAF is creating for the army in central political spheres, protesters returned to the streets of Tahrir on April 8, 2011 to demonstrate against army corruption (for example, the detention and torture of activists, abuse of women by mandatory virginity tests and detention, and military trials)[26] and the delays of the trials of Mubarak and his associates. The security forces attacked the overnight sit-in with over two hours of shooting. On April 9, 2011, uniformed defectors from the Military Police joined protesters who took to the streets the day before, reestablishing "*id waHda*" as a possibility with those who support and protect the people, those who are of the people.

The SCAF ordered the arrest of the defectors, bringing them before military court for trial. As for protesters, they vowed to continue demonstrating until the army's abuse stopped, and Mubarak and his family were brought to trial on corruption charges. Families and average citizens are claimed on popular talk shows to have demanded: "The chaos at Tahrir needs to stop, but the government needs to bring Mubarak's family to trial." This time and after encountering a discrepancy and challenge to its own institution, the SCAF did not cite the language of unity or its reservoir with the people; it unwaveringly responded that it would use "firmness and force" to clear protesters.

On June 28, 2011, protesters were demanding the rights of martyrs and their families; they were later severely attacked by the Central Security Forces. And on June 29, 2011, as the army stepped in to break overnight clashes between protesters, who were often accused of being thugs, and the Central Security Forces; the army was hesitantly greeted by some with "*id waHda*." In fact, many protesters were angrily chanting back: "*al-Sha'b yurid isqat al-mushir*" ('The people demand the fall of the field marshal [Tantawi]'). Protesters vowed to end police brutality, and promised the martyrs and their families that they will not be forsaken. They will not rest until accountability, justice, and retribution are achieved.

The shift in the SCAF's role is especially important in understanding the distinction between the army and the institution, as well as the ongoing challenge to the concept of unity. At first, the council appeared to be comprised of national superheroes with members like General al-Fangary saluting the martyrs on national television, and General al-Ruwaini standing among protesters in Tahrir on February 10, 2011, who had been patronized and threatened in the speeches of Omar Suleiman and Mubarak. However, as events continued to unfold, unlike the soldiers on the ground, the members of the council became largely inaccessible, especially Field Marshal Tantawi. While some members such as al-Fangary and al-Ruwaini were featured on talk shows such as Mona al-Shazli's "The 10 PM Show," and asked "if they are *real* people," they were still appearing as individuals representing the seemingly supernatural council. This shielded, rather distant form of appearance gave rise to a determinative moment at the discursive level between the SCAF and the army: while some members finally descended to earth, so to speak, as rumors

Protesters (in the form of 'asham) showing the army officers empty tear gas and rubber bullet canisters fired at them by the Central Security Forces. Photograph by Michael Kennedy

spread about their institution's intentions, people began to distinguish between the council as an entity and a power structure, on the one hand, and on the other, the soldiers on the ground as still 'their' army.

Conclusion

In April of 1824, a rebellion of thirty thousand men and women in Upper Egypt took place against the injustices of Muhammad Ali.[27] Newly conscripted Egyptian troops were deployed to quash the rebellion to test their loyalty to the pasha and their regiment. Many of the soldiers were from Upper Egyptian villages. While the new soldiers attacked, some joined the rebels, becoming defectors to be killed before the eyes of other soldiers. The rebellion was put down in two weeks, leaving four thousand people dead, and the newly conscripted army proved its loyalty and efficiency.[28] After all, they fought the rebels (some of whom were their own family members and neighbors) without question or hesitation.

Fast forward to April 9, 2011: soldiers were deployed by their institutional command to put down "a clash" between protesters (rebels) and security forces. Some joined protesters while others attacked. And the SCAF (the command) was merciless in dealing with its defectors, ostensibly teaching all soldiers a lesson: 'Dare not consider disobeying your command; you are now outlaws; you are no longer of us—this institution.' Yet, what conditions make possible such loyalty/disloyalty? How were the defectors deemed disloyal if they were enacting the slogan upon which the army was founded: 'of the people,' 'a single hand,'—"*al-Sha'b wa-l-gish id waHda*." Here, rhetoric is challenged by the lived: those soldiers deployed to attack fellow nationals are facing a crisis of some sort. Could it be one of recognition or of discourse?

How do we translate the use of slogans in simultaneous support and opposition to the army? Does mention or utterance here separate itself from conditions of its use? Are these conditions (their contradiction) performative or do they reflect the complexity of the relationship between the people and the army? If the aim is to meet the above-stated goals, why were protesters willing to engage violently with other security forces, but not the army—even though the latter is thought to either be passive or complicit in relation to violent acts and lack of accountability?

The army, its conscription, its engagement with and meaning to the people are all called into question, leading to the unmaking of unity between people and the army, and in some ways the varying perceptions of the army, despite violent encounters. Do the people (non-protesters and even some protesters) want to have a trusted loyal body on which they can depend or does the need for 'nonviolence' project this faith in the army? Furthermore, are protesters tapping into a reservoir of moments in collective memory whereby the army indeed acted as protectors so as to shame the new self-appointed body (the SCAF—citing itself as "redeemer" of popular credit and reputation) into protection?

The ongoing evolution of the army and the SCAF since January 28 signifies the following: an inexperienced military establishment, unfamiliar with the mechanics of civil rule, and uncomfortable with its role as the authority on matters of everyday life, especially when dealing with a continuously resisting and protesting public. As a pseudo-disciplinary institution turned sovereign, creating conditions for an indispensability typified by its unity with the people against the Mubarak regime, the SCAF is most concerned with order, or rather its ability to restore order at whatever cost. The SCAF's authoritative institutionalism hinders its ability to deal with ongoing demonstration and dissidence on civil matters without resorting to the uninhibited use of military order, policing duties, and violence.

I have spoken here about the chain of events since January 25, 2011 as ephemeral moments during and after the first eighteen days of the revolution. For instance, the January 28, 2011 encounter has given rise to a new discourse by which protesters can further differentiate the character of the army for future accountability and leveraging during moments of violence. Yet, the on-and-off presence of the army in the streets since January 28, ongoing expulsion of public demonstrators from Tahrir, and other encounters condition this kind of negotiation and leveraging. August 1, 2011 marked one of the most violent disbands by the army and the Central Security Forces of a public sit-in, which was calling for the rights of martyrs, political prisoners, and the restoration of civilian rule in place of "*Hukm al-'askar*" (reign of the soldier). It is then that Field Marshal Tantawi (visibly absent from the public sphere) finally appears to congratulate his troops on successfully occupying the square and ridding it of the demonstrators—whose status as revolutionaries has been slandered and revoked by the SCAF. Indeed, we can see how the slogan "*al-Gish wa-l-sha'b id waHda*" becomes a fetishized myth, as the notion of unity between the two bodies (people and army) continues to be annulled.

One cannot ponder semiotics and rhetoric without confronting the most recent, most violent set of attacks on protesters by army soldiers. On October 9, 2011 (known as the "Maspero Massacre"), the army fired live ammunition and deployed tanks at demonstrators marching against the destruction of the newly constructed Melibar church in Aswan, and the lack of permits given to the construction of churches countrywide. Over twenty demonstrators, predominantly Coptic, were killed and hundreds were injured. In an effort to silence the dissonant voices, army rifles were fired, and soldiers ran tanks over demonstrators, crushing skulls and pinning bodies to the ground.

Although the army had previously resorted to the use of force on February 25, March 9, and August 1, the magnitude and visibility of violence on October 9 were unprecedented. Not only did the SCAF audaciously claim (through reports on state television) that agents instigating violence infiltrated the demonstration, it called for an investigation against all who were involved directly, by way of incitement, or indirectly, in triggering the army to use force. Much commentary in private newspapers and talk shows labeled state television as "the broadcasters of the military, not the people." On October 10, 2011, many commented and chanted: "The credit that the military received from the people in Tahrir Square just ran out yesterday." Regardless of rhetorical debates over who instigated what, the SCAF appeared incoherent, unable to coopt or bank on its *rasid* ('credit') or unity with the people to legitimize its failure to transition the country to stability, reform, and nonviolence. It could also no longer straddle this unique position between militarism and civility vis-à-vis its unity with the people: voices and bodies were indeed silenced by the rifle.

Notes

1   The law was activated after the 1967 War and has been used by the Mubarak regime to suspend constitutional rights, any non-governmental political activity including protests, and to legalize indefinite imprisonment of individuals.

2   Although many believe the 1952 Revolution led by the Free Officers against King Farouk's monarchy to be a military coup, it is still perceived and cited in nationalist consciousness as the big revolution that freed Egyptians from foreign and corrupt rule. See Samia Mehrez, *The Literary Life of Cairo: One Hundred Years in the Heart of the City* (Cairo: American University in Cairo Press, 2011).

3   See James T. Siegel, *Fetish, Recognition, Revolution* (Princeton, NJ: Princeton University Press, 1997). The events offer "the possibility of hearing what had always been present but now seemed if not mysterious, at least intensely interesting" (Siegel, *Fetish, Recognition, Revolution*, p. 6). As events continue to intensify, language as a mode of communication and deliverance is controlled, used, and broken down. Bringing messages and stories (past to present) results in creating bound collective frames of unity leading to an uprising. Resulting from a history of hearing and overhearing, speech acts and gestures often conceptualize a reclaimed independence (from all that is alien) to an Egyptian origin that once fought colonialism, monarchy, and brutality. Throughout the three episodes, protesters seek to supplement these referents (subtle, hidden, muted) to *origin*, as they demand the removal of a corrupt regime, which already offers a kind of recognition (through past and present identification, diplomas, and passports). Recognition and identification achieved, crafted, and monopolized by the state, is desired, negotiated, and *rewritten*. To free their identity from the state and its monopolization, protesters awaken references that were not intended, from a prior place and time—what Barthes defines as a kind of mythical distortion of the real.

4   Timothy Mitchell, *Rule of Experts: Egypt, Techno-Politics, Modernity* (Berkeley: University of California Press, 2002).

5   Here, the process of translating is not literal, but rather to interpret the events while seeking to analyze a given meaning in a slogan or chant as different from its original use, its new form of citation and respective lexical features. To better grapple with these features, two analytic issues must be explored: the danger of interpretation here as reductive, and the relationship between speakers and language. If we were to interpret the citation of either past (as descriptive) or possible (as prescriptive) discourse in slogans and chants, we might consider translation here as an attempt to interpret and transfer intention and consciousness during moments of verbal or bodily exchange. See Jacques Derrida, "What Is a 'Relevant' Translation?" in *Critical Inquiry* 27, no. 2 (2001): 174–200.

6   The combining of text and image is done to offer the readers an emotive and sensory experience, following what John Berger calls "another way of telling." See John Berger and Jean Mohr, *Another Way of Telling* (New York: Pantheon, 1982). I do not offer the text and images as a re-creation of the experiences of the revolution but a different avenue through which the theoretical questions in the text might be

approached. Zooming in on particular events of Tahrir, theatrics is at the heart of creating this montage and its selection of frameworks. In some ways, I see its modes of storytelling and commentary as a kind of quotation from a contested reality. What is revealed in a photograph cannot easily lend itself to articulation. Nevertheless, photographs call for lexis: they are imperative, and as shot, snapped, or manipulated provide meaning to their object of production. Combining the aesthetic with the empirical here allows the two media to give an image distinction to a social function of interpretation and commentary; see Walter Benjamin, *Illuminations: Essays and Reflections* (New York: Schocken Books, 1968). In turn, the text is not describing the content of the photograph, but both forms can be seen as attachés to an alternative interpretation of the events in Tahrir, which were at times abrupt, disorienting, and ambiguous.

7   Roland Barthes, "Myth Today," in *Mythologies*, ed. and trans. Annette Lavers (New York: Hill and Wang, 1972).

8   M.M. Bakhtin, *The Dialogic Imagination: Four Essays*, ed. Michael Holquist, trans. Caryl Emerson and Michael Holquist (Austin and London: University of Texas Press, 1930s/1981). See also M.M. Bakhtin, *Speech Genres and Other Late Essays*, trans. Vern W. McGee (Austin: University of Texas Press, 1930s/1986); Ludwig Wittgenstein, *Philosophical Investigations* (New Jersey: Blackwell Publishing, 1953/2001).

9   Khaled Fahmy, *All the Pasha's Men: Mehmed Ali, His Army, and the Making of Modern Egypt* (Cairo: American University in Cairo Press, 2003).

10 Fahmy, *All the Pasha's Men*, p. 80.

11 Gamal al-Ghitani, *Hikayat al-gharib* (The Chronicles of the Stranger) (Cairo: al-Hay'a al-Misriya al-'amma li-l-Kitab, 1976).

12 See Mubarak's and Omar Suleiman's speeches throughout the eighteen days.

13 Reuters, "Egyptian Vice President Omar Suleiman Speech," February 10, 2011, http://www.reuters.com/article/2011/02/10/us-egypt-suleiman-speech-idUSTRE71990120110210

14 There is ephemerality to the events, a history (that is cited or invoked) to the establishment of new relations between the people and the army (Barthes, *Mythologies*, p. 121). It can be seen through the materials and modes of representation assimilated to language (photographs, songs, rituals, and objects) used to create a new discourse that negotiates the events (Barthes, *Mythologies*, p. 114). These materials are reduced to a

signifying function, endowing speech with a mythical form of signification, but not an active one that necessarily involves a kind of embodiment. For instance, a constant play on the meaning and function of language through the form of speech (slogan or song) or gesture defines this mythical speech, and the signification of its qualities, its values, and its intentions creates a locus of associative, spatial relations between the familiar and the uncanny (Barthes, *Mythologies*, pp. 118, 122).

15 "The weightlessness of a language that is severed from culture makes it less intimidating," offering an opportunity for a certain "excursion" with a new identity, authenticated through such colloquial or popular forms of speech (Siegel, *Fetish, Recognition, Revolution*, p. 15). This is precisely what I mean by citation: in *quoting* certain ideological and semiological language, speakers become characters in the story of speech, intending to signify a new form of political consciousness in establishing new relations (Barthes, *Mythologies*, p. 110). And knowledge in a given mythical concept "is confused, made of yielding, shapeless associations" at times inapplicable to a present context (Barthes, *Mythologies*, p. 119). Here, there is a difference between speaker and interlocutor as the original speaker becomes blurred in the process of revival of old discourse (that is, resistance) as a new one is created (Siegel, *Fetish, Recognition, Revolution*, p. 19).

16 Joseph Massad, "Liberating Songs: Palestine Put to Music," in *Palestine, Israel, and the Politics of Popular Culture*, ed. Rebecca Stein and Ted Swedenburg (Durham, NC: Duke University Press, 2005), pp. 175–201, especially p. 178.

17 Abdel Halim Hafez, "Hikayit sha'b," YouTube, http://www.youtube.com/watch?v=nof1vbCcJzU

18 Abdel Halim. "Sikit al-kalam," YouTube, http://www.youtube.com/watch?v=-6nleFSw3jI

19 Marcel Mauss, "The Gift: Forms and Functions of Exchange in Archaic Societies," in *Sociologie et Anthropologie* (Paris: Press Universitaires de France, 1950). Also see James T. Seigel, *Naming the Witch* (California: Stanford University Press, 2006), pp. 2–10. Although social reciprocity can be thought of in many ways, Marcel Mauss's notion of the gift is useful in thinking about the ways in which verbal and non-verbal exchanges renegotiate the relationship between social groups. In this context, the exchange of chocolates, kisses, roses, gestures (a protester's arm around the shoulder of a soldier) signifies, even performed an association: *al-Nas dul ma'ana* (these people are *with* us, and are on our side), responding to the speculation in the

chant: "*Ya 'askari yabu bundu'iya, inta ma'aya walla 'alaya?*" (You! Soldier with a rifle, are you with me or against me?). Yet the army officers mostly stood silent or unmoved in an effort to uphold their orders of neutrality.

20 The army's restoration of order has at times such as 1986 also depended on violence.

21 Mercenary-like or private security forces usually hired in an unofficial capacity by Mubarak and former National Democratic Party members to execute unlawful deals and interests at a distance from the state.

22 Nermine Hammam, *Dystopia*, artist's statement for art exhibit in Paris, July 2011.

23 Supreme Council of the Armed Forces, "Official Facebook page of the Armed Forces," Facebook, February 2011 to present, http://www.facebook.com/Egyptian.Armed.Forces?ref=ts&sk=app_4949752878

24 Walid El Hamamsy, "BB = BlackBerry or Big Brother: Digital Media and the Egyptian Revolution," *Journal of Postcolonial Writing* 47, no. 4 (2011): 454–66.

25 Supreme Council of the Armed Forces, "Official Facebook page of the Armed Forces," Facebook, Statement 69, July 23, 2011, http://www.facebook.com/photograph.php?fbid=244871462199777&set=pu.19111 5070908750&type=1&theater

26 See "Yawmiyat taHt Hukm al-'askar," August 29, 2011, http://tahrirdiaries.wordpress.com/; see also testimony about military courts on YouTube, August 11, 2011, http://www.youtube.com/watch?v=qXkZ jZTCcZY&feature=share

27 Fahmy, *All the Pasha's Men*, p. 95.

28 Fahmy, *All the Pasha's Men*.

8

Global Translations and Translating the Global: Discursive Regimes of Revolt

Sarah Hawas

In memory of Vittorio Arrigoni, and all the other martyrs,
who dared to stay human.[1]

In the months following Mubarak's resignation, a process of translation
has been occurring in which the temporal and cultural specificity of the
revolutionary moment in Egypt has traveled across the world to command the hearts and minds of non-Egyptians. This process connected
individuals across the world—who were protesting against union restrictions, austerity measures, job precariousness, housing crises, the financial
system, and the military-industrial complex—with protesters in Egypt,
articulating a politics of solidarity, recognition, and in many cases shared
class consciousness. Governments and international organizations, too,
have been engaged in a very particular process of translation, the invisibility of which, like the fabled invisible hand of the free market, is less and
less stable with every protest movement in the global north that actively
uses Tahrir as a framing device. This chapter seeks to examine with equal
interest what it means to think about—and, therefore, to translate—*revolution* in the twenty-first century. I am specifically interested in the way
certain representations of dissent, revolution, and the political travel (or
do not travel) at a 'global' level, and the multiple possible implications of
these processes. The chapter is divided into two parts: the first seeks to
examine the traveling representations of revolution at a consciously global
level, while the second seeks to examine the implications of the same at
the 'national' level, a category that is becoming increasingly unstable. I
argue that while protesters sought, from the very beginning of the uprising, to translate themselves to a global imaginary, they simultaneously

did so as an act of resistance to an essentializing impulse which would otherwise impose a specific translation (one of actuality, of homecoming, or of 'arrival') at the expense of new translations (ones of potentialities, ruptures, and dissonance) that might privilege process over inclusion in a preexisting narrative. Against prevalent narratives—which I variously refer to as mis- or distranslations—that construe the Arab Spring as a wave of 'pro-democracy' revolutionary movements, I argue that a truly revolutionary translation would seek not to communicate—or contain— elements of an uprising that are a priori intelligible on the world stage, but rather seek to reveal the potentiality for ruptures and new narratives that also capture a global imaginary in equal measure.

The global context of translation, as the global context of revolt, which framed the Egyptian uprising, is one in which texts themselves are read differently owing to the structural transformations of their production and reception. Under globalization, technological transformations affecting both space and time reduce the costs of communication, positing English as an international lingua franca while simultaneously creating a pressured demand for translation for the drastically sped-up circulation of information. Consequently, the speed at which restructured capital reproduces itself is such that translation becomes mechanized. From the instant, automated, and often user-generated translations of Internet pages to the ever-increasing sophistication of translation software, and the professionalization of translators for the reproduction of stock interpretations employed by the mass media, language is petrified into a communicative function drained of agency.

Especially in a postcolonial context, however, translation and the theories that inform it are laden with their own specific political challenges and cultural anxieties: translators are tasked with negotiating nation and nationalism, colonialism and its 'Others,' and the problematic stakes and possibilities of grappling with and translating (or not translating) subalterity.[2] These tasks are particularly compelling in the present political moment, in which neoliberal transfigurations and homogenizations of political and social subjectivity render translation increasingly invisible and seemingly redundant or otherwise underappreciated. At this juncture, we find that an occupation, role, or practice—that is, translation—traditionally regarded as arbitrary, mechanical, or otherwise derivative and therefore subordinate to more so-called 'original' cultural practices, becomes even more professionalized. It therefore also becomes more naturalized and, ironically, less visible and less critical. Neoliberal shifts to deregulated markets, expanded spatial and compressed temporal conditions of work, and short-term contracts breeding self-discipline and hyper-individualized entrepreneurship dissolve the boundaries of the nation-state—informalizing all sectors including cultural production, of which translation is an integral part—and, at the same time, conceal the labor of translation and its own autonomy, agency, and political choices in the reproduction of texts and other cultural artifacts.[3]

By focusing on a limited number of sites of translation, I seek to examine the ways in which the Egyptian Revolution has been translated at the global level and therefore *made intelligible* to global capital. By drawing attention to the particular teleologies that guide selected sites of translation, in which 'democracy,' 'secularity,' and 'sovereignty' come into play with no regard for the structural conditions of a global capitalist system, the object of my analysis, therefore, is partially to reveal the way in which contemporary structural conditions determine the ways in which we imagine—and then translate—revolution. I also attempt to examine some of those nodes of agency in which a politically committed translation can affect revolutionary potential itself. Sites of translation are variously nodes of familiarity or difference in which signification undergoes a challenge conditioned by the linguistic, cultural, and ultimately political realities specific to time, space, and place. I aim to theorize the political stakes inherent in the global project of translating the Egyptian Revolution, as well as the conditions of (im)possibility presented in the task of translating the *global* as an unstable social construct without universal currency. I argue that the process of translation continues to be instrumental in shaping the current political landscape within Egypt and without, and that the languages and registers that constitute this process can and should be situated politically in order to limit and subvert the universalizing impulse of 'invisible' translation. The impulse toward invisibility in the translation process is characterized by a desire to obtain fluidity, appropriating and naturalizing text from its source language to a target one. The tendency to search for—and find—the self in the Other is a classical gesture in translation, whereby the foreign is tamed and domesticated in terms favorable to the target language and culture, terms that proceed to penetrate their subjects and supposedly 'enrich' them with new signification. Moreover, translation—with all its violences—does not necessarily always and only take place between languages but also within them, between experience and memory. After all, modern languages are constitutionally unstable and guided by different hegemonic narratives that shape the register and referential world of any given speaker (or, for that matter, non-speaker). In a moment of revolutionary fervor, though, the impulse to read a particular notion of the political can often override the very political commitment that we imagine guides us to translate—that is, recognize and reproduce—texts, subjects, and events of any kind. We often gravitate toward the familiar and hence desirable, in the process silencing anything which is not, and dismissing its potential to challenge power and to do so effectively.

Against this approach, I seek to demonstrate both the nodes of familiarity in which resistance comfortably resides and travels across borders, but also the tensions that constitute the same forms of resistance, and which subvert the universalist assumptions of 'invisible' translation. I also argue that in the global translation of a revolution, the choice of territorializing signification (and therefore, essentializing it) cannot be but a violent act aimed at neutering and privatizing, to various extents, revolutionary desires and momentum.

Globalizing therefore depends on and requires the localization (or nativization) and containment of citizenship in the creation of the 'exceptions.'[4] By valorizing notions of fidelity and loyalty to an 'original' text, the present trajectory runs the risk of increasing invisibility, and this has the unfortunate consequence of displacing the social and cultural contexts that are inherently part and parcel of the translation process, at the levels of production and consumption. The task, therefore, is to insist upon a revised understanding of translation at the theoretical—or philosophical—level but also at the level of power and politics, so that the concerns of the translator bypass notions of language and linguistic difference and transcend concepts of register to enlist an ethnographic interrogation of discourse and ultimately ideology, teleology, and structural conditions themselves.

Gayatri Spivak, writing on the gendered politics (and the politics of gender) in translation, highlights the complex role of identity politics in contemporary translation work, particularly from postcolonial, ostensibly "dominated" languages into a dominant language such as English.[5] Contrary to what Lori Chamberlain has identified as an outdated fidelity complex privileging intimacy between the translator and the author—in an eroticized practice of protecting the potentially infidel female text—Spivak calls for an intimacy, indeed "submission" by the translator to the text itself, in an active effort to avoid the valorization of the native or indigenous.[6] Spivak recounts numerous illustrations of blind intimacy between translator and writer (in which the translator defers to the 'author' of the text, rather than to the text itself) that have occasioned the unquestioning reproduction of hegemonic subjectivity rather than a critical, political engagement with the text itself as subject, which would necessitate an intimate, virtually eroticized knowledge of the mother tongue which the 'author' herself might not betray. These are examples of the dangerous—or otherwise absent—use of ethnographic impulses to justify, legitimize, or otherwise make legible translations from the third world.[7]

The process of translation inevitably and necessarily involves a repetition and reinterpretation within a particular field, situating a particular text not only within a certain register but also within a wider semiotic field of consciousness: here, for example, 'Egypt' and 'revolution.' Just as we cannot speak of the events that took place in Egypt from January 25 until February 11, 2011 without attending to a discourse of 'revolution' despite structural arguments to the contrary, we are compelled to examine what was in fact revolutionary about these events, or in retrospect, not. This is a direct consequence of translation—not from a purely linguistic level, but at the semiotic level because language itself is the product of translation. To the extent that an act of protest seeks to translate political and social desires into structural reality, the language used seeks to effect the realization, or translation, of a potentiality into concrete reality. The act of cementing meaning and translation into a particular epistemology is by nature a failed experiment, as it only begs the translation of new sites and possibilities. I am therefore interested in examining both the stakes and possibilities of this process of reification, but also and at once its implications, that is, what potentials for meaning or being (non-being) are left out in the process of reinterpretation.

The centrality of a politics of difference to the translation process that I am practicing *and* proposing lies in the social reality of difference, whereby people paradoxically both fear and depend on difference. History and memory function in the creation of national identities—that is, imagined communities—through the usually failed or otherwise exaggerated performance of 'othered' language and culture.[8] Translation is thus pivotal to the generation of consciousness, national or otherwise. It is the process through which memories, histories, identities and social formations are transported and transplanted, and it is frequently in this process—of suspended subjectivity—that a subversive freedom beyond the nation-state is located. Jacques Derrida's famous rereading of the biblical story of the Tower of Babel proposes, among other things, much the same sentiment.[9] Treating the biblical story as the classical metanarrative, Derrida explores the origin of the multiplicity of mother tongues as a consequence of the imperial imposition of a singular language for all of humanity. As punishment, God subsequently makes impossible the singularization of a unique and universal genealogy, imposing instead both the necessity and constant impossibility of pure translation. This results in an anxiety surrounding the communicative nature (or lack thereof) of any text, but equally endows the translator with a duty and responsibility to engage the same.[10] Language, in the process of translation, can free us from the will of the nation-state, generating a borderland in which multiple desires can be constructed and in which the contours of language are stretched to reveal the inner contradictions and inconsistencies of the national claim to stability and cohesion. After all, translation does not merely take place from one language to another, but within language itself: between experience and memory.

Translating Empire from Tahrir to Tel Aviv

One of the most pressing demands in translating Egypt's Revolution is the reproductive temporal and geographical aspect of these events and their framing. As historians, translators, and critics we are already complicit in the structural management of a political movement under the false dichotomy of the sovereign nation-state versus the world. What, indeed, did it mean that "*al-sha'b yurid isqat al-nizam*"? Which *nizam* was under attack, and how is it challenged—or not—by the continued uprisings? Already, translation issues arise. *Nizam* can variously translate to 'system,' 'order,' 'regime,' or all three at once. Where does a domestic system of government begin and end, and how do we think of this differently from a global political order, and how can we separate any of these things from a prevailing superstructure and *way of life* against which the vast majority of Egyptians fought and which many continue to resist?

The 'Arab Spring' is in large part a global construct that has been translated by regional Arab media outlets to refer to the various uprisings at large. However, insofar as 'Arab Spring' is a naming tool, it is also a way of compressing and managing the anxieties of regionalism and its opposites, reflecting an ongoing mistranslation of sociopolitical movements into the prepackaged historical narrative of the 'Prague Spring' and the fall of the Berlin Wall, respectively bookending the popular unraveling of the Eastern Bloc and the end of the Cold War.

In contemporary teleologies of the political, the conflation of political liberalism with economic liberalization is a necessary and inevitable consequence of neoliberalism and the subsumption of both the social and the political. Its transposition, however, in this case also marks the Arab world as an exception to an otherwise advanced stage of modernity. Alternatives to the present regime of globalization are immediately non-translatable owing to the hegemonic discursive hold of a particular—and inevitable—understanding of globalization, tied intimately as it is to free markets. As Saroj Giri writes, "Even leaders and ministers do not really need to *believe* in neoliberalism, in capitalism or anything else. They just need to submit, or so the story goes, to the 'realistic objective workings' of the market and economy. Politics itself is declared over."[11] Democracy is translated unequivocally in the image of a historical imaginary in which a kind of collective amnesia paves the way for a procedural performance of the 'political' without paying any heed to the structural conditions of global capitalism.

In the case of Egypt, US and other western media, along with academics and civil society at large, entertained the performance of this particular revolt and engaged in their own particular translations, employing a politics of the intelligible to translate and in doing so, domesticate or adopt the revolution, through particular nodes of familiarity at the global level. 'Politics of the intelligible' means here the translating into a preexisting imaginary of what constitutes the political or actual, rather than allowing for the translation process to open up new potentialities.

With Obama's second speech as representative of the much-too-late reading of the Egyptian uprising, and by quoting the word '*silmiya*'—Arabic for 'peaceful'—he also goes out of his way to valorize a false image of indigeneity, selectively choosing what to translate, foreignizing it, and allowing the aforementioned familiar agents to be his source texts. Obama's translation—and the many that followed—of an indigenized *silmiya* as a universal principle upon which the legitimacy of any political movement must be founded completely misreads the fact that *silmiya*—chanted repeatedly by protesters in the early days of the demonstration when confronted and corralled by Central Security Forces—is and was used as a tactic, not a principle.

Much gets left out of the translation—specifically, the multiple layers of subaltern narrative in which the uprising was anything but peaceful, in a thoroughly violent context of protesting against a regime willing to use live bullets (most of which are manufactured and paid for by US corporations, and donated as part of US financial aid packages). Likewise, the hundreds upon hundreds of dead martyrs and their families, who would go on to become mascots of liberation, regularly threatened with violence from thugs hired by former and current Central Security Forces, are nowhere to be found in that translation. It also fails to convey the capital strikes made against the Egyptian people through the closure of banks. This translation does not acknowledge the withdrawal of the police or what came to be known as the 'Battle of the Camel,' which resulted thugs were unleashed to assault protesters in the Tahrir encampment, silently observed and sanctioned by the military troops deployed around the square. The translation above does not recognize their attempt to terrorize neighborhoods into adopting pro-stability positions, which would then be used to police other Egyptians away from Tahrir Square. Finally, the nationwide blackout of Internet and telephone services, and much, much more violence that would follow in the months ahead, are also not translated through the above interpretation of events.

As Rabab El-Mahdi writes:

In the case of Egypt, the recent uprising is constructed as a youth, non-violent revolution in which social media (especially Facebook and Twitter) are champions. The underlying message here is that these "middle-class" educated youth (read: modern) are not "terrorists," they hold the same values as "us" (the democratic West), and finally use the same tools (Facebook and twitter) that "we" invented and use in our daily-lives. They are just like "us" and hence they deserve celebration.[12]

Punctuating notions of nonviolence are, as El-Mahdi points out, certain conceptions of modernity. Underpinning all of these translations, there is the assumption indeed that not only was this *thawra sha'biya* (a popular revolution) but also and especially a *thawrit shabab* (a revolution of the youth). In a country where the youth constitute over half the population, the Mubarak regime's policies impacted everyone equally, with the exception of the very rich. This should not be conflated with the images of modern civil disobedience that El-Mahdi rightly criticizes. Yet even if smart phones are not yet the privilege of the majority, the Internet—not just as an instrument of organization, but as consciousness itself—reaches most, in part constituting a truly unprecedented decentralized, leaderless, and popular revolution. The common translation has tended to be one in which the "youth" are posited a priori as global participants, in contrast to previous generations, rather than simply a dispossessed demographic majority that dares to imagine radically different paradigms for change.

The liberal winds of change were by no means confined to the borders of Egypt. Let us briefly examine the case of Amina Arraf—the fictional persona behind the "Gay Girl in Damascus" blog, who would later turn out to be Tom MacMaster, an American based in Edinburgh.[13] Mona Anis, in her *Al-Ahram Weekly* column, addresses the interface of transnational human rights agendas with the manufacturing of xeno-phobia resulting in the legitimization of Arab dictatorships.[14] This analysis is rightly wary of western agendas of homonormativity.[15] Maya Mikdashi is more concerned with the embeddedness, within prevalent transnational human-rights regimes, of transnational lesbian gay bisexual transgender (LGBT) discourse—what they variously refer to as pink-washing in hegemonic liberalism, with the implications of a western LGBT agenda—specifically one which inflates the "threat of Islamism" to similarly cement western hegemonic control over the region and stunt revolutionary desires. While these analyses are accurate in their articula-tion of how rights-based regimes—particularly those based on personal rights—are not only complicit but in fact symptomatic of imperial con-trol, they nevertheless participate in the reproduction of progressively "queered" bodies, albeit ones whose identities (as queered bodies) should not trespass or limit their belonging to a community undergoing real and very serious structural repressions, both racial and economic.

Missing from Mikdashi's analysis, however, is an appreciation of the epistemological violence at the heart of notions of sexual identity. Here, Joseph Massad's work[16] is instrumental: he has shown how—building on Foucault's thesis that sexual identity, indeed, sexuality itself, was invented in Europe over a century ago as a biopolitical vehicle of control—sexuality in the Arab World was similarly constructed as identifying episteme par excellence to map, control, orient, and repress Arab desires and practices. Massad further demonstrates the role played by translation—particularly in the rewriting of Arab history and social science—during the Nahda, or Arab Renaissance, at the turn of the century, otherwise known as the liberal age, which was spearheaded in Egypt. Queer politics is itself the most recent identity-based discourse to occupy a place in internationalist literature on the Middle East, particularly in response to Israel's pink-washing campaigns. The underlying logic is that by adopting a politics of solidarity under 'queer,' activists bypass the heteronormative function of mainstream LGBT discourse both in the US (its home) and abroad, reclaiming 'queerness,' under the umbrella of LGBT existence, and reconfiguring it in radical opposition to Israeli apartheid and its imperial context, rather than an instrument thereof. Knowingly, at best these activists and their allies deliberately universalize queerness as a challenge both to instrumental homonormative assemblages as well as the allegedly heteronormative function of anti-colonial resistance. In doing so, activists overstate the universality and alleged symbolic capital of queer identification by dispensing first with a historical understanding of queer epistemology,[17] and secondly, with a practical understanding of gender as process and performance, and not static identity. The practice of labeling—that is, regulating—is inherently fraught with problematic power dynamics that are historically rooted in racist, colonial mechanisms for mapping and policing social behavior. Sexual identity must therefore always be understood as originating in its own particular historical and geographical context. The a priori translation of sexuality as sexual identity, be it queer or otherwise, is itself part of a larger project of rendering intelligible, and visible, that which is not and need not be so.

At the heart of the Arraf case was the blogger's professed love for fantasy and fiction. Indeed, by writing the blog—and gaining an eager following composed of spectators and journalists alike—MacMaster indulged in the classic fantasy of most liberals: a young, good-looking, moderate Muslim homosexual female with perfect English communicated via the Internet to the world not only her desires for the anti-Assad uprising to succeed, but also her father's solidarity and protection of her, and what's more, the embodied potential of a demilitarized and impotent state apparatus that could be shamed into ceasing their violent arrests. This fantasy posits Arraf—with all the aforementioned attributes—as the 'woman who needs saving,' par excellence. Indeed, it makes the Syrian uprising—and the Arab Spring at large—*intelligible* to a particular sensibility. While Mikdashi covers most of this well, she insists on adopting the subjectivity of "progressive queer" as the opposite of comprador native informant, but meanwhile reifies a seemingly inevitable corruption of the translation process, putting forward the false notion that *translation need necessarily be about communication*. The epistemic violence incurred in the process of translating so-called 'non-normative sexuality' to 'queerness' or the qualified 'progressive LGBTs' or any other subjectivity cannot be underestimated, for it does a great disservice both to the aforementioned history, signification, and cultural economy around 'queer' (and similarly, LGBT) as well as those of 'sexuality' itself. A truly emancipatory politics must recognize first and foremost the role of power and privilege in the permission to speak and thus the formulation of a particular social subjectivity that carries symbolic capital, but would also then proceed to acknowledge these subjectivities as products and progenitors of a relatively recent form of capital flows named variously 'globalization,' 'late capitalism,' or 'neoliberalism.'

But so are there other translations of the global. Labor union organizers, workers and teachers went on strike in Wisconsin shortly after Mubarak's ouster, carrying signs that read "Walk Like an Egyptian."[18] Echoes of Tahrir Square were distinctly articulated by the anti-austerity movement in Syntagma Square in Athens,[19] and in Madrid, Spain, where the same tropes (youth, precarity, unemployment, the economy) were heard and protesters self-consciously drew comparisons to the Egyptian and Tunisian revolutions.[20] Meanwhile, Tahrir-inspired uprisings raged throughout the Arab world, and met with considerably different translations.

Most compellingly, Israeli society has not been immune to the economic grievances sweeping the world's populations.[21] Beginning on July 14, 2011 a steady stream of mass demonstrations—which came to be known as the J14 Movement—occupied cities all over Israel proper, in a display of social struggle unprecedented in the history of the state's existence. From the very earliest days of the J14 movement, protesters consciously and visibly chose to translate their demands in the language of Tahrir, much to the chagrin of many Egyptian activists, who used social media to disavow the demonstrations in various ways.[22] The demands of the Israeli protesters, after all, have centered on largely bourgeois economic concerns, in particular the suffocating costs of living and housing, and the shortage of affordable housing in any of the major cities. Little mention has been made in mainstream coverage of any conscious politicization of the protests with respect to Israeli occupation of the West Bank and the Golan Heights, as well as the siege on Gaza. In fact, the leadership of the movement has been so sensitive to the historically divisive topic of the occupation that the majority of protesters, centered at the heart of Tel Aviv on Rothschild Boulevard, insisted on avoiding a confrontation with the state, limiting their demands to tangible socioeconomic deliverables rather than making an explicit connection between economic disposses-sion and the continued colonization of Palestinians.

In emphasizing a movement for social justice, the protesters appear to reify the very particular nature of the Zionist social compact, which depends on cohesion and, as Defense Minister Ehud Barak would later put it, upholds that "life itself precedes quality of life."[23] Having been boy-cotted by the right-wing populist Tea Party-style Im Tirtzu movement, the J14 protesters, clamoring for mass approval and support, resurrected as a unifying mascot of Israeli identity and social cohesion the figure of Gilad Shalit, a single soldier abducted by Hamas, reaffirming the Zion-ist narrative in what Max Blumenthal and Joseph Dana would go on to describe as a consistent "cognitive dissonance."[24] Yet, despite the familiar and surreal racist paradigms governing much of the movement, it has vis-ibly and regularly translated—or otherwise borrowed or derived—many of the signs, slogans, chants, and songs from Egypt first and foremost, and much more so than from the 'Arab Spring' at large. It therefore has selec-tively and consciously chosen to translate the Egyptian uprising in terms of social justice. Ironically, this contains immense revolutionary potential, as it reintroduces class consciousness in the rewriting of a new narrative that breaches Zionist hegemony, drawing closer, as it does, to the intra-Jewish function of racism that threatens the hegemonic narrative of the early Israeli state.[25] Meanwhile, the heated process of translation that has taken place over the last several months in Egypt has been one in which the over-politicization of the 'democracy' complex by political elites came at the expense of widespread contempt for social struggle and efforts by the same bourgeois process of co-optation to neuter their divisive realities.

The translation process that took place between Tahrir and Tel Aviv, and which continues to guide protest movements the world over, is emblematic of precisely the kind of *potentiality* that confronts any politically committed translator.[26] The contemporary nature of revolt, given the multiplication in conditions of precarity and dispossession, but particularly in a context of solidarity and recognition across such uneven territory as Egypt and Israeli-occupied Palestine, is such that it posits itself as open, and as the agents of dissent respond to oppression in those terms most tangible to them, so the interface between language and signification becomes visible. Translating the Egyptian Revolution across time and space therefore requires an interrogation of what constitutes the very notion of the political, and with that, questions of statehood and sovereignty.[27]

Translating Sovereignty Between the Secular and the National

What is at the heart of geographical abstractions that discriminate between the 'social justice' protests of Israel's J14 movement and the heavily politicized imaginary of the Egyptian Revolution? What leads us to frame our readings of dissent in terms of the 'internal' and 'external,' the political and the social, and the 'national' versus the 'global'?[28] How useful is the concept of the 'nation' as a mobilizing force, and what is the nature of this subjectivity in relation to the state? What are the limitations to translating the national as a site of resistance, and how do we variously translate 'the state' as an object of the political?[29] Two sites of translation in the context of the ongoing Egyptian uprising are particularly illustrative of these tensions: the debates around 'the secular' and those around 'national interest.'

Narratives of secularism and secularity (or, indeed, *secularizing* narratives) in the contemporary political moment in Egypt need to be explored in light of the translation process in order to explain and account for multiple political imaginaries that orient themselves around 'the secular' and which have been and continue to be produced, developed, and deployed throughout the ongoing Egyptian Revolution. Categories such as 'Islamism' or 'secularism' are constantly malleable and contingent on very specific narratives, as are their multiple attendant subjectivities. The contours of these imaginaries are not always divorced from official discourse, and are almost always bound to internationalist discourse. Like terrorism, secularism appears to be without opposite, and yet this somehow functions as a point of strength, dehumanizing other ways of being.[30] In the neoliberal moment, and particularly when both state and citizenship are less than static or known concepts, 'to be secular' is to enter an aggressively globalizing imaginary whose constituents include, but are not limited to: cosmopolitanism, multiculturalism, diversity, democracy, pluralism, co-existence, and most intriguing of all, *tolerance*.[31] The secular being is variously construed as a progressive subject, modeled after urban, modern, and capitalist ideals, while the debates around the secular—or civil—character of a state as opposed to a religious—specifically Islamic— state are mistranslations of a much more complex reality in which the chief antagonism has been one surrounding the structural integrity and meaning of a democratic and sovereign state in the twenty-first century. By transliterating Enlightenment concepts into the present political moment in Egypt, reactionary discourse dispenses with any kind of material, class-based analysis rooted in the present, in favor of a series of abstractions. On the one hand, the brand of cultural and moral anti-imperialism brandished by the Muslim Brotherhood posits itself as the cultural guardian of Muslim populations, thereby divorcing itself from the structural realities depriving those populations of self-determination or enfranchisement, and on the other hand, liberal political opposition orients itself toward the 'secular,' 'civil' state as the sole political imaginary for progress and democratic practice, equally blind to the realities of postcolonial statehood in the neoliberal moment and in denial of its complicity in maintaining the material, structural limitations to political participation.

An examination of the secular as a site of mis- and distranslation therefore begs the question of *who are the translators and readers* participating in this project and, on the other hand, *who does not* participate in this discourse and therefore becomes merely an object of its interpellation in a highly specific and profound *incitement to discourse* rather than a cohesive and stable hegemonic universe. I argue that secularism, in its multiple negotiations, is variously a fundamental tool of orientation toward a specific construct of the 'global' and therefore a highly potent mechanism of depoliticization and ultimately subjugation. Its potency lies in the fact that it is a myth. Frequently, the 'secular' (like the 'moderate Muslim') does not exist outside of an imagined containment of 'extremism' and 'intolerance'; in other words, Al-Qaeda-style tendencies in the Arab-Islamic imaginary. This normative discursive translation has attained the power of a myth, which is repeated so often it becomes empty of signification, and yet manages—through its prolonged life expectancy— to reify itself at every political juncture.

Indeed, since Mubarak's departure, the acting leadership of the Muslim Brotherhood, the internationalized signifier of Islamism par excellence, has formed a close alliance with the ruling Supreme Council of the Armed Forces (SCAF). On the one hand, this alliance has allowed the SCAF to access a broad and deep grass-roots network of influence and consent. At the same time, the intersection of the interests of the leadership of the Muslim Brotherhood and the military institution has surfaced in their joint campaign to outlaw protests and labor strikes and to morally shame Egyptian society into obedience. The earliest symptom of this alliance was evident on March 17, 2011 during the constitutional referendum's voting process, in which members of the Muslim Brotherhood and resurfaced Salafi activists all but coerced a large percentage of the voting population to vote in favor of the amendments rather than against them (the latter of which would have otherwise led to the dissolution of the constitution, postponement of parliamentary and presidential elections, and the establishment of a thoroughly new constitution).[32] But it is the widespread contempt displayed by the Muslim Brotherhood's leadership for ongoing protests and for the labor movement in particular that illustrates their political and economic investment in the state, having regularly discouraged and mostly boycotted sit-ins and actively supported the SCAF's criminalization of protests and strikes.[33]

By translating dissent in economic terms, both the self-identified Islamist vanguard and the ruling SCAF perform the edicts of neoliberal capital, variously supported by the United States government, Saudi Arabia, the World Bank, and the IMF. Indeed, the discourse of *'agalit al-intag*—that is, the wheel of production—coupled with the proliferation of fears and anxieties concerning sovereignty and national security, have historically been the two most notorious pillars of Mubarak's regime, which presided not only through rigged elections but equally through the demonization and *takhwin*—(the charge of treason)—of political opposition. The biopolitical force of millions of Egyptians mired in urban poverty, vulnerable to state propaganda about "economic consequences" and the sovereignty of the Egyptian military—which occupies a cherished place in popular Egyptian memory—has translated repeatedly into divisions within the revolutionary movement as well as the generation of a definitively organic pro-stability movement that would later take it upon itself to literally police the Egyptian street and neuter dissent.[34] The 'wheel of production' must therefore be translated not only as the legitimate and natural concern of the masses of working people who depend on daily wages, but also as the fetishization of normalcy, stability, and indeed the status quo, all in a moment of revolution, of confrontation with structural injustice, and class struggle.

In tandem with the 'wheel of production,' *fulul al-nizam* ('remnants of the regime') emerged in the early weeks following Mubarak's departure.

Students and faculty occupied the campuses of public universities and hundreds of workers began to organize to resume or prepare for multiple strikes. These activists insisted on the cleansing of all institutions, academic and otherwise, from the control of administrators with close ties to the regime. In contrast, the less ambiguous *rumuz al-nizam* ('symbols of the regime') refers to ousted politicians and business owners, whom the movement deemed must be held accountable. The former, *fulul*, is a more general reference to bureaucrats, administrators, managers, university deans, and editors-in-chief, whose corruption and exploitation were characteristic of the environment created and upheld by Mubarak. It is no wonder, then, that it would come to accumulate symbolic capital among everyone who sought to change the prevailing code of conduct—in which bribery, thuggery, and 'might-is-right' reigned freely—and therefore become a moralizing force on its own. Indeed, as with the overused term *baltagiya* ('thugs'), the term *fulul* has been abused by anyone who wishes to delegitimize the presence of certain actors. In this way, state media would discourage people from joining protests by associating them with the presence of thugs, a mystifying term that came to denote everyone from paid infiltrators to street children and street vendors.

An open-ended sit-in was launched on July 8, 2011 to demand prompt trials for Mubarak and other *rumuz* and the immediate enactment of measures to curb social inequality, such as the institution of a legal minimum wage. Protesters fought hard to dispel the myth of the *baltagiya*, but were in turn met with the equally disturbing discourse that identified them as *gawasi*s ('spies') and *'umala* ('foreign agents'). In late July 2011, the SCAF released a communiqué that specifically targeted the April 6 Youth Movement for agitating against the military. The tone of the communiqué rapidly devolved into accusations, claiming that activists were serving foreign agendas and therefore represented a potential threat to Egypt's national security and sovereignty. Meanwhile, an increasingly enraged pro-stability movement named Asfin Ya Rayyis ('We Are Sorry, Mr. President') became visibly organized in response to the continued sit-in. Members of this organized group would go on to kidnap Amr Gharbeia and accuse him of espionage.[35] (Gharbeia is a popular human rights activist and researcher with the Egyptian Initiative for Personal Rights, and formerly with Amnesty International.) He was kidnapped while participating in a march through Abbassiya toward the Ministry of Defense on July 26, 2011, a march that intended to provide its own translation of cultural and historical memory in celebrating the 1952 Military Coup under Gamal Abdel Nasser by exacting its own revolutionary demands and pressures on the same institution. After being captured, Gharbeia was paraded around the street for a short time, while his captors chanted "Here is the spy! Here is the spy!" before driving off to hand him over to the first in a series of different authorities.[36] One of his captors would later announce in a televised phone call with a popular talk show host and commentator that "the Egyptian army is a red line," a trope that has been echoed by a seemingly countless number of the ruling military's loyal supporters throughout the last seven months.

What this incident exposed, in contrast to the discourse surrounding *baltagiya*, was the willingness of the regime to arouse dangerous suspicions and disseminate harmful accusations that would prey on the nerves of the most vulnerable members of society and coalesce with the interests of a ruling class deeply experienced in crowd control, thereby wrenching society apart. But what it also reveals is the role of translation in the creation and maintenance of a permanent crisis of authenticity in order to regulate authorship and therefore, citizenship. Indeed, the construction of xenophobic fears has been the most tried and tested tactic of regime control under dictatorships. Just minutes before the kidnapping of Gharbeia, the Asfin Ya Rayyis movement posted a composite photograph on their Facebook page in which a real photograph of Gharbeia was juxtaposed with a photograph of Ilan Grapel, an Israeli-American arrested weeks earlier and charged with spying for Israel, and in which Grapel posed next to an individual with features similar to Gharbeia's. The captions on the photograph alleged that the person posing with Grapel was Gharbeia himself. The photograph circulated virally, reaching millions of Egyptians over the following twenty-four hours. The case of Grapel's arrest and charges is itself reminiscent of an antiquated regime tactic that has for decades legitimized a state of emergency.[37] It is no wonder, then, that when the Asfin Ya Rayyis movement opted to enhance the military's chauvinistic tone, they resorted to inventing associations with the accused Israeli-American.[38] It is in this context that a military institution, which is heavily subsidized by the United States, enters into an alliance with a sociopolitical movement largely populated by businessmen with close financial ties to Saudi Arabia, and both proceed to articulate sovereignty (and, it follows, legitimacy) in terms of economic stability and national security.

Similarly, let us look at the discursive management of the plans to commemorate Nakba Day on the weekend of May 15, 2011. Though by no means signifying grass-roots organization, popular consciousness in the months following Mubarak's ouster was definitively oriented toward regional events, and regular—though by no means consistent or popular—protests took place outside the embassies of Libya, Syria, Yemen, and Bahrain to establish solidarity with other Arab uprisings. Indeed, Nakba Day was marked by a mass reoccupation of Tahrir Square in a colorful performance of solidarity and memory to confirm popular commitment to the Palestinian cause and to pressure the Egyptian government to abide by its promise of—and expose its lies about—opening the Egyptian–Palestinian border crossing at Rafah.[39] That is, until some activists dared to journey to the border itself. Though many of the activists reached the border and even camped out there in order to assert their demands, many were also prevented from reaching the crossing and were confronted by the Military Police and Central Security Forces before reaching Ismailiya.[40] The resulting state narrative insisted that activists were undermining Egyptian sovereignty and national security, despite the fact that it is the Camp David Accords and the prevailing peace treaty between Egypt and Israel that has legally prevented the Egyptian military from having any substantive presence in Sinai. Even more interesting was the state's reaction to a mass protest staged outside the Israeli embassy that same weekend, in which over three hundred people were arrested, and dozens more seriously injured by the Military Police. This event was promptly narrated by state media as an attempt by the Central Security Forces to prevent protesters—often dubbed *baltagiya* as well— from declaring war on the state of Israel by removing the Israeli flag. In keeping with the SCAF's first and foremost reassurance to the international community, that the peace treaty with Israel would remain untouched, the ruling council proceeded to defame and demonize popular will and alienate pro-Palestine activists by describing them as a menace to national security. It is notable that the Egyptian military has since been deployed in Sinai, in numbers unprecedented in the Camp David era, only to stem the rising tide of allegedly Islamist-led armed resistance among Bedouin communities, who have succeeded in bombing the Egypt–Israel gas pipeline at least ten times as of the time of writing.[41] It is also interesting to note, however, that several months later, when the Israeli army shot dead five Egyptian army conscripts in Sinai, triple the number of Nakba protests laid siege to the building housing the Israeli embassy in Cairo. An unlikely hero, later dubbed Flagman on social media, succeeded in scaling the building to remove the Israeli flag, burn it, and replace it with the Egyptian flag.[42] The Israeli flag was restored to the embassy within two days' time, along with a new wall built to protect the compound. A few days later, protesters spontaneously dismantled the wall and raided the embassy, sending the Israeli diplomatic corps, along with Israeli workers from Delta Galil (a QIZ company) fleeing the country; the emergency law was reinstated.

If the disguise of national security to protect US and Israeli interests and the defamation of the April 6 Youth Movement and various activists engaged (and in many cases, entangled) in transnational human rights regimes should come as no surprise at the hands of a state whose illegitimacy and increased lack of sovereignty have become fully visible, then even more intriguing was the tirade performed by General Hassan al-Ruwaini of the SCAF against Tamim Al-Barghouti—a celebrated poet and political scientist, who is also a symbol of (and for) young revolutionaries throughout the Arab world. In response to a program that featured Al-Barghouti as a guest, and in which he criticized Egyptian foreign policy among other things, al-Ruwaini characterized him as someone speaking with "a strange accent . . . whose features were not very Egyptian" and proceeded to chastise him for daring to "dictate foreign policy" to the Egyptian state, in a country of "86 million Egyptians," a country, he insists, that has been responsible for the reconciliation of Palestinian factions and which, we are no doubt expected to conclude, is leading the Israeli–Palestinian peace process.[43] Al-Barghouti is not only half-Egyptian—he is the son of acclaimed Egyptian novelist and professor Radwa Ashour and Palestinian poet Mourid Barghouti—he also holds a PhD in political science and has written and lectured on political theory for years. He was deported from Egypt in 2003 (as was his father, in the 1970s) for participating in protests against the US-led invasion of Iraq and Egypt's complicity in it. But all of this aside, what is particularly troubling in al-Ruwaini's tirade against Al-Barghouti is not so much his racialized intervention, which smacks of the Sadat- and Mubarak-era policy of isolating Egypt from its Arab neighbors, but specifically the founding implications of the argument. These implications have resonated and continue to underpin much of the counterrevolutionary discourse within and without Egypt. First, "national security" and "national sovereignty" are considered to be values that are superior to Arab identity, political solidarity, and human rights. Second, the Egyptian revolution is separate and distinct from regional concerns—above all, the Zionist colonization of Palestinian lands and daily massacre of Palestinians. Third, anyone who dares to criticize these values or policies is necessarily "less Egyptian," if not altogether an arm of destabilizing foreign intervention. This distranslation of citizenship and sovereignty along explicitly imperial fault lines, and the intricate marriage of those concepts to the neoliberal lexicon of work, productivity, and the myth of economic stability, is a powerful policing device. When it is translated back among Egyptians it results in reactionary, post-nationalist assemblages of loyalty and responsibility, as seen in the Asfin Ya Rayyis movement and even among many supporters of the revolutionaries. In effect, communiqués issued by the SCAF echoing decades of scapegoating by Mubarak's regime and a police apparatus and warning against the threat of western and Israeli designs for fostering "instability," must be translated seriously. They should not be translated only as fictive distractions from real problems, but also and equally as reflections on the waning sovereignty and economic interests of the Egyptian political-economic elite—including the Egyptian military—as well as that of Israel and the United States.

Global Translation or Translation of the Global?

In his seminal paper, "Grassroots Globalisation and the Research Imagination," Arjun Appadurai calls on academics to address the massive gap between transnational intellectual work on globalization, and the vast majority of people affected by globalization.[44] Given that both the knowledge and theory generated by intellectual labor in the academy are symptoms of an increasingly privileged and isolated few, who are separated from the rapidly growing mass of multiple excluded subaltern objects of the same academic production, Appadurai encourages scholars and researchers to investigate ways for the counter-hegemonic redistribution both of resources and knowledge. We are invited, then, to be highly critical of the knowledge economy in which our own scholarship—whether as students or paid professors and researchers—is complicit in the continued generation of a skewed and highly uneven knowledge society, with real implications for both the nature and the ethics of academic work. We are compelled, in light of this call, to examine both the way in which the present structures of globalization shape our epistemology and guide our research imaginations. We are also compelled to examine the moral, theoretical, political, and ultimately strategic conditions imposed upon us by globalization and its implications for regimes of justice and social change. This entails the inclusion of a critical geography of globalization and knowledge, as well as an active engagement with both subaltern epistemologies as well as their formerly dispossessed bourgeois counterparts in the academic imaginaries specific to those locations.

In the spirit of this call for a critical geographical imaginary, I emphasize that understanding neoliberal subjectivity is of enormous relevance to the task of translation, not only because translation concerns itself with the cultural and therefore sociopolitical significations that overwhelm language, but also because translation is a process and practice of occupying the interstitial borderlands *between* language and culture. This is not to suggest that the object of translation must always necessarily be marginal and peripheral (with the oft-cited corollary that translators, like Orientalists more generally, are tasked with the burden of finding the limits of language) but rather that translation is inevitably always an impossible act. To translate is to reach for the impossible.

The present political moment in Egypt must be translated as part of a wider political moment throughout the world. Political commitment means attending not only to the cultural field itself, or to the political field, but rather, recognizing the false dichotomy that posits them as separate and distinct fields. In the same way that political economists today are faced with the ever-growing task to constantly challenge the separation of economics and politics, translators are tasked with the responsibility to do away with bourgeois literary and cultural divestment of language from its political content. Translators must therefore constantly challenge an industry and field that renders them in all cases as workers without authority or responsibility, neutering the act of translation of its political essence, its urgency, and its inherent instrumentality.

This chapter should not be read as its own distinct translation of the ongoing Egyptian Revolution, its sister Arab revolutions, or social movements throughout the world, but rather as a modest and limited engagement with the role of translation in the rendering of these multiple narratives and their inclusion or exclusion in a narrative of globalization and its imagined opposites or alternatives. Rather than argue for a particular reading or translation of the global, I wish to emphasize that attention to the structural conditions of neoliberalism are crucial to our understanding of what constitutes, effectively, the political, and moreover, the revolutionary, and what is automatically excluded from this rendering. My hope has been to illustrate that despite the harrowing restrictions that beset revolutionary movements in the twenty-first century, the particular context of the Egyptian narrative over the past year has equally exposed both the capacity of translation and its fact as daily labor in the rendition of counter-hegemonic notions of the global. The chief task for contemporary translators, which this volume has engaged, must be a consciousness of the very fact of their subjects' own engagement in the practice of translation. By reading subjects as political agents with their own potentialities, our own engagement is repoliticized and newly endowed with a responsibility to analyze necessary structural contexts.

The task before us is not so much to translate the Egyptian Revolution, then, as it is to produce and engage *revolutionary translations* themselves. For it is only through the recognition that language and culture contain the potential for social transformation that we recognize our own agency, as translators and cultural workers, in effecting the same.

Notes

1   Vittorio Arrigoni is lovingly remembered by all who knew him as a friend, a comrade, a Palestinian by choice, and a martyr. Having devoted much of his young life to resistance in solidarity with Palestinians, Vik was murdered in Gaza on April 15, 2011. Immediately following news of his death, a delegation of Italian activists made their way through Cairo to Gaza, naming the action "Stay Human." The first of this summer's boats to sail to Gaza was deliberately given the same name. It is a translation of "Restiamo Umani," the title of a book containing a collection of Vik's writings from Gaza. He will always be remembered for his raw courage and dreams. He taught us the revolutionary power of reclaiming our humanity in the face of an increasingly dehumanizing global reality. He will remain a humbling inspiration and proof that, indeed, other translations are still possible.

2   Tejaswini Niranjana, *Siting Translation: History, Post-structuralism, and the Colonial Context* (Berkeley: University of California Press, 1992).

3   The political and economic conditions of cultural production, particularly under a dictatorship, render culture increasingly invisible. In doing so, they paradoxically generate new forms and standards of cultural productions, laying the ground for dynamic and often volatile culture wars in which state patronage, the private sector,

and notions of popular culture and art are increasingly contested sites for the expression of autonomy and sovereignty. For the landmark text engaging these intersections, among others, in Egypt, see Samia Mehrez, *Egypt's Culture Wars* (London: Routledge, 2008). For an influential economic anthropology exploring the intersections of market-based regimes of governance, international finance, the state, and popular culture, see Julia Elyachar, *Markets of Dispossession: NGOs, Economic Development and the State in Cairo* (Durham, NC: Duke University Press, 2005).

4 My principal understanding of the contemporary sociological and philosophical rendition of the 'state of emergency' is informed by Giorgio Agamben's *State of Exception* (Chicago: University of Chicago Press, 2005). Agamben's influential thesis has built on Carl Schmitt's and Hannah Arendt's articulations of the refugee experience during the Second World War and beyond. Agamben's contribution to both social theory and continental philosophy stems from his application of political philosophy around the 'state of emergency' to the present condition of neoliberal statehood and its attendant discourses of sovereignty, which are increasingly tied less to liberal state function and more to those state apparatuses that police and regulate citizenship through the identification of its negation. Here, I am seeking to explore the cultural field and, through a discursive analysis of its internal logic and the state and non-state structures that shape it, demonstrate the centrality of critical geographies to the practice of translation. Also see Aihwa Ong, *Neoliberalism as Exception: Mutations in Citizenship and Sovereignty* (Durham, NC: Duke University Press, 2006). In this book, and in her preceding work more generally, Ong's ethnographies detail the implications of neoliberal structural transformation for the rearticulation of citizenship and claims on state sponsorship, as well as attendant discourses of sovereignty. Drawing on the work of Schmitt and Agamben, she analyzes neoliberal statehood and citizenship through the creation of differentially regulated bodies of labor and middle-class formations, as well as exceptional claims on the state. The process of exceptionalism is central to contemporary analyses of the nation-state more generally, and to culture wars specifically, and is one of the fundamental processes inspiring my analysis of some of the translations in this chapter.

5 Gayatri Chakravorty Spivak, "The Politics of Translation," in *The Translation Studies Reader*, ed. Lawrence Venuti (London: Routledge, 2000), pp. 397–416.

6　Lori Chamberlain, "Gender and the Metaphorics of Translation," in *The Translation Studies Reader*, ed. Lawrence Venuti (London: Routledge, 2000), pp. 314–30.

7　Disciplinary currents in the social sciences and humanities, but particularly in postcolonial studies and anthropology, have historically grappled with questions of self-reflexivity and indigineity. Translation studies in this context re-read the history of translation through the late colonial encounter, in which the construction of national narratives is deeply rooted in the process of orientation around 'othered' constructs. The favored antidote to Orientalism has been the uncritical valorization of the native, in which subjectivity is reproduced blindly, if not in the image of a dominant language and referential world, then in the image of the author him/herself. In general, the accepted tendency among translators has frequently been to polarize languages and cultures rather than explore the potential contribution of the translator's own subjectivity and its capacity to enrich, through critical engagement with the 'original' text, and produce a thoroughly new text.

8　See Judith Butler, *Gender Trouble: Feminism and the Subversion of Identity* (London: Routledge, 1989) for the seminal work on performance theory, the role of 'othering' and its contribution to gender identity and experience. The role of performativity in the construction of gender and sexuality, particularly during the late colonial encounter, was pivotal in the construction and preservation of national narratives; see Joseph Massad, *Desiring Arabs* (Chicago: Chicago University Press, 2007).

9　Jacques Derrida, "Des Tours de Babel," in *Difference in Translation*, ed. Joseph F. Graham (Ithaca and London: Cornell University Press, 1985).

10　Derrida, "Des Tours de Babel," p. 184.

11　Saroj Giri, "End of 1989?" *Open Democracy*, March 1, 2011, http://www.opendemocracy.net/saroj-giri/end-of-%E2%80%981989%E2%80%99

12　Rabab El-Mahdi, "Orientalising the Egyptian Uprising," *Jadaliyya*, April 11, 2011, http://www.jadaliyya.com/pages/index/1214/orientalising-the-egyptian-uprising

13　Catriona Davies, "Will Gays Be 'Sacrificial Lambs' in Arab Spring?" CNN, June 13, 2011, http://www.cnn.com/2011/WORLD/meast/05/27/gay.rights.arab.spring/

14　Mona Anis, "Marginalia: Manufacturing Xenophobia," *Al-Ahram Weekly*, June 23–29, 2011, http://weekly.ahram.org.eg/2011/1053/cu212.htm

15   See Jasbir Puar, *Terrorist Assemblages: Homonationalism in Queer Times* (Durham, NC: Duke University Press, 2007), in which she builds on similar ground to Massad's in *Desiring Arabs*, and charts the post-9/11 re-inscription of terrorist bodies through the establishment—by the US government, transnational rights networks of organizations and activists, mass media, and the tourism industry—of a homonormative patriotic subject. In the few years since 2007, the linkages between hegemonic transnational LGBT discourse and imperial control of the Middle East have been well established and widely accepted by both scholars and activists. Less examined has been queer theory itself and new movements of the last half-decade, both in the US and Europe as well as the region, that consciously inscribe themselves as part of a global justice movement and in opposition to Israel's pinkwashing campaigns, for instance.

16   Massad, *Desiring Arabs*.

17   The term 'queer' was "reclaimed" in the early nineties in the United States, in the context of the Queer Nation organization, a movement of AIDS activists who sought to counter anti-gay hate crimes and violence through confrontational methods that included outing people without their consent. The term 'queer' has since evolved to be used either interchangeably with LGBT(Q) or frequently as an alternative to gender binaries in heteronormative western contexts.

18   Jim Worth, "Walk Like an Egyptian," *The Huffington Post*, February 17, 2011, http://www.huffingtonpost.com/jim-worth/walk-like-an-egyptian_b_824329.html

19   Gerry Emmett, "Greece: Tahrir Squared," *News and Letters*, July–Aug. 2011, http://newsandletters.org/issues/2011/Jul-Aug/wivGreeceJul Aug_11.asp

20   Michelle May, "How the Egyptian Revolution Inspired Protests in Spain," *Mediashift*, June 10, 2011, http://www.pbs.org/mediashift/2011/06/how-the-egyptian-revolution-inspired-protests-in-spain161.html

21   Sarah Hawas, "Translating Revolution between J14 and the Israeli Embassy in Cairo," September 19, 2011, http://mondoweiss.net/2011/09/translating-revolution-between-j14-and-the-israeli-embassy-in-cairo.html

22   Noam Sheizaf, "Some Arab Twitterers Use Anti-Semitic Tag in Discussing J14," *+972 Magazine*, August 8, 2011, http://972mag.com/arab-tweeterers-use-anti-semitic-tag-in-discussing-j14-232819-77/

23   Sami Peretz and Ora Cohen, "Barak: Israel Can't Cut Defense Budget to Meet Social Demands," *Ha'aretz*, September 1, 2011.

24 Max Blumenthal and Joseph Dana, "J14: The Exclusive Revolution,"
    +972 *Magazine*, August 26, 2011, http://972mag.com/the-exclusive-
    revolution
25 For a comprehensive historical overview of the sociology of the J14
    movement, see Max Ajl, "Social Origins of the Tent Protests in Israel,"
    Monthly Review Zine, August 16, 2011. For a wider academic take on rul-
    ing-class formation in Israel, see Jonathan Nitzan and Shimshon Bichler,
    The Global Political Economy of Israel (London: Pluto Press, 2002).
26 I argue for a consideration of potentiality as articulated by Giorgio
    Agamben, whose idea of potentiality as a condition of human existence
    is not necessarily defined dialectically in terms of potentiality/actuality,
    but is rather defined by the possibility of its negation, specifically its
    impotentiality. By replacing potentiality with impotentiality as a condi-
    tion of becoming (or actuality), Agamben invites us to consider the lack
    of actualization as a unique and present constitution in its own right.
    See Agamben, *Potentialities* (Stanford: Stanford University Press, 1999).
27 Agamben's proposed exercise is useful to the analysis of hegemonic
    regimes of social change, development, and progress precisely because
    it echoes the very process of literary translation itelf: the impregna-
    tion of potentiality with an idea of actualization, which is arrived at
    prior to any consideration of its others or opposites, is very much the
    epistemological paradigm that governs the narrative of neoliberal-
    ism, from the divergence of markets from the local to the global and
    the forced industrialization of communities in the global south, to the
    proliferation of regimes of immaterial labor and the self-exploitation
    of productive capacities. Furthermore, market-based transformations
    in our subjectivities lead to the annihilation of other conditions of (im)
    potentiality, rendering a multitudinous precariousness as the final con-
    dition of belonging. The concept I am drawing on, of immaterial labor,
    as well as formal and real subsumption by capital, is obviously traced to
    Karl Marx, *Capital*, vol. 1, but in this context I refer to contemporary
    literature by political economists, philosophers, and anthropologists
    who theorize present-day forms of work and precarity in light of the
    widespread post-industrial shift to service industries as the primary
    site of economic activity. See for example Michael Hardt and Antonio
    Negri, *Empire* (Cambridge, MA: Harvard University Press, 2000) and
    additional articles by the same authors. I am especially interested in
    technology and social media as sites for new and vast pools of uncon-
    scious and automated immaterial labor. For the seminal text on this, see
    Mark Cote and Jennifer Pybus, "Learning to Immaterial Labour 2.0:

MySpace and Social Networks," *Ephemera* 7, no. 1 (2007): 88–106. See also the seminal work informing contemporary debates around immaterial labor: Maurizio Lazzarato, "Immaterial Labour," *Generation Online*, undated, http://www.generation-online.org/c/fcimmateriallabour3.htm

28 The denationalization characteristic of the contemporary moment misleads many to imagine the nation-state as irrelevant or arbitrary; in other words, the marginalization and near-death of the nation-state under neoliberal regimes of market liberalization, along with the attendant spatial and temporal flows of the global cityscape, might suggest to many the withering away of the state as a useful category of social or cultural analysis. See Saskia Sassen, *Losing Control? Sovereignty in an Age of Globalization* (New York: Columbia University Press, 1996).

29 The 'success' of neoliberalism, if any, lies precisely in its capacity as a dominant regime of flexibility in rewriting the global geographical imaginary and making invisible all of the processes of production and reproduction, the gendering of labor practices, the dissolution of class boundaries in the global north along with the depiction of increased labor migration as class mobility (and its attendant domesticated finance and market-based regimes of development and consumption) in the global south. See Pierre Bourdieu, "The Essence of Neoliberalism," *Le Monde Diplomatique*, December 8, 1998, http://mondediplo.com/1998/12/08bourdieu. Even with the effective structural death of the welfare state in the post-Cold War decades, and with the exacerbated erosion of national identities, the military and police apparatus of these very same states are only strengthened through privatization, and their regulatory functions coincide with ruling-class interests (albeit transnational ones)—which, in the context of Egypt, include the political elite harnessed by the Mubarak administration over the last thirty years—to regulate citizenship through renationalized and reterritorialized exceptions. What this means for translation and translators, particularly in a postcolonial context like Egypt, is that a practice that was for much of the modern period (between the eighteenth and the twentieth centuries) instrumentalized by national discourses and the birth of a bourgeois ruling class is today faced with the same transformations that beset the nation-state, and must accordingly deal with multiple culture wars that reveal more about class—albeit an increasingly transnational and complex category of class—than they do about nations and their 'others.'

30 For a well-known contemporary treatment of this, see Joseph Massad, "Introduction: The Opposite of Terror," in *The Persistence of the Palestinian Question* (New York: Routledge, 2006).

31   For an in-depth examination of the political economy of 'tolerance,'
      see Wendy Brown, *Regulating Aversion: Tolerance in the Age of Identity and
      Empire* (Princeton, NJ: Princeton University Press, 2008).
32   http://english.ahram.org.eg/newsContent/1/64/8023/Egypt/
      Politics-/Egypt-constitutional-referendum-blow-by-blow-accou.
      aspx. The most frequently cited motive for the Muslim Brotherhood's
      behavior was a fear that the second constitutional article, identifying
      Islam as the official religion of the state, might be removed in a
      future constitution. The history of this particular article, put in place
      in the 1970s by Sadat in order to appease Islamists, attests to the
      symbiotic relationship between the Muslim Brotherhood and the
      outgoing regime, in which the biopolitical role of the organization
      through its experiments in moral economy served to govern dissent
      through the formation of a new ruling class, anti-imperial in dis-
      course and aesthetics but deeply experienced in the protection
      of economic activity. For a detailed and holistic analysis of the
      debates surrounding the March 2011 constitution, its historical
      context, and the particular interests of the Muslim Brotherhood,
      see Tom Francis, "Egypt's Legal Revolution," *Open Democracy*,
      August 17, 2011, http://www.opendemocracy.net/tom-francis/
      egypts-legal-revolution
33   Hesham Sallam, "Striking Back at Egyptian Workers," *Jadaliyya*, June
      16, 2011, http://www.jadaliyya.com/pages/index/1914/striking-back-at-
      egyptian-workers
34   Sarah Carr, "Mubarak Loyalists Bring Old State-run Media Ethos to
      the Web," *al-Masry al-Youm English Edition*, August 10, 2011, http://
      www.almasryalyoum.com/en/node/485174
35   Zeinab El-Gundy, "Searching for Amr Gharbeia and Others Miss-
      ing from Abbasiya Battle," *AhramOnline*, July 24, 2011, http://english.
      ahram.org.eg/NewsContent/1/64/17174/Egypt/Politics-/Searching-
      for-Amr-Gharbeia-and-others-missing-from.aspx
36   See Amr Gharbeia's televised appearance on *Baladna Bil Masri*: "Shaha-
      det Amr Gharbeia 'an ikhtitafuh fi ahdath al-Abbasiyya," July 25, 2011,
      http://www.youtube.com/watch?v=R2NKdk1024o
37   Jon Leyne, "Egypt Divided over 'Israeli Spy' Ilan Grapel," *BBC
      News*, June 22, 2001, http://www.bbc.co.uk/news/world-middle-
      east-13868160
38   For just a few select, prominent examples of the discourse, see Amr
      Moustafa's tirades, for example on the talk show *Fasel 'Al Hawa*, http://
      www.youtube.com/watch?v=19j7aIphyaI

39 "Thousands Rally in Egypt's Tahrir Square," *Al Jazeera English*, May 13, 2011, http://english.aljazeera.net/news/middleeast/2011/05/201151394331855329.html

40 Salma Shukrallah, "Egyptian Convoy Bound for Rafah Banned," *AhramOnline*, May 14, 2011, http://english.ahram.org.eg/NewsContent/1/64/12093/Egypt/Politics-/Egyptian-convoy-bound-for-Rafah-banned-.aspx

41 The history of the complex relationship between local Bedouin communities in the Sinai and the Egyptian state is too long to detail here and warrants its own treatment, but suffice it to say that Sinai Bedouin have long struggled to retain some sense of autonomy over their lands in the face of a brutal tourism-industrial complex that has colonized them since the Israeli withdrawal in 1979. The Egyptian military owes it to Israel to protect their gas supply but also owes it to itself, as an institution, to protect its rather generous share of the tourism industry as well.

42 Zeinab El Gundy, "Man Scales 13 Floors to Bring Down the Israeli Flag," *AhramOnline*, August 22, 2011, http://english.ahram.org.eg/~/NewsContent/1/64/19349/Egypt/Politics-/Egyptian-young-man-scales--floors-to-bring-down-th.aspx

43 Ola El-Saket, "General's Statement against Palestinian Poet Angers Egyptian Intellectuals," *al-Masry al-Youm English Edition*, July 20, 2011, http://www.almasryalyoum.com/en/node/478896

44 Arjun Appadurai, "Grassroots Globalisation and the Research Imagination," in Joan Vincent, ed., *The Anthropology of Politics: A Reader in Ethnography, Theory and Critique* (Malden: Blackwell Publishers, 2002).

Appendix 1
Arabic Text of Quotes Cited in Chapter 2,
"Of Drama and Performance"

Asmaa Mahfouz Vlog , January 18, 2011
http://www.youtube.com/watch?gl=EG&v=SgjIgMdsEuk

Asmaa Mahfouz, quote 1, p. 76:

أربعة مصريين ولعوا في نفسهم، من الذل و من الجوع و من الفقر و من
البهدلة إللي شايفنها بقالهم تلاتين سنة. أربعة من المصريين ولعوا في نفسهم
قالوا يمكن يحصل زي إللي حصل في تونس، قالوا يمكن نبقى بلد حرة،
بلد فيها عدل، بلد فيها كرامة، بلد الإنسان فيها إنسان بجد، مش عايش
ك..ك..كحيوان.

Azmaa Mahfouz, quote 2, p. 77:

أنا نزلت و كتبت إن أنا بنت و هنزل ميدان التحرير و هقف لوحدي و هرفع
يافطة يمكن الناس تحس و كتبت رقمي يمكن الناس تنزل. ما حدش نزل إلا تلت
شباب، ما حدش نزل إلا تلت شباب و تلت عربيات أمن مركزي و كان الباقي
جي في السكة، و عشرات من البلطجية و ظباط و كانوا جايين بمنتهى الرعب،
فضلوا يتكلموا معانا بعدونا عن الناس يمكن بقسوة شوية، بس أول لما انفردوا
بينا قعدوا يقولولنا حرام عليكو كفاية إحنا منكوا إحنا من الشعب الناس إللي
ماتوا دول عندهم حالة نفسية.

Asmaa Mahfouz, quote 3, p. 77:

و كل واحد في البلد ديه شايف نفسه راجل، يبقى ينزل. وكل واحد في البلد
ديه بيقول البنات إللي بتنزل مظاهرة بتتبهدل و ما يصحش إن هي تنزل و حرام،
يخلي عنده نخوة و رجولة و ينزل يوم ٢٥. لو انت عندك كرامة و إنسان و راجل
في البلد ديه، يبقى تنزل، تنزل تحميني و تحمي أي بنت تانية.

Amaa Mahfouz, quote 4, p. 78:

إوعى تقول مفيش أمل. طول ما انت بتقول مفيش أمل يبقى مفيش أمل. طول ما انت بتنزل و تسجل موقف يبقى فيه أمل. إوعى تخاف من الحكومة، خاف من ربك. ربنا بيقول «إن الله لا يغير ما بقوم حتى يغيروا ما بأنفسهم»، ليه؟ مش عشان إن انت تبقى كويس و قاعد في حالك و ماشي جنب الحيط.

Quran (13:11)
Asmaa Mahfouz, quote 5, p. 78:

(ترفع لافتة) أنا نازلة يوم ٢٥ و هقول للفساد لأة و للنظام لأ.

Mubarak's second speech (Arabic transcript)
http://www.iraq4all.org/ShowNews.php?id=6199

Mubarak, quote 1, p. 80:

إن الوطن يتعرض لأحداث عصيبة واختبارات قاسية بدأت بشباب ومواطنين شرفاء مارسوا حقهم في التظاهر السلمي تعبيراً عن همومهم وتطلعاتهم .. سرعان ما استغلها من سعى لإشاعة الفوضى واللجوء إلى العنف والمواجهة وللقفز على الشرعية الدستورية والانقضاض عليها.

تحولت تلك التظاهرات من مظهر راق ومتحضر لممارسة حرية الرأي والتعبير الى مواجهات مؤسفة تحركها وتهيمن عليها قوى سياسية سعت الى التصعيد وصب الزيت على النار واستهدفت أمن الوطن واستقراره بأعمال إثارة وتحريض وسلب ونهب وإشعال للحرائق وقطع للطرقات واعتداء على مرافق الدولة والممتلكات العامة والخاصة واقتحام لبعض البعثات الدبلوماسية على أرض مصر.

Mubarak, quote 2, p. 81:

نعيش معا أيام مؤلمة وأكثر ما يوجع قلوبنا هو الخوف الذي انتاب الأغلبية الكاسحة من المصريين وما ساورهم من انزعاج وقلق وهواجس حول ما سيأتي به الغد ولذويهم وعائلاتهم ومستقبل ومصير بلدهم. إن أحداث الأيام القليلة الماضية تفرض علينا جميعاً شعباً وقيادة الاختيار ما بين الفوضى والاستقرار.

Mubarak, quote 3, pp. 81–82:

إن مسؤوليتي الأولى الآن هي استعادة أمن واستقرار الوطن لتحقيق الانتقال السلمي للسلطة في أجواء تحمي مصر والمصريين وتتيح تسلم المسؤولية لمن يختاره الشعب في الانتخابات الرئاسية المقبلة. وأقول بكل الصدق وبصرف النظر عن الظرف الراهن إني لم أكن أنتوي الترشح لفترة رئاسية جديدة فقد قضيت ما يكفي من العمر في خدمة مصر وشعبها. لكنني الآن حريص كل الحرص على

أن أختتم عملي من أجل الوطن بما يضمن تسليم أمانته ورايته ومصر عزيزة آمنة مستقرة وبما يحفظ الشرعية ويحترم الدستور.

Mubarak, quote 4, pp. 82–83:

أيها الأخوة المواطنون ستخرج مصر من الظروف الراهنة أقوى مما كانت عليه قبلها وأكثر ثقة وتماسكاً واستقراراً سيخرج منها شعبنا وهو أكثر وعياً بما يحقق مصالحه وأكثر حرصاً على عدم التفريط في مصيره ومستقبله. إن حسني مبارك الذي يتحدث إليكم اليوم يعتز بما قضاه من سنين طويلة في خدمة مصر وشعبها. إن هذا الوطن العزيز هو وطني مثلما هو وطن كل مصري ومصرية فيه عشت وحاربت من أجله ودافعت عن أرضه وسيادته ومصالحه وعلى أرضه أموت وسيحكم التاريخ علي وعلى غيري بما لنا أو علينا.

Wael Ghoneim interview
http://www.youtube.com/watch?v=VlBAzvX9Xw4&feature=related

Wael Ghoneim, quote 1, p. 86:

إحنا فينا شباب أغنيا جداً، عايشين في أحلى بيوت، راكبين أحسن عربيات، أنا مش محتاج أي حاجة من أي حدّ، وماكنتش عايز أي حاجة من أي حدّ. كل الحاجات اللي كانت بتتعمل كانت بتعرض حياة كل واحد فينا للخطر.

Wael Ghoneim, quote 2, p. 87:

أول حاجة أنا عايز أقول لكل الناس الأمهات والأبهات اللي ولادهم ماتوا: البقاء لله، وربنا يتقبل ولادكم من الشهداء سواء كانوا مواطنين سواء كانوا ضباط سواء كانوا عساكر، أي حدّ مات دا شهيد. أنا لو كنت خاين، على فكرة أنا كنت حاقعد في الفيلا بتاعتي في البيسين في الإمارات وأنبسط وأعيش حياتي. أنا باقبض وكل شوية المرتب بتاعي عمال يزيد وعايش حياتي.

Wael Ghoneim, quote 3, p. 87:

بُصي حضرتك، إحنا عشان مابقيناش نسمع بعض الف.. أنا أنا عايز الأول أقول على حاجة، ودا، أنا عارف إن دا دلوقت، موسم.. ممكن أسميه موسم التخوين.

Wael Ghoneim, quote 4, p. 87:

حرام، حرام إن يبقى أبويا بيشوف بعين واحدة وممكن يخسر العين التانية ويقعد ١٢ يوم مايعرفش إبنه فين (crying) ليه؟ ليه؟

Wael Ghoneim, quote 5, p.88:

فأرجوكم يا جماعة، مافيش أبطال. الأبطال همّ الناس اللي في الشارع. الأبطال هم كل واحد فينا. مافيش واحد. مافيش النهاردا واحد راكب الحصان هو اللي بيضرب السرج ويحرك الناس. أوعى حدّ يضحك عليكو ويقول لكو كدا. دي ثورة شباب الإنترنت، دي ثورة شباب الإنترنت اللي بقت بعد كدا ثورة شباب مصر اللي بعد كدا بقت ثورة كل مصر. ومافيش بطل فيها ومافيش واحد هو اللي المفروض ياخُد الـ scene كلنا كنا أبطال.

Wael Ghoneim, quote 6, p. 88:

إحنا عندنا في مصر بنحب نعمل أبطال، أنا مش بطل. أنا كنت نايم ١٢ يوم. الأبطال هم اللي كانوا في الشارع، الأبطال همّ اللي نزلوا المظاهرات الأبطال هم اللي ضحوا بحياتهم، الأبطال هم اللي اتضربوا، الأبطال همّ اللي اعتقلوا واتعرّضوا لمخاطر. أنا ماكنتش بطل.

Quote from Mubarak's third speech, which is contrasted with Wael's discourse, p. 89. http://www.youtube.com/watch?v=XOiXKqPiPVw

لقد كنت شابا مثل شباب مصر الآن، عندما تعلمت شرف العسكرية المصرية والولاء للوطن والتضحية من أجله.. أفنيت عمري دفاعاً عن أرضه وسيادته، شهدت حروبه بهزائمها وانتصاراتها، عشت أيام الانكسار والاحتلال وأيام العبور والنصر والتحرير.. أسعد أيام حياتي يوم رفعت علم مصر فوق سيناء، واجهت الموت مرات عديدة طياراً وفي أديس أبابا وغير ذلك كثير، لم أخضع يوما لضغوط أجنبية أو إملاءات، حافظت على السلام، عملت من أجل أمن مصر واستقرارها، اجتهدت من أجل نهضتها، و من أجل أبنائها، لم أسع يوماً لسلطة أو شعبية زائفة.. أثق أن الأغلبية الكاسحة من أبناء الشعب يعرفون من هو حسني مبارك، ويحز في نفسي ما ألاقيه اليوم من بعض بني وطني.

Wael Ghoneim, quote 7, p. 90:

أنا آسف بس دي مش غلطتنا، والله العظيم دي مش غلطتنا. دي غلطة كل واحد كان ماسك في السلطة ومتبت فيها. أنا عايز أمشي...

Omar Suleiman's statement announcing Mubarak's resignation, February 11, 2011, p. 91. http://www.youtube.com/watch?v=ph8e11KR8mk

بسم الله الرحمن الرحيم. أيها المواطنون، في هذه الظروف العصيبة التي تمر بها البلاد قرر الرئيس محمد حسني مبارك تخليه عن منصب رئيس الجمهورية و كلف المجلس الأعلى للقوات المسلحة بإدارة شئون البلاد. و الله الموفق و المستعان.

Major General Mohsen al-Fangary, third military communiqué, p. 94.
http://www.youtube.com/watch?v=ayeU6XebjTg&feature=related

أيها المواطنون في هذه اللحظة التاريخية الفارقة من تاريخ مصر, و بصدور قرار السيد الرئيس محمد حسني مبارك بالتخلي عن منصب رئيس الجمهورية, و تكليف المجلس الأعلى للقوات المسلحة بإدارة شئون البلاد في هذا الصدد, فإن المجلس الأعلى للقوات المسلحة يتوجه بكل التحية و الإعزاز لأرواح الشهداء [stops to salute] الذين ضحوا بأرواحهم فداءً للحرية و أمن بلدهم و لكل أفراد شعبها العظيم. و الله الموفق و**المستعان**، والسلام عليكم و رحمة الله و بركاته.

Appendix 2
Poems Quoted in Chapter 6

Tamim Al-Barghouti, "Ya Masr hanit wi banit," p. 227

تميم البرغوثي

يامصر هانت وبانت كلها كام يوم...

نهارنا نادي ونهار الندل مش باين
الدولة مفضلتش منها إلا حبة شوم..
لو مش مصدق تعالى علي الميدان عاين
ياناس مفيش حاكم إلا من خيال محكوم..
واللي هيقعد في بيته بعدها خاين

Hisham al-Gokh, "A View of Midan Tahrir," pp. 227–28

هشام الجخ

مشهد رأسي من ميدان التحرير

خبئ قصائدك القديمة كلها. مزق دفاترك القديمة كلها و اكتب لمصر اليوم شعراً مثلها
خبئ دفاترك القديمة كلها و اكتب لمصر اليوم شعراً مثلها
لا صمت بعد اليوم يفرض خوفه و اكتب سلام النيل مصر و أهلها
عيناك عيناك أجمل طفلتين تقرران بأن هذا الخوف ماض و انتهى
كانت تداعبنا الشوارع بالبرودة و الصقيع و لم نفسر وقتها
كنا ندفئ بعضنا في بعضنا و نراك تبتسمين ننسى بردها
وإذا غضبتي كشفت عن وجهها و حياءنا يأبى أن يدلس وجهها
لا تتركيهم يخبرونك بأنني متمرد خان الأمانة أو سهى
لا تتركيهم يخبرونك بأنني أصبحت شيئا تافها و موجه
فأنا ابن بطنك وابن بطنك من أراد ومن أقال ومن أقر ومن نهى
صمتت فلول الخائفين بجبنهم وجموع من عشقوكي قالت قولها

313

Abul Qasim al-Shabbi, "Iradat al-Haya," p. 229

أبو القاسم الشابي

إرادة الحياة

أبو القاسم الشابي

إذا الشــعبُ يومًــا أراد الحيــاة فــلا بــدّ أن يسـتجيب القــدرْ

ولا بـــدَّ لليــل أن ينجــلي ولا بــدّ للقيـد أن ينكسـرْ

ومـن لـم يعانقْـه شـوْقُ الحيـاة تبخَّـرَ في جوِّهـا واندثـرْ

فـويل لمـن لـم تَشُـقهُ الحيـاة مـن صفْعـة العـدَم المنتصـرْ

كــذلك قـالـت ليَ الكائنـاتُ وحـدثني روحُهـا المسـتترْ

Ahmed Abdel Muti Hijazi, "Iradat al-Haya:
A Tribute to Abul Qasim al-Shabbi," p. 230

أحمد عبد المعطي حجازي

إرادة الحياة

إلى أبي القاسم الشابي

إذا الشعب يوماً أراد الحياة

فلابد أن يتحرر من خوفه

ويحمل في كفّه

روحه

ويسير بها موغلاً في الخطر

إلى أن يستجيب القدر!

إذا الشعب يوماً أراد الحياة

فلابد من أن يقوم العبيد

قيامتهم

يصبرون على عضة الجوع

لكن على عضة القيد لا يصبرون

يموتون في أول الليل، إن كان لابد من أن يموتوا

لأنهم سيقومون في مطلع الفجر

كي يولدوا في غد من جديد!

فيا أيها الميتون انهضوا

أيها الفقراء الأرقاء قوموا قيامتكم

أيها الساكنون اللحود!

فقد طالما انتظرتكم حياة تظل مؤجلة

وشموس بلا عجج لم تروها!
ومرت عليكم عصور، وأنتم رقود!

Abdel Rahman al-Abnoudi, "al-Midan," p. 232

عبد الرحمن الأبنودي
قصيدة الميدان

أيادي مصرية سمرا ليها في التمييز
ممدودة وسط الزئير بتكسر البراويز
سطوع لصوت الجموع شوف مصر تحت الشمس
آن الآوان ترحلي يا دولة العواجيز
عواجيز شداد مسعورين أكلوا بلدنا أكل
ويشبهوا بعضهم نهم وخسة وشكل
طلع الشباب البديع قلبوا خريفها ربيع
وحققوا المعجزة صحوا القتيل من القتل
إقتلني قتلي ما هيعيد دولتك تاني
بكتب بدمي حياة تانية لأوطاني
دمي ده ولا الربيع الاتنين بلون أخضر
وببتسم من سعادتي ولا أحزاني

ZAP Tharwat, "Our Morning is Dew," pp. 233–34

زاب ثروت ZAP Tharwat
صباحنا ندي

على كلام البرغوتي أنا جاي اكمل
يا مصر هانت و بانت معلش نتحمل
صباحنا ندي
و صباح الندل مش باين
يا ابو كاب و دبوره بقى دمي عليك هاين
يمكن نكون أصحاب .. أخوات .. أو يمكن متعرفنيش
بس أنا عارف لو تعرفني بسلاحك متضربنيش
سلاحك ده ليا أمان مش ضرب وإهانة
يا مصر احنا ولادك ولا انتى بيعانا
فجأة بقينا أبطال الناس تحيينا
مظاهرة والتانية الناس تنادينا

وفجأه قلبوا علينا و لعنوا أسامينا
ومنهم اللي حاول بالجزمة يدينا
بتقولوا ضحكوا علينا ؟
إنتم بقى فاهمين
ما كنتم لسه معانا و جنبنا نايمين
وإيد فى إيد شابكين مسلم و مسيحيين
طلعنا خونه وعملاء وأخوان وإيرانيين
وأجنده حمرا وخضرا وكتاب وكراستين
ما تنزل تشوف بالعين
إسالهم إنتم مين
وليه كده قاعدين
جعانين ومش خايفين
وعلى البرد ليه صابرين
وفي وشهم واقفين
إسالهم إنتم مين
هتلاقي رد جماعي ياعم مصريين
والله مصريين
خايفين على بلادنا
على الظلم مش راضيين
لدم كل شهيد فاكرين ومش ناسيين
رجالة ستات أعمارنا مختلفين
فينا تلاقي شباب وفينا مسنين
تجمعنا كلمة مصر
وعنوانا فى التحرير

Amr Katamish, pp. 235–36

عمرو قطامش
شعر "Arabs Got Talent"

دلعي نورا وإسمي عزة
ويقولون بأني مزة
كل بناطيلي ديقة
كي أبدو كوزة
لو أمشي ويراني شاب

ينظرلي بعيون بزة
لكن بعد الثورة لما امشي اتصورني معزة
لا أسمع بسبس او ما ما
لا أرى شاب يغمز غمزة
ولهذا افتخر ببلدي وعرفت هنا معنى العزة
وتيقنت بأن يوما وقريبا سنطهر غزة

كنت وزيراً
أحب حياتي
أسرق دوما ما يحلولي
لكن بعد نجاح الثورة
قد زادت للموت ميولي
ماذا أفعل يا دكتور
أخبرني لأشوف حلولي

Sayyed Higab, "Catfight," p. 238

سيد حجاب
وصلة ردح

قالوا لسمه إيه
ياسمك إيه
تنحى
متنح ليه
قال إسمه إيه
أصله إيه
كرامته ناءحه عليه
بقى ده عنده كرامة؟
ده خسته في عنيه
وعمرنا ودم أولادنا إتسفح بإيديه
إذا ده عنده كرامة ليه نهبنا ليه
وليه خربها ليه
وخان ترابها ليه
وقتل شبابها ليه
لو أبونا خاين ولص نجيب عاليه في واطيه
وندفنه بعاره ولاحدش يصلي عليه

Appendix 3
Songs Quoted in Chapter 6

Abdel Halim Hafez, "Watan al-akbar," p. 222

عبدالحليم حافظ

الوطن الأكبر

وطني يا مالك حبك قلبـــــــي
وطني يا وطن الشعب العربـــــي

يا اللي نديت بالوحدة الكبـــــرى
بعد ما شفت جمال الثـــــــورة

إنت كبير .. وأكبر كتيــــــــر ..
من الوجود كله .. من الخلود كلـه
يا وطني ..
وطني حبيبي

Shadia, "Ya Habibti ya Masr," p. 223

شادية

ياحبيبتي يا مصر

يابلادي
يا أحلى البلاد
يا بلادي
فداكي

319

أنا والولاد
يا بلادي
ياحبيبتي
يا مصر
يا مصر
ياحبيبتي
يا مصر
يا مصر
ياحبيبتي
يا مصر
ما شافش الأمل
في عيون الولاد
وصبايا البلد
ولا شاف العمل
سهران في البلاد
والعزم اتولد
ولا شاف النيل
في أحضان الشجر
ولا سمع
مواويل
في ليالي القمر
أصله معداش على مصر

Naguib Shihab al-Din, "Ya Masr umi," p. 224

نجيب شهاب الدين
يا مصر قومي

يا مصر قومي وشدي الحيل
كل اللي تتمنيه عندي
لا القهر يطويني ولا الليل
آمان آمان بيرم أفندي
رافعين جباه حرة شريفة
باسطين أيادي تأدي الفرض
ناقصين مؤذن وخليفة

Muhammad Mounir, "Ezzay?," pp. 225–26

محمد منير

إزاي

إزاي ترضيلي حبيبتي

إزاي ترضيلي حبيبتي
أتمعشق إسمك وانتي
عماله تزيدي فى حيرتي وما انتيش حاسه بطيبتي إزاي ؟

مش لاقي في عشقك دافع
ولا صدق فى حبك شافع
إزاي أنا رافع راسك وانتي بتحني في راسي إزاي ؟

أنا أقدم شارع فيكي
وآمالك م اللي باليكي
أنا طفل اتعلق بيكي فى نص السكة وتوهتيه

أنا لو عاشقك متخير
كان قلبي زمانه اتغير
وحياتك لفضل أغير فيكي لحد ما ترضي عليه

إزاي سيباني فى ضعفي
طب ليه مش واقفة في صفي
وأنا عشت حياتي بحالها علشان ملمحش فى عينك خوف

وفى بحرك ولا فى برك
إزاي أحميلك ضهرك
وأنا ضهري فى آخر الليل دايما بيبات محني ومكشوف

وازاي ترضيلي حبيبتي

Umm Kulthum, "Ana-l-sha'b," p. 231

أم كلثوم
أنا الشعب

وصاح من الشعب صوت طليق
قوي، أبيّ، عريق، عميق
يقول : أنا الشعب والمعجزة
أنا الشعب لا شيء قد أعجزه
وكل الذى قاله أنجزه

Ahmed Mekky, "January 25," p. 234

أحمد مكى و محمد محسن
٢٥ يناير

كرامة المصري تساوى عنده كتير ، نفسه يرجع كرامته والفساد يطير
شهر يناير يوم خمسة وعشرين، أعظم تاريخ ثورة مصرية على مر السنين
شباب رفع رأس مصر لفوق ،مش لابس طوق عاوز حقوقه الشرعية وطلبها بكل ذوق
خدلك لفة ولفلف واتفرج في ميدان التحرير, حتلاقي وشك إبتسم قلبك قرب يطير
شباب فهم معنى الوحدة ،إتحد عمل تغيير, إيني المصري النهاردة بعد الثورة أكبر بكتير

Ramy Essam, "IrHal," p. 237

رامي عصام
إرحل

كلنا إيد واحدة طلبنا حاجة واحدة إرحل إرحل إرحل
كلنا إيد واحدة طلبنا حاجة واحدة إرحل إرحل إرحل
قولي قولي
كلنا إيد واحدة طلبنا حاجة واحدة إرحل إرحل إرحل
كلنا إيد واحدة طلبنا حاجة واحدة إرحل إرحل إرحل
يسقط يسقط حسني مبارك (رجع)
يسقط يسقط حسني مبارك
يسقط يسقط حسني مبارك
يسقط يسقط حسني مبارك
الشعب يريد إسقاط النظام
الشعب يريد إسقاط النظام

الشعب يريد إسقاط النظام
هو يمشي مش حنمشي
سامع!
هو يمشي مش حنمشي

Ramy Essam, "al-Gish al-'arabi fin?," p. 240

رامي عصام
الجيش العربي فين

واحد اتنين الجيش العربي فين
الجيش العربي في مصر
ساكن في مدينة نصر
بيصحى من النوم العصر
وبيفطر شاي ومنين

واحد اتنين الجيش العربي فين
الجيش العربي في سوريا
حالق عالموضة كابوريا
وعلى طريقة فكتوريا
خلّى الترماي بدورين
واحد اتنين الجيش العربي فين
الجيش العربي الليبي
زيّ الفن التكعيبي
كله بتنجان يا حبيبي
الظاهر واخد عين

واحد اتنين الجيش العربي فين
الجيش العربي خليجي
ما فيه حيل لا يروح ولا ييجي
وده صمت استراتيجي
إيه فيك يا غراب البين

واحد اتنين الجيش العربي فين
الجيش العربي في تونس

أخضر مثل البقدونس
وعزيزة بتعشق يونس
يبقى الحروبات بعدين

واحد اتنين الجيش العربي فين
الجيش العربي سوداني
سامع رنّته بوداني
هو انا هاهجم فرداني
يالا ارجع يا ابو حسين

واحد اتنين الجيش العربي فين
الجيش العربي اتهان
يوم ما انضربوا الأفغان
وسكت في البوسنة زمان
وقبل ياكل بالدين
واحد اتنين الجيش العربي فين